PETERSON'S

HANDBOOK

FOR

COLLEGE

ADMISSIONS

The essential family guide to

selecting colleges ❖ *visits and interviews*

applications ❖ *financial aid*

the freshman ye

D0869458

THOMAS C. HAYDEN

Vice President, Oberlin College

Peterson's

Princeton, New Jersey

4th edition

Library of Congress Cataloging-in-Publication Data

Hayden, Thomas C.
    Peterson's handbook for college admissions : the essential family guide to selecting colleges, visits and interviews, applications, financial aid, the freshman year / Thomas C. Hayden. — 4th ed.
      p. cm.
    Includes index.
    ISBN 1-56079-428-3
      1. Universities and colleges—United States—Admission. I. Title
    LB2351.2.H38   1995
    378.1'056'0973—dc20   95-33208
                                              CIP

Editorial direction: Carol Hupping
Copyediting & production:
  Bernadette Boylan
Proofreading: Marie Burnett
Composition: Gary Rozmierski

Creative direction: Linda Huber
Cover design: Greg Wozney
Cover photograph:
  Richard Hutchings
Interior design: Cynthia Boone

Printed in the United States of America

10 9 8 7 6 5 4 3 2 1

Visit Peterson's Education Center on the Internet (World Wide Web) at http://www.petersons.com

To 4,000 or so Exies and their parents,
who taught me as they learned
about the college admissions process.

CONTENTS

INTRODUCTION

This is a guidebook for high school students and their families as they seek to plan for that complicated journey toward college: a journey that involves selecting a suitable list of schools, gaining admission to many of them, paying for and enrolling in, and adjusting successfully to one of them.

Although this book cannot promise its readers that they or their children will gain admission to the college of their choice, it can and does pose the significant questions that families and students ought to be asking themselves as they go through the college search process. It also provides a wealth of practical advice about sources of information on various aspects of college selection and college financing; it offers numerous strategies that can be employed to make the most of your talents and accomplishments, and it suggests tactics that can be used to make *the system* work for you.

As you move into the world of college admissions and college financing, you enter a world shrouded in vagueness and misconception. Before you can really understand the college admissions system and how it can work for you, you must first clear up some of the confusion and the myths associated with it.

The first myth might be called difficulty equals quality. And it is not true. The difficulty of gaining admission to a school does *not* determine its quality or prestige. You need to look beyond the selectivity or difficulty of admission in the guidebooks to find the numerous other indicators of quality—and the best fit between the school and the student. The real challenge is to find a college or university where your talents will be stretched at the same time that your success will be assured.

Another myth that circles around the heads of students and families is that of the "prestige" college. Prestige is often defined as the number of applications a school receives and consequently the number of students it can turn down. It often stems from the notoriety of one or two of its graduates. Frequently it arises from a national image promoted by a school's vigorous public relations office. Whatever the particular combination of forces that produces prestige, you will soon discover that there is often little connection between the fame of a school and the quality of the educational experience there.

The third myth is called the single factor myth. Students and families who embrace this myth will be inclined to believe that one factor is the be-all and the end-all of the college admissions process. It might, for example, be the interview: Prepare frantically for an interview and make a good impression there, and you're in! Standardized testing is another example: If you can get a high enough score on the SAT I and/or the SAT II, then a particular school will undoubtedly admit you and ignore other flat spots in your admissions folder.

Nothing could be further from the truth. The college admissions process, even at nonselective schools, takes into account a variety of factors in your application: grades in high school, standardized testing, school recommendations (counselor and teachers), your own part of the application, and your essay. All of these factors are brought together in a balanced judgment; there are no single factors—there are multiple factors.

The fourth myth is particularly pernicious: The best kids get into the best colleges. This myth suggests that the selective college admissions process does in fact find the best candidates. But it ignores the fact that although admitting students is a very personal one, admissions officers are like the students they admit—not perfect. They do not make correct judgments all the time. They are not clairvoyant and able to see how the students they do admit are going to perform. You need to bear in mind that admissions officers are not admitting and rejecting people, they are admitting and rejecting applications! So, a year or more from now, when the results come in from the colleges to which you applied, remember that if you are rejected, it was *your application* that was rejected, not *you*. There is still a "right" college for you.

If you find yourself accepting any of these myths, try to move beyond them. Indulging in any of them often brings on cynicism and occasionally frivolous or devious behavior. This book was written in reaction to these four myths—to try to cast light on what can be an orderly, rational, at times humorous, and always educational process for parents and students alike.

*   *   *

This book, now in its fourth edition, is designed to serve as a guide, and something more. For students, it is designed to help them find a new appreciation for their talents and their potential—not just for college work itself but also for establishing themselves as worthwhile, contributing citizens of their community, as growing, independent individuals. It is hoped that this book will also give you a glimpse of the dynamic role that a college education will play in illuminating your path toward an interesting, productive, and happy life.

For parents, the book is meant to show them how they can personally benefit from the college admissions process. By treating your children as equals in the college decision making and planning process, by crediting ideas and behavior that are new and different, and by sharing the values and experience of your own lives with them, you can form the basis of an adult relationship with your children.

For students *and* parents, I hope this book will show you that the process of finding the appropriate college affords a very practical form of education for every individual. Some of this education will come from parents and students actively listening to one another; some will come from reading between the lines, from catalogs and conversations with college admissions people, from finding out what these institutions and their representatives are really saying to you about themselves. Part of it will come from trusting one's own instincts to act in a way that is different from the norm.

As rational as we try to make the process, there is always room for creativity and calculated risk. Part of this education will come with dealing adroitly with the unexpected—the flat tire on the way to the interview, a new way of financing college costs, and a host of others. Be assured there will be some surprises in finding the right college. Be assured that there will be some fun too and that when it comes you will make the most of it.

The advice in this book comes from a decade of my involvement with and observation of particularly interesting groups of students and parents—on both the college side and the secondary school side—coming to grips with the vagaries of the admissions and financial aid process. I have tried to distill that experience into a coherent and readable form and to write the text from the candidate's point of view. I am attempting to reach those students and families who want to make the most of the student's abilities and use the opportunities available in the marketplace to help that student gain admission to an institution that will develop his/her potential to its fullest. That approach means you will find much in this book that assumes some traditional American ideals: an interest in the academic enterprise, a reliance on hard work, and a commitment to using knowledge in some way to serve society.

This book also comes from two decades of observation of 100 of the nation's most prestigious colleges and universities and how they make decisions. It relies also on an insider's knowledge of one of those schools in particular, Oberlin College. It draws on candid and informative conversations with countless college admissions officers around the country, with high school counselors, and detailed discussions with financial aid, admissions, and research officers at Oberlin. To all of these individuals I am deeply indebted.

In writing this book, I have sought to be fair to all the institutions mentioned and to my readers. For any errors or misinterpretations that mortals make, I am responsible—I hope they are few. I hope too that readers will find in this book a store of useful advice and that in the course of following it, they will realize during their college years and beyond, the best that is within them.

Thomas C. Hayden
June 1995
Oberlin, Ohio

O N E

Thinking
About College . . .

Travelers to the ancient city of Delphi who sought to find out what the future had in store for them were often puzzled by the vagueness of what the priests of the temple had to say. Many of those travelers would have been less confused had they read the motto inscribed over the temple's entrance: "Know thyself."

That motto is classic; its meaning holds as true for us today as it did for the Delphinians and their guests. And it's good advice for all young people pondering the galaxy of questions that surround the decision of where to go to college. You must "know yourself."

All too often students who are absorbed in their college planning dwell on the importance of getting accepted by a particular school rather than on the important questions that should be answered before they select schools.

As you begin your college planning, you first need to think objectively about yourself, your interests, and your needs. Only then can you focus on the school that will best suit those particular educational and social needs. You should begin with a self-assessment—perhaps your first—before you even think about specific colleges. This self-assessment may be one of the most valuable learning experiences of your whole college-search process, for it will enable you to see yourself, your goals, and the routes to those goals with a new degree of clarity and understanding. Ask your guidance counselor if one of the following personal inventory tests is available at your school: Myers-Briggs, California Psychological Inventory, or the Minnesota Multiphasic Personality Inventory.

Several years ago a professor at Haverford College studied the backgrounds of successful graduates of his institution. He found that one of the key elements of success in later life was the presence, at a young age, of a strong and realistic self-awareness.

DOING A SELF-ASSESSMENT

Every person has a unique combination of skills, personal traits, goals, values, aptitudes, habits, and beliefs. Let us explore some of the ways you can discover your unique combination and wisely use this knowledge to find the colleges or universities that will be best for you.

The method that I'm going to suggest you use for this self-discovery into your skills, your values, and your personality will take a little time and some concentration, but I feel sure you'll find that it will be worth the effort. To begin, get out a sheet of paper and a pen and eliminate any distractions around you. Then settle back and begin.

Look at some of your current skills. You might not be aware of how many you already have. Start by making a log of all your activities during the past 24 hours. Divide your log into two columns, one for the activity itself and a second for the skills it involved. After you have looked at the day just past, continue down the left-hand column of your log with the activities you have found enjoyable and productive over the past year. Then skip a few lines and make a short list of some of the things you would like to do in the future.

When you have completed your list of activities present, past, and future, let your list cool for a while. Return to it tomorrow and then beside each activity write down the skills that activity involved. For example, your list might look like the one on page 7.

A brief glance at your activities shows that you already have mastered a number of skills and are in the process of perfecting others. A look at the list also reveals that you have reason to feel good about yourself and your potential. As you think about college, add some activities to the last section of the list and itemize the skills that you would like to perfect over the course of the next four years.

Your Own Values

Next, consider your personal values and the role they inevitably play in your daily life. You may not be aware of how strongly you believe in some values and how uncertain you are about others. To find out, try this fanciful

ACTIVITIES	SKILLS INVOLVED
◆ **Yesterday & Today**	
French homework	Memorization, writing, and speaking another language
Chem lab report	Understanding complex molecules and physical forces of bonding
Took out trash	No skill I can think of
Cheerleader practice	Physical coordination, sense of balance and motion, and cooperation with others
Trumpet lesson	Digital facility, knowledge of scale and melody, awareness of harmony and some theory, integration of instrument within orchestra
◆ **Last Summer**	
Camped in Maine woods	Reading maps; building fires; cooking simple meals; learning how to pack and walk with a heavy load and how to observe nature; persuading parents to let me go
Repaired family stereo	Digital facility, knowledge of electrical circuitry and theory of sound reproduction
Learned to sail	Elementary navigation, physics of wind and water, observation of weather and water patterns
◆ **The Future**	
Dismantle a jet engine	Knowledge of engineering physics, digital facility, sense of planning and organization in sorting the parts, and understanding how those parts function together
Run a marathon	Physical conditioning, setting the proper diet, understanding the physics of the foot as it encounters running surfaces, planning for extensive training

experiment called a *Value Auction*. First, write down the following values and add to the list any others that may occur to you:

Health	Religion	Security
Family Travel	Power	Marriage
Justice	Personal recognition	Honesty
Love	Personal autonomy	Friendship
Emotional well-being	Good appearance	Knowledge, wisdom
Pleasure	Charity	Achievement

Second, assume a budget of $1,000 to spend on "purchasing" some or all of these values for $100 to $200 each. Now spend the $1,000 on the values on your list and see where your money goes.

What values emerged as most important to you? Which ones were less so? Which did you omit, and why? Rank your values in order of their importance to you and keep your list firmly in mind as you explore various colleges, talk to undergraduates and admissions personnel, and look over the college literature you receive. At some point further down the road, you will want to align your personal values with those of the institution where you will be spending the next four years.

To begin this assessment of how an institution might affect your values and your direction positively or negatively, fantasize for a few moments. (Researchers have found that fantasies have a high degree of correlation with our personal needs and ultimately our career decisions.) Imagine what you would like to have written about you in your obituary. What achievements would you choose to be remembered? What weaknesses would you like concealed or dealt with gently?

Jot your thoughts down on paper and keep them private. At the same time, consider what type of educational and career plans you might have to make to achieve the noteworthy results you outlined in your "obituary." What values would you have to adhere to? Think about the type of college that might best help you to meet your objectives and to refine the values you care about.

Your Personality

A third area of self-assessment lies in the domain of personality. What type of person are you? What kind of working and learning environment suits you best? Socially? Intellectually?

Richard N. Bolles, in his clever and helpful book *What Color Is Your Parachute?* offers a model for us to consider. He asks us to imagine a party at which people with the same or similar interests gather in six different areas of a room. As the newcomer, you are asked to identify the group with which you feel a natural affinity, the one you would enjoy being with. As you stand at the door of the party and consider which group you would like to join, you see six interesting groups:

Group A: People with athletic or mechanical ability who prefer to work with objects, machines, tools, plants, or animals or to be outdoors

Group B: People who have clerical or quantitative ability who like to work with data and like to carry things out in detail or follow through on others' instructions

Group C: People who like to work with others, influencing, persuading, leading, or managing them as they seek organizational goals, particularly financial ones

Group D: People who like to work with others, to inform, enlighten, train, develop, or cure them, or who are skilled with words

Group E: People who have artistic, innovative, or intuitional abilities and like to work in unstructured situations using their imagination and creativity

Group F: People who like to observe, learn, investigate, analyze, evaluate, or solve problems

Make a note of the group you would most like to join. Then imagine that the group breaks up for some reason and its members go home. Which group would you join next? Which would be your third choice? Having made these decisions, write them down. Note the skills that were associated with your first choice of group. Also note how your personal values were underscored by your choices. Then proceed to your second and third choices, noting the skills, values, and degree of personal fulfillment those choices would reinforce, were this a real-life situation.

Now you should consider making it just that, a real-life situation. Whom do you know and admire who fits into the groups you have just chosen? Make a list of their personality traits and values. Describe their work and the social and physical features of their working environments insofar as you know those details. Consider calling one of them to get as much detail as you can about his or her life and work.

You should be aware that there is room for people from more than one of the listed groups in any given field. For example, in the field of medicine, members of Group D obviously would make good family doctors, but those in Group A might specialize in surgery or some aspect of medicine involving mechanical skills. Students who are interested in medicine and are most comfortable in Group F might find fulfillment as research doctors in a large hospital or university.

THE WORLD OF WORK

After attending the hypothetical party and considering the ways in which individual skills, values, and personality need to combine comfortably and productively with the group settings, you need to carry your process of self-evaluation into its next phase—consideration of the world of work.

Your exploration of the world of work need not be extensive at this point. Having identified your skills, interests, and preferred environments, you want to gather information about possible careers or fields of work in which you might function well in the future.

The ideal way to begin would be to ask your guidance counselor to let you take the Jackson Interest Inventory Test or the Holland Self-Directed Search Test and then to go over the results with you. The armed services offer a test called the Armed Services Vocational Aptitude Battery (ASVAB), and it too can be interpreted by your guidance counselor. These tests will help you identify the fields of work for which you may have an affinity, but they are by no means conclusive predictors of future performance. Properly understood and utilized, they can help you identify your skills and aptitudes and focus on possible career goals.

To explore ways of reaching these goals, go to the library and look for two useful works: the *Dictionary of Occupational Titles* and the *Occupational Outlook Handbook*. Pick two careers that might be of interest to you and read about their requirements in the *Dictionary of Occupational Titles*. Then turn to the *Occupational Outlook Handbook* and consider the projected need for new workers in those fields. If the prospects look promising, make a list of all the requirements for those career choices, leaving space for other related careers.

From this list you should develop a set of questions about the careers you have chosen to investigate. Perhaps you've had some experience in job situations that will help you formulate your questions. The following will help you prepare for an interview with a person in your chosen career field.

Working Conditions: What are the hours of work? Is the environment clean/dirty/dangerous/noisy/quiet/safe?

Duties: What are four typical duties you might be expected to carry out?

People: To what extent does your job involve working with other people? Is it satisfying to you in this respect?

Education: What special training or certification did you have to get? To what extent did your education and previous jobs help you to find and obtain this one?

Benefits: What are the salary and benefits associated with your work, including travel, use of a company car, research facilities, health insurance, and the like?

Disadvantages: What do you dislike about your work and is there anything you can do to change it?

Personal Qualities: What are the most important personal qualities people should have to succeed in this line of work?

General: Do you have any particular advice for me if I become interested in entering this career—contacts I should make, experience I should seek?

Having drafted a list of questions such as these, try to interview someone in each of the fields of interest you have designated. It may sound difficult, but the benefits of personal contact with adults working in the field are considerable, not to mention the experience you'll gain in arranging a meeting and conducting an interview. Interviews often can be conducted informally with family members or friends who are involved in careers that interest you. You might ask to "shadow" someone for a day. For example, you could accompany your doctor uncle on his rounds and then interview him in the car on the way to and from the hospital.

In the best of all possible worlds your final step in exploring the world of work is to actually do a little work related to the field or fields that interest you, perhaps in a summer job. If you find engineering interesting, apply for a summer job in the local computer or stereo store. Does it look like medicine is for you? Volunteer in the local hospital, clinic, or nursing home. Thinking about getting into a business field? Get out into the business world, even if it means taking a job as a waitress or waiter, sales clerk, shipper, or even factory worker.

In each instance, looking for a job that suits you will be made easier by the insights you already have gained about your skills and interests and the kind of work environments best suited to developing them.

THINKING ABOUT MAJORS

Somewhere in the course of this odyssey dedicated to identifying your strong qualities and directing them toward a career, you will begin to develop some ideas about a possible college major. You do not need to make a final decision about a college major in high school; you may want to sample a broad range of subjects in your freshman year. However, at this stage it is useful to consider possible fields of study and how they might relate to the careers you are considering.

Your uncle, the doctor, may encourage you to pursue a liberal arts program as the best preparation for dealing with the variety of individuals that a doctor encounters and must understand. On the other hand, if you want to be a pilot, you may want to major in electrical engineering and get on with the acquisition of the technical knowledge that will be required further down the line. If you aspire to be a journalist, you may be told to continue with your interest in mathematics—because of the technological changes that are sweeping over our lives—and at the same time keep on writing. This could lead you to the science editorship of a major newspaper one day.

When you have identified particular subjects or majors you might want to pursue, you can turn to a number of standard sources that will direct you toward colleges that have strengths in those areas. The College Board publishes *The Index to Majors*, and Peterson's has its *Guide to Four-Year Colleges*. In addition, both have computer programs that enable you to locate colleges offering a particular major.

Before choosing a college, however, you have to frame a set of questions that will help you discover whether a proposed major is suited to your skills, values, and learning style. In addition, you will need to know whether your choice of major will allow you the flexibility to explore other areas of knowledge while pursuing your career goals.

At your college interview you should try to get answers to the following questions:

♦ What skills are needed to pursue this major successfully? What high school courses will help me prepare myself? (A good question to ask if you're interviewing in spring of your junior year, when you still may have time to make adjustments to your senior year class schedule.)

♦ What fields of work do students in this major enter?

♦ Is there room for students to branch out into related areas while pursuing this major? Examples?

♦ What college courses are commonly taken in conjunction with this major? If I major in history, will I be encouraged to take political science and economics?

♦ Are there any special programs within this major, such as work-study, foreign study, or internships, that could help me refine my interests and perfect my abilities?

♦ To what extent is graduate school necessary to acquire real competence in this major?

♦ What satisfactions and dissatisfactions might I experience as a student with this major at this college?

♦ What kind of people typically enter this major and do well in it? (Think back to the groups at the "party" on page 9.)

As you get answers to such questions from college interviewers, alumni representatives, or students at the college who are majoring in your field of interest, think back to your own self-assessment. Your skills, values, personality, and learning style should roughly coincide with those of the students majoring in your field; if they do not, then you should keep an open mind and look into other majors that might be a better fit for you. If you do decide to consider another school, remember that the learning environment is important, and you shouldn't let a weak department lead you to reject a school that is in all other respects a positive place for you to live and learn.

Let us look at the example of George Matthews, who is 17 and wants to be a lawyer. George has a keen interest in history. He does some research on Donaldson College and is pleased to hear that 60 percent of the history department's graduates took the Law School Admission Test last spring. He is equally impressed by several courses that focus on the role of law in society. He makes a list of the skills he would need to be successful in history and, ultimately, law. He recognizes that his strong writing abilities would help him, as would his ability to organize data and make hypotheses about them. However, he would have to concentrate on his research and note-taking skills because there are lots of lecture courses and research papers in the history department at Donaldson.

George has already taken two history courses in high school and would welcome the opportunity to study the allied field of political science in college. He also wants to understand rudimentary economics and perhaps take some courses in fiscal management. He discovers that these options are available at the college.

In assessing Donaldson's strengths and drawbacks, he finds he could live with the crowding at the library reserve desk and the fact that history professors are often away on sabbatical in Washington, D.C. He knows he would find satisfaction studying a subject in which he has always been interested and one that is obviously favored by the college. (The best-teacher award has gone to a member of the history department in three of the past five years.) The Donaldson history department would provide him with stimulating professors whose national reputation might enhance his application to law school or graduate school.

Finally, as George considers the type of social and intellectual situation he likes most—working with and managing people as they seek organizational goals—he becomes convinced that history is the major for him, and Donaldson is the college where he should study.

THE OTHER YOU:
EXTRACURRICULAR LIFE AND INTERESTS

After you have chosen your major(s) you will want to consider your extracurricular and creative interests. Pursuing those activities and interests is an important part of college life. The history student who is also a good football player and likes to play the violin will want to locate a school where all those talents can be nurtured—one with a good history curriculum, a strong football team, and an expansive music program that welcomes amateurs as well as experienced musicians. Similarly, the student who loves to cook, someday hopes to own a catering business, and plans to study economics will have to look carefully at a college's culinary arts facilities as well as its academic ones.

Both of these students need to consider their extracurricular activities in some kind of social context, too. The accomplished cook who used to perform cooking miracles at home will have to rely on the college's equipment now and share it with members of the Gourmet Society. This sharing may necessitate relating to other people more than in the past. An interest in cooking can thus lead to friendships outside the dormitory and the classroom. For the football player who was lionized in high school, getting to know his new teammates off the field—in the classroom and in the dormitory—will be important. As a person who likes music and plays it on occasion, he may want to act as liaison between the football team and the band in the fall, then join the band as an instrumentalist during the winter and spring.

Whatever their choices, both cook and athlete need to find a school where academics are of primary importance but their special talents are appreciated as well.

ACADEMIC ABILITIES

By now you've assessed your personal skills, the learning environment that suits you best, your career interests, potential major, and extracurricular talents, but your self-evaluation is not complete without a frank appraisal of your academic abilities. Look over the list of academic-related skills below and see how you rate. Be honest with yourself. If you know that you're weak in any particular areas, work on improving them during your remaining time in high school.

Note-taking

Not only should you be able to take notes on a lecture, but you also should be able to capture the main ideas in a reading assignment. This includes summarizing the message of the text, defining the author's key terms, and restating the author's point of view and biases in your own words.

Organizing information for papers

Look at your high school course description booklet. Find a course that promises to teach you how to conduct research and write an analytical paper based on an array of data. This course will help you to put together a bibliography, take notes on note cards, evolve a thesis, and organize an outline. An added bonus of the course might be instruction on use of the computer to assemble all your information in an attractive and well-organized format.

Oral discussion skills

Although many freshman courses meet in large lectures, classes tend to become smaller as students progress and specialize. Ideally you will have at least one freshman seminar class in which you can use your oral discussion skills. These skills can be practiced in high school classes or in ordinary conversation with friends.

A crucial oral skill is the ability to keep your attention on the main point of the conversation and not be distracted by digressions. When having a serious discussion with a group of people, try to keep them on track by asking them to define any new terms they employ or, when they go off the track, try to return them to the main point.

Oral discussion also calls for the ability to present ideas that may contradict without alienating others. Learning to do this naturally and smoothly comes from practice; it is an art too elaborate for description here but one that is well worth having. Referring positively to something that a speaker has said and then relating it to your own comment and to the topic in general often will avoid offense.

At the end of a group discussion, you should practice synthesizing the various opinions that have been expressed and then pose some new questions that might not have been considered.

Not all of these techniques come easily, but don't undervalue the role of the spoken word in your educational growth. Whether in all-night bull sessions or in an introductory course on Western political tradition, your oral skills will help you clarify your own ideas, assimilate new ones, and present yourself to college interviewers and job recruiters, later on.

Basic writing skills

Most of today's high school students haven't mastered the ability to write with clarity, coherence, and style. High school curricula have shifted emphasis away from writing courses and teachers assign too few written exercises. Television has fostered the preeminence of the spoken over the written word. Eleventh graders planning to apply to a four-year college should therefore make it a priority to concentrate on developing effective writing skills before their freshman year of college.

A conference with your English teacher is the first step in improving your writing skills. Your teacher can help you identify any weaknesses and suggest ways to remedy them. Perhaps the suggestion will involve something as simple as learning the rule for the correct use of who and whom, or how to avoid split infinitives. Or it may involve more complicated skills: vocabulary building, outlining your thoughts before writing, studying the various ways of subordinating ideas in a sentence.

For an indication of your level of writing ability, look at a pamphlet called *Taking the SAT II Subject Tests* (published by the College Board and available from your high school guidance office). Under the section on the Writing Test, you will find a sample essay question from the exam. One recent version asks students to formulate a written response to the proposition: People seldom stand up for what they truly believe in; instead they merely go along with the popular view.

Following the statement are four responses, which represent a good, an average, a below-average, and a poor response for a high school senior. You may want to write your own response to the sample question before looking at the examples. Then, when you have made your own comparisons, ask your English teacher to rate your efforts and suggest possible improvements.

Word processing and computer know-how

Word processing sounds like such a simple matter, and it is—unless you don't know how! Most college courses require typed papers, and, moreover, students who can produce their own papers gain time in which they can put their papers through additional revisions before they are due. Many students also know the fundamentals of constructing a spreadsheet. Try to master both a word and spreadsheet program before you get to college.

Remember that in many college environments you will not even put your thoughts on paper. You will "write" them on a screen, send them by local area network to your professor and get your critical comments and grades back via the same route.

In addition to its editorial function, the computer has touched all aspects of learning in the past decade. Historians use computers to study the demography of communities, formulating theories about social and political change. With them, political scientists study voting patterns and predict elections. Economists use computers to analyze the stock market, and even language teachers use them to test their students' knowledge of grammatical forms.

If students understand the elementary principles of computing, how to use the computer to collect data, how to operate word processing programs, and how to connect a school or personal computer with networks like the Internet, CompuServe, America Online, Prodigy, and other such services, they will find these skills useful when they are in college. Knowing what kinds of questions the computer can answer and how to make it supply those answers will be enormously beneficial.

YOUR FAMILY'S ROLE

No self-evaluation, however honest and far-reaching, should ignore the importance of your family in shaping the college decision. Thinking about college involves thinking about your parents' expectations for you and about its finances. Plan to have some long discussions with your parents and anyone else who may be helping to pay some of your college costs.

Often students find that their families have very high expectations of them. Parents sometimes believe that their son or daughter should pursue a particular major and, even worse, apply pressure on their offspring to do so at a particular college or university. Parents need to know more about the realities of the college admissions process. Students may have to arrange a meeting with their guidance counselor for this purpose, thus introducing an objective third party to help the family conduct a reasonable conversation and bring them much-needed information.

On the other hand, some families may have expectations that are not high enough. They may not realize that you are as capable and focused as you are and do, indeed, have the potential to reach your goal of becoming a doctor. Parents sometimes also use financial limitations to mask their lack of confidence in their children or their ignorance of the real value of a college education. In both cases—high expectations and low—students should gather as many facts as they can so they can inform their families of the importance of choosing the right college. Having such information can be very helpful in addressing the concerns of a cost-conscious parent who has a jaundiced view of the need for a liberal arts education followed by graduate school.

For example, saying, "Dad, when I interviewed Dr. Soldowski, he told me that a four-year liberal arts education with a few science courses sprinkled in is the best preparation for medical school that he could possibly think of," can help carry the argument for a small liberal arts college as opposed to a very large, less expensive state university. Being able to rebut the argument that you must go to a particular Ivy League school because your parents' friends' children go there with the statement that "the aeronautical physics department at the University of Texas is better" will help defuse the high expectations argument advanced by some parents.

Once parents know specific facts about the colleges their children are considering and understand how reasonably they are approaching the subject in general, they tend to delegate considerable control over the college selection process to them. Parents will undoubtedly ask to be kept informed—they will offer their opinions from time to time—but they will play a supportive yet subordinate role. (See Chapter 8 for more on parents' roles in the entire college selection and admission process.)

PHILOSOPHICAL CONSIDERATIONS

A four-year college education begins a lifelong process of learning and changing. College is not a finite experience; it stays with you throughout your life. What you are looking for in a college is something beyond good grades, rewarding extracurricular activities, a particular expertise, a degree, and a "ticket to the big life." You want to find a place that will enhance your capacity to think independently, to appreciate the variety and complexity of the world around you, and to move comfortably within it. As a college student, you should seek not only to acquire knowledge but to develop a creative and disciplined mind that allows you to be adventurous in thought and action while at the same time feel secure and committed.

Think for a moment about the enormous differences between high school and college; try to imagine the immense freedom that college brings. There is no freer period in a person's life than the four years of college. Away from home and family, able to set your own schedule of work and play, free to take a wide variety of courses and to engage in any number of social and extracurricular activities, and—with luck—free from major financial worries, you have an unlimited opportunity to construct and furnish an intellectual, spiritual, and social home of your own. It is important, therefore, that you realize why you want to be at college in the first place so that from its innumerable options you make wise choices.

Let us be a bit more specific. You and your family are investing a great deal of time and money in this experience. Therefore, it makes sense to set some standards for yourself that ensure that you make the most of the opportunity. Having some expectations for yourself and reaching *your* goals will help you deal with the variety of attitudes and behavior you may find on your college campus. For instance, you may find that some fellow students will be indifferent to rules and common sense. They may overindulge in drugs or alcohol or sex. Or they may focus intently on preparing for their careers and compiling good grades for graduate school at the expense of sharing ideas and experience with fellow students. Whatever happens, making some decisions about where you stand on these particular issues will help you make the most of your particular college experience.

In the end, what really matters is that you actively choose a college and course of study for the right reasons. As long as your decision is an active one and takes into consideration your own skills, interests, and personality based on a realistic self-assessment, then yours will be the right decision. Too often we look at only one side of Robert Frost's poem about the roads diverging in the yellow wood:

> *I shall be telling this with a sigh*
> *Somewhere ages and ages hence,*
> *Two roads diverged in a wood, and I,*
> *I took the one less traveled by,*
> *And that has made all the difference.*

We are inclined to believe that the less-traveled path is the right path. In other words, it is better to be a poet than a banker. But Frost did not say exactly that, for elsewhere in the poem he writes:

> *. . . both that morning equally lay*
> *in leaves no step has trodden black.*

Frost is emphasizing the need for free choice in our life's decisions. Like the poet, you will come to many junctions and have to make choices. The freedom to make the choices involved in going to college does not come merely from the absence of restraint; it rises from a realistic self-evaluation, a sincere commitment to the educational process itself, and an awareness that a college education imposes a certain responsibility on you. As we look ahead to the remainder of this century and the first years of the next, we can readily see that our society will require the maximum development of individual potential.

Ernest Boyer, head of the Carnegie Foundation for the Advancement of Teaching, explained the task well when he wrote:

> This nation and the world need well-informed, inquisitive, open-minded young people who are both productive and reflective, seeking answers to life's most important question. Above all, we need educated men and women who not only pursue their own personal interests but are also prepared to fulfill their social and civic obligations. And it is during the undergraduate experience . . . that these essential qualities of

mind and character are refined. (*College: The Undergraduate Experience*. Ernest L. Boyer. New York: Harper and Row, 1987, p. 7.)

The decision to go to college, then, entails a special commitment to the larger society as well as to yourself. Like all real decisions, it represents both a freedom and a responsibility.

Choosing Colleges

"Choosing the right college for yourself involves using both sides of your brain, the rational left side and the instinctive right side, to arrive at a decision about which college or university best suits your needs."

Judith H. Harper, Associate Director, College Counseling,
Phillips Exeter Academy

Selecting a college entails blending the factors you have developed through your self-evaluation with other important criteria. It combines a look inside yourself with a look beyond yourself. In Chapter 1 you had an opportunity to think about your skills, values, and learning style, and as a result you may have already chosen a possible field of work and the college major that will best prepare you for that field. Now you need to seek the advice of three groups of people:

People working in the field you wish to enter

Let us assume you want to enter the medical field as either a physician or veterinarian. If your high school does not have a career day, make arrangements yourself to spend the day shadowing a doctor or a veterinarian. See if you like what they do. Discuss the advantages and disadvantages of their work. Ask their advice on the best preparation, schools, and courses for their professions.

Your guidance counselor

She can steer you to the various electronic and printed directories that describe the requirements for various career fields and list the prerequisites you have to meet in college. Some directories will list the colleges or universities that provide the best training in a particular field. Make notes on what you discover, and then check out your impressions with your guidance counselor.

From this conversation you hope to develop a list of undergraduate institutions that would best prepare you for your career goals.

Trusted friends

Your peers and your adult friends—perhaps even your parents—can help you judge the fit between you and schools on this early list. Keep an open mind at this point and listen to all opinions, especially those based on facts or personal experience. You'll have plenty of time later to make your own decision.

FACTORS FOR YOU TO CONSIDER

Now, keeping in mind the advice you have received, you will want to make a list of the factors that will affect your selection of schools. With each school in turn, focus first on the academic programs. This is, after all, your main criterion.

Does the school offer strong programs in your field of interest? Are there small classes where you can receive individual attention? Are there internship programs that will allow you to gain practical experience in a laboratory or job setting. Are there programs abroad that you may wish to take to complement the classroom experience?

If you also want to be near home—or in a particular region—then location might be your second major consideration. You may have some preconceived notions about how large or small a college you want to attend, so size is a third criterion. Then comes the very significant category of your extracurricular activities: sports, drama, music, nationally ranked chess club, or whatever is important to you.

You should be sure that there are interesting activities to engage you outside the classroom as well as inside it. For some, such activities will figure very prominently in the college experience. This will be a fifth category.

Next comes the important and complicated matter of cost and what kind of financial aid you will need to pay for college (see Chapter 7 for a discussion of college money matters). And finally you will need to consider the difficulty of admission—how selective the school is in admitting applicants.

BOOKS, SOFTWARE, AND VIDEOS

Once you've established some basic criteria for yourself about colleges, use some of the many sources of information available today to learn more about the colleges that interest you. Choose your medium:

Directories

Look first at the large college directories. These contain in-depth objective descriptions of all or most of the colleges in the United States. Most also have charts and cross-indexes that allow you to see at a glance schools by state or region, by size, by majors, whether they are private or state schools, and so forth. *Peterson's Guide to Four-Year Colleges* and the *College Handbook* of the College Board are the two most popular directories.

Subjective guides

You may also want to look at some of the subjective guides. They usually rank the colleges and describe the schools in qualitative terms that are designed to leave an unmistakable impression on the reader. You'll want to gather as much data as possible from an objective guide before turning for assistance to a subjective one.

Computer software

There are also software packages available that allow you to create selective lists of schools that meet your criteria; these can be very helpful and are growing rapidly in availability. *Peterson's College Selection Service* and the College Board's *College Explorer Plus* can be found in many libraries and high school counseling offices.

Some colleges have key academic, admissions, and financial aid information on CD-ROM and will send you a disk if you call them. Others have signed on with companies like College View to make their school information available on CD-ROM; ask at your high school counseling office to see whether you can have access to the College View Program and through it to some of the colleges and universities you may be interested in. You can contact College View directly to find out what CDs it has available for your use (800-927-VIEW).

College videos

Videos are another source of information about colleges. Call the 800 number of the schools that interest you and ask for a video. Also consult your high school counselor's reference shelf for videos. Remember to use videos in combination with other information in making your assessment of the match with a particular school.

The Internet

Many colleges and universities are accessible on the Internet. Call the admissions offices of the schools on your list and ask if it has a home page. If it does, its address will look something like: http://www.oberlin.edu. If you're a subscriber to one of the on-line services like Prodigy, CompuServe, or America Online, check out college electronic bulletin boards there for school information. If you have one of these services, you can also use it to access Peterson's Education Center: http://www.petersons.com, which will provide you with profiles of four-year colleges across the country.

CATALOGS AND VIEWBOOKS

Once you've narrowed your choices down, you will want to take a closer look at the schools on your list. Get a copy of the catalog for each school you're interested in and study it carefully, keeping your own selection criteria in mind. Sometimes colleges will not send catalogs with their first mailing since they are expensive to publish and to mail. However, they may have placed their catalog on an electronic database that you can access through the Internet on the World Wide Web. Look for the web address in your literature from the college or call the school and ask for it. Then "surf" the catalog yourself.

Alternatively, colleges may send you a viewbook. Smaller and less costly than a catalog, a viewbook gives you an overview of the college's history, programs, and philosophy of education. It also contains numerous pictures of the campus, school facilities, students, and faculty. Viewbooks can be quite factual and informative. If you find one that is not, your school counseling office or library may have the school's catalog for you to borrow. Or ask around; a friend may have a copy to lend.

In examining the catalog, look first at the academic programs in which you are interested:

♦ Are there a fairly large number of courses you could take in your chosen academic area?

◆ Are there special programs that would be accessible to you and that would enable you to craft your course of study so that you have marketable skills as well as mastery of a particular discipline when you graduate?

For example, if you are interested in majoring in the history of art and possibly going on to a career as a museum curator, does the college or university offer programs that involve students with nearby museums? Does it offer a study-abroad program that would enable someone like yourself to examine the art treasures of Florence and Rome firsthand? Can a major in the history of art be joined with a minor in business management?

Let us assume you are interested in majoring in engineering and want to minor in business so that you will be able to move into business from engineering later in your career, should you wish. Look at the requirements for engineering. Do they allow you to take a half-dozen courses in economics, marketing, and organizational behavior? Is there a specific program for people who wish to combine engineering with a related field? (Some schools offer a combined degree in liberal arts and engineering called 3-2 programs.) Does the college or university offer internships—college-sponsored job opportunities—so that you can acquire hands-on experience in your intended field of interest?

If the academic programs at a specific college or university look interesting, then ask yourself these questions:

◆ How accessible will these courses, programs, and faculty really be to me?
◆ Does the catalog give the average class size for the introductory courses taken by freshmen?
◆ Are there mandatory or optional freshman seminars with senior faculty or are seminars reserved only for majors who are juniors and seniors?
◆ If you intend to major in a science, you will want to pay special heed to the size and frequency of laboratory periods: How many instructors supervise the laboratory sessions?
◆ If you see that classes are large, will the professors be available outside of class to answer questions and give guidance?
◆ Are profs required to hold office hours? Do they maintain contact with their students by computer? Are they encouraged by the administration to entertain students informally in their homes?

GETTING ANSWERS

In reading catalogs, surfing through a database, or examining other pieces of printed and visual information provided by colleges, you should keep in mind that such documents have two purposes.

One, they are designed to convey information, and two, they are shaped to give a favorable impression of the institution. Be aware of college image making—and don't depend upon the information or images you see on paper or a computer screen to give you complete information about schools. Ask questions until you feel you've gotten all the answers you need before making final application.

If the catalog does not answer all of your questions, write them down to raise later—during your campus visit, in a letter addressed to the office of admissions, in a talk you might have with an alumnus or present student, or even through e-mail (some schools have set up Internet links for just this purpose).

If you've taken special advanced classes in your particular field of interest, you'll want to know whether a college or university grants credit for advanced placement (AP) courses taken in high school or for courses taken at a local community college. If a college has a progressive policy for AP or college courses, you may be able to amass enough credits to graduate early and save a year's tuition. If you're intending to move through a university at an accelerated pace, you may also want to know if it is possible to take graduate courses at the university while you're still an undergraduate.

On the other hand, the budding physicist who has recently discovered the glories of literature will want to be assured that the physics department will allow him to take a number of courses outside the department, perhaps to double major. Talented athletes will have to look carefully at programs with rigid laboratory and class schedules that may interfere with team practice.

Having established that the college has both sufficient flexibility and opportunity in the department you're most interested in, you should next look at the quality of the education being offered there. Ask the admissions office for a detailed description of the department(s) in which you intend to take a substantial number of your courses. These descriptions are often called *department and program fact sheets* and are useful because they describe offerings in great detail, give the names and areas of interest of the faculty, and often cite statistics about the placement of students in graduate school. Here's a list of questions about the quality of education that you should ask:

The Academic Program

♦ Do the course descriptions in the catalog sound exciting?

♦ Is there a commitment to teaching undergraduates? What is the number of professors compared to number of students in the department? Are seminars available?

♦ Are the facilities adequate? Laboratory equipment, practice rooms, departmental library, computer access to faculty and to sources off campus: these will all make a difference in how well and how fast you will learn.

♦ Is the teaching satisfactory or even better? Ask current students this question, and then find out if there is a *student underground guide* to courses and instructors. This publication, frequently photocopied and sold in the college's bookstore, assesses each course's difficulty and quality, evaluates the books used, summarizes assignments, and appraises the quality of the teaching of the professor and teaching assistants.

Some other ways to evaluate a department:

♦ Pick a topic within your field of interest, such as cellular biology, and then ask a professor in the department of biology about the research opportunities at the school for a student interested in that particular area of biology.

♦ If you're interested in American history, you could scan the index to the *American Historical Review* to see if the names of any of the history faculty at a particular school appear.

♦ Contact someone practicing in your career field of interest, someone perhaps teaching at a local college, and ask for an opinion of the academic departments of the schools you're considering. For instance, if you're a potential business major and you have an aunt who majored in economics in college and is now a personnel manager for a large corporation, ask her what she thinks of the economics departments of College X and University Y.

The Academic Facilities

Library

Viewbooks and catalogs describe an institution's academic facilities. Pay careful attention to the information about a school's library, particularly to the accessibility of the library's collections, its computers, and study areas. What parts of the collection circulate to students? How long can books circulate? Does the library have an ample reserve collection so that high demand volumes are always available to students?

What are the library's hours? This question is very important, for there may be times when the dormitory becomes too noisy for study. Is a certain section of the library open all night, for instance? You should determine the number of seats in the library in relation to the number of students. If there is room for no more than 10 percent of the total student population, then the library will undoubtedly be overcrowded around exam time.

Are there other libraries or study centers on campus that are open to students? Do dormitories have small libraries, or do individual departments allow students to use their books?

Does the library have a good collection of primary sources? History buffs will want to know if the library has the *New York Times* on microfilm and perhaps some other major paper as well—the *Chicago Tribune*, for instance. Musicians will want to know the number of classical music recordings and whether tapes and CDs are available for loan to students.

Computers

All college students will be using the computer in one form or other, and you'll want to determine the number and location of terminals that can be used by students. At many schools computer facilities are more than adequate, and you will not have to purchase equipment of your own. At others computers are included in the tuition. At nearly all colleges and universities, computers and software can be purchased at a substantial discount through the book store.

Laboratories and Studios

If you're interested in science or the arts, you will want to study these facilities carefully. If there are, for example, 50 stations in every introductory chemistry lab or 50 soundproof music practice rooms and over 500 students are enrolled in each department, crowding will invariably result. Limited access to such laboratory and studio space can hamper the vital time for experimentation and practice that are needed in these important areas.

Special equipment

Special instructional equipment, especially that available for use by undergraduates, can make one school stand out over another. Prospective mechanical engineers should be impressed by an engineering department that boasts a giant stress machine. This device will be an asset when they test the models they build in the laboratory. Similarly a practice room for the baroque organ or a series of theatre spaces can give one school a particular advantage.

Once you have completed your survey of a college's facilities, you should record your impressions in a notebook. Eventually you will want to refer to your notes when comparing one college's facilities with those of another.

Extracurricular Activities

Extracurricular activities must be evaluated, too. If you've got a particular talent that you plan to pursue in college, you will want to ask questions about extracurricular activities similar to those asked about academic programs. Quality and access are your key themes.

Interaction with faculty and staff

How much contact is there with coaches or directors? Can you get a sense of the institutional commitment to your particular activity? How much space is allocated to it, how many staff and students, what are the opportunities for competition or involvement with other students and schools? Are there road trips? tournaments?

Facilities

Athletes will want to move beyond the glitzy athletic video and make sure that there are on-campus facilities for their sport. Divers need to know if there is a separate diving pool or if the divers and swimmers share the same one. Ham radio operators will be interested in the wattage of the shortwave radio station's transformer. Clarinetists will want to be sure that the orchestra is large enough to accommodate a few new players every year. Budding actresses and actors will want to read about theater facilities: Is there a practice theater or an experimental theater?

Opportunities for involvement

Is it possible for students interested in a particular activity to perform in the community or to travel to a nearby city to observe professionals in their particular area of interest?

Attending a professional soccer match, or hearing a world class symphony orchestra, or attending an intercollegiate debate are all logical extensions of an individual's interest. Are such opportunities available and encouraged?

If you're considering taking up new extracurricular activities in college you should make sure that there are opportunities and programs open to beginners and that participation is not limited to those with higher levels of skill. If you would not qualify for the varsity tennis team, are there junior varsity and intramural teams that would allow you to continue to enjoy your sport and be challenged by other players?

Students interested in acting might look into other opportunities if they do not get a role in a major production. Are there student-directed plays offered in a smaller theater? Are there such things as dormitory or house plays in which they could participate? In other words, be sure that there are different levels of a given activity so that students of differing abilities can participate.

Campus Life

College is not all books and activities, though. You should give serious thought to the social life and the social climate you'll find on campus.

The student body

What kind of students attend the particular college or university? These are the people you may be living with for four years. It is crucial to discover whether you will be comfortable and happy in their company. In order to focus on the students, their interests, and their personalities, consider the following suggestions:

♦ Read closely what the catalog has to say about dormitories. Are there a variety of living arrangements, both coeducational and single-sex? In particular, is there enough space? How many students are assigned to a room? Do a fair number of students move off campus for some reason, and why? Is it crowding, or expense, or both?
♦ Is there a chance to change roommates if you need to?

♦ What about fraternities and sororities? Are they encouraged or discouraged? What percentage of the students are members? (If more than 50 percent of students join fraternities or sororities, you can assume that these groups are a major force in campus life.)

♦ Does the college have a variety of meal plans and can students experiment with cooperative housing arrangements?

The sense of community

Moving beyond the living conditions on campus, you should try to discern what the social climate of the campus is. How do students treat one another, on the paths in dormitories, in class, at parties? What is the relationship of faculty members to students?

Do faculty and students see a lot of one another or not? Under what conditions, formal or informal? What is the relationship between the college students and the local community? Finally, do the members of this community value their opportunity to share a common experience? Do they treat each other fairly and with mutual respect?

The social life

Try to find out what students do in their free time. Do many of them own cars? If so, do they vacate the campus on weekends? Are there big campus events such as a rites of spring celebration or winter carnival? Do most students participate? If not, who is left out and why? What is the role of athletics on campus? Does football dominate the fall and therefore define the social life of that season?

Develop some sense of the cultural life on campus. Is there a current list of visiting lecturers, concerts, and plays? Are students involved in planning these affairs, or are they the responsibility of a faculty committee? If you attended that particular college, could you be involved in the decision making that shapes campus life?

Photographs in the catalog and viewbook will tell you something about the college's social climate. Do they portray a variety of social activities? Do they show informal student interactions as well as more formal ones, such as dances or excursions? As you look at the photos, study them closely and be discriminating; remember that they have been chosen to show you what the school wants you to see! Do the pictures appear staged or not?

Let me give you an example to illustrate my point: One suburban school in the East recently devoted ten full pages of its catalog to pictures of life on campus, but if you looked closely at the shots, you'd see that they had actually been taken in a nearby city, where another prominent school happens to be located.

These photos give a false impression of the campus and could be misleading to readers who don't know the school at all.

This sort of lack of candor is quite common, as schools attempt to show their best faces in videos and slick brochures. So read catalogs and judge videos and photographs critically. Generalize from both what you see and what you don't see.

Here's another example: A catalog from a small college in upstate New York has only two pictures out of thirty showing snow. This school is not being honest about the weather, since the average snowfall for that region is about 40 inches a year! Students interested in an unfamiliar location should ask questions about its annual rainfall and average temperature, the percentage of sunny days per season, and the presence of any local peculiarities, such as snow or smog or pollen.

It goes without saying that a visit to the schools you're most interested in will give you a much better sense of the campus, the students, and the overall environment than any brochure or video can. (You'll find more about campus visits in Chapter 3.)

THE COST OF COLLEGE

You and your family will surely be interested in the cost of the schools on your list. To calculate college costs accurately you need to know how to compute the total cost to the family—not just rely on the fees stated in the catalog. There are often extra or "hidden" costs, such as:

♦ Transportation to and from the college; this will obviously vary from student to student.
♦ Student activity fees may not be added in tuition costs.
♦ Athletic facility fees are sometimes separate. So are lab fees and music lessons.
♦ Deposits for rooms and labs. When are they credited to the student's account—in the first semester, or possibly the last?
♦ There may be other fees as well. Does one incur penalties for living off campus or for not taking a full course load? Are there charges for exceeding a course load limit and graduating early? What are the charges for having an automobile and parking it on university property?

Add all these together and you have the actual cost of attendance that you and your family will have to pay.

With respect to the actual, stated charges, it is important to find out what the school's plans are for raising student charges over the next four years. Is there an institutional commitment to price moderation?

Questions about Financial Aid

If you're counting on getting financial aid you will need to develop a list of additional questions to ask of each school you're considering. (To get a more complete understanding of the difference between loans and grants and how schools award financial aid to applicants, see Chapter 7.) You'll want to know:

♦ How much grant aid is actually available from the college, in dollars and as a percent of the total aid given to students?

♦ What is the average grant per student?

♦ What is the ratio of college grant aid to government and college loans in the average financial aid award?

♦ What is the availability of need- and merit-based aid? Need-based aid means the funds that would be available to meet your particular financial need, which is determined by an established formula described in Chapter 7. Merit-based aid refers to aid above and beyond your actual need. Merit scholarships are often given to students who have special academic or personal qualities that the college or university wants to have on campus.

♦ Merit scholarship aid will be of particular interest to you if you and your family do not qualify for need-based aid.

♦ You need to ask the financial aid office about its outside scholarship policy. If you win a scholarship from the local chapter of the Knights of Columbus, will the college make you substitute it for other grant monies you might have received or reduce your loans? Some parents will want to know about parent loan programs and the availability of long-term financing and be pleased to learn that most colleges have very specific literature on all these topics and that there are a number financing options available to them (again, see Chapter 7 for more detail).

SCHOOL SIZE

Just like deciding on a pair of shoes or a coat, look for a good fit. When shopping around for a college, start out with an open mind, and don't fall prey to any of the several myths concerning school size:

Myth #1: Large schools are more diverse than smaller ones.
This is also not necessarily so. Some large schools see their mission as serving a particular region of the country or type of student. Others are genuinely committed to finding a very diverse student body.

Myth #2: Small schools have the advantage when it comes to forming close and varied social relationships.
This is also not necessarily so. Some large schools nurture the same degree of closeness among their students.

Myth # 3: The smaller the school, the greater the access students have to professors.
Candidates often believe that large schools encourage students to work on their own and leave professors to their own research, while at small schools professors are obliged to have an open-door policy. This is not always true.

Myth # 4: The smaller the school, the greater the access students have to classes and extracurricular activities.
Don't assume that attending a large school means that access to classes and extracurricular activities will be more difficult than attending a smaller college. Intramural sports, for instance, may be supported more vigorously at a large school than at a small one. Large schools may have seminar programs featuring major professors, just as the smaller colleges do.

If you set aside such preconceptions about school size, you can more realistically determine the real and varying impact of size as it relates to your own needs. Read catalogs carefully, talk to students and professors, and keep your eyes and ears open! You may well find that there are several different types of schools—large, mid-sized, or small—that would suit you well.

ADMISSIONS DIFFICULTY

The final criterion to consider is difficulty of admission to the colleges or universities you've chosen. Most college reference books have a paragraph and some statistics about their admissions requirements. They will tell you something about Scholastic Assessment Test (SAT) or American College Testing (ACT) Program scores for the entering class, in words something like this: "Of those admitted, 60 percent had an SAT verbal score above 560." Begin with these statistics; then ask your guidance counselor to react to them and to assess the likelihood of your being accepted.

Your counselor may have a third source of information: the Class Profile that most colleges produce for secondary schools. Profiles give mean SAT I and SAT II results (see Chapter 4 for more about tests) for the entering class; they also show the relationship of class rank to admission. In addition, geographical distribution, minority enrollment, and yield statistics (percentage of students who accept the college's offer of admission) are reported.

Beyond what these statistics relate, you will want to find out from your counselor or from the college (in your interview or group information session) something about the admissions process itself:

♦ how folders (or student files) are read and evaluated
♦ the role of the interview
♦ the number of students admitted compared to the total number of applications
♦ the median financial aid package and whether or not the admissions decision is related to the level of the student's financial need

Not Just Numbers
The difficulty factor for you is determined by how closely your qualifications line up with the admissions standards of the college. The wider the difference, the harder it will be for you to gain admission.

Keep in mind, however, that the difficulty factor at the most selective colleges goes beyond mere numerical comparisons between your profile and that of the college. Because the selective colleges have so many applicants, their perceptive admissions staffs apply a variety of nonnumerical criteria to each candidate.

Admissions officers at the selective schools are very interested, for instance, in personal qualities such as character and leadership potential. They frequently move beyond test results and grades to look for individual creativity in the arts, or special contributions students may have made to their communities, or to research in a particular field.

Because the few highly selective colleges are deluged with applications from outstanding candidates, the summary figures for SAT and

ACT scores, class rank, and the like will be impressive and daunting. However, the selection process is more complex than just looking at the numbers.

YOUR PERSONAL STRATEGY OF SELECTIVE APPLICATIONS

After reading the catalogs, visiting the colleges that look most interesting, and talking to a member of the admissions staff, students at the college, parents, guidance counselors, and friends, you come face to face with the task of selecting the schools you will ultimately apply to. How many will there be? And which ones?

Before you answer these questions, consider the *strategy of selective applications.*

Since it is highly probable that you will not gain admission to all the colleges to which you apply, you should select a range of colleges that will guarantee you a choice of acceptances. You can assume that the easier the admissions standards of your selected schools, the more schools you'll be accepted at. The tougher the schools, the fewer acceptances you can expect. Remember, too, that for many students, acceptance doesn't just mean being admitted to a school; it means being admitted to a school and being granted an adequate financial aid package. In following the strategy of selective application, remember there are limits. It would be folly, for instance, for you to apply to one "safe" school and a parcel of very difficult ones.

This may very well leave you with only one choice in the end: the safe school. Rather, you should try to gain admission to at least three of the five schools you choose—a 60 percent acceptance rate. If this happens, you'll have genuine choices in April of your senior year. You will feel much better about attending the college you eventually select than perhaps one you're forced to choose because you have no other options.

Establishing an order of preference for your college applications is a bit like playing the game of diplomacy. The diplomat makes a list stating what his government most wants to extract from negotiations with a foreign power; then he makes three or four more lists stating what he would accept if his first proposals were to meet with resistance. These additional demands are arranged in order of preference, from most preferred to least preferred. By arranging the colleges you have selected from your first through fifth choices, you, like the diplomat, will then know your preferences in advance.

Rate the Schools on Your List

First, focus on the admissions criteria for each of your colleges. Develop a rating scale of one to five. Number one should be the "toughest" school; number five, the "easiest." In determining this rating, you will want to consider the SAT and ACT scores of candidates accepted in the previous year (the big college directories include such information in each school's profile), your class rank, the difficulty of the program you have pursued in high school, and, finally, the types of students from your school who have been selected by the college in the past. At this point it might be helpful to write a brief admissions profile of yourself:

Your Admissions Profile

Academic: SAT I Reasoning Test—math 590, verbal 640; SAT II Subject Tests: Writing 620, Math II 700, American History 640; Grades in high school: B average (3.6); top 15 percent of high school class in a highly rated suburban school. National Merit Semifinalist, National Honor Society. Want to major in history in college and become a lawyer.

Extracurricular: Goalie for boys' varsity soccer team, Life Scout, camp counselor for three summers, construction worker for one summer, play the trumpet well in school band, and won a regional talent show last year. Do some acting and like it, want to continue in college. Also write music and drama reviews for school's newspaper.

Personal: Liked and admired by friends; enjoy being with people and managing them; also value family, personal honesty, and hard work (according to the values clarification exercise discussed in Chapter 4). While not always a leader, I am conscientious and well-organized in everything that I do. People turn to me for advice and ask me to take charge.

Now write the colleges that you are interested in along the left-hand margin of a piece of paper, arranging them in descending order of difficulty of admission. List your criteria across the top, as in the sample chart on the next page: Academic Program, Location, Size, Extracurricular Activities, Cost, Level of Difficulty, and Total.

In the first column rate the quality of the academic program of each college on a scale from 1 to 5, with 1 standing for the strongest and 5 for the weakest. Do the same for the attractiveness of the location and the size of the school. If a school is attractive in all respects except that its size is too large for you, then it must receive a size rating of 4 or 5.

The extracurricular category refers to the availability of activities that you will want to become involved in at college.

For instance, if you are a moderately good field hockey player, and the college's team had a fair season last year and will probably be looking for players, then the college gets the highest rating of 1.

Cost comes next. Remember to figure in the average financial aid award or discount. The cheapest school gets a 1, the most expensive a 5. (There is a chart explaining how to analyze your financial aid offer and arrive at the true cost of attending a school in Chapter 7.) The last on the list is the level of difficulty of admission, the D-factor. Your toughest school gets a 1, your easiest a 5. Then total each college's ratings.

Reducing Your List to Five

You are now ready to make distinctions among the colleges and reduce your list to five choices. Already you know that Hanover is going to be your toughest school to get into. Last year the students who were accepted from your school had scores in the high 600s and were in the top 10 percent of their class, except for the varsity basketball center, who was accepted from the waiting list. Even so, you may be able to impress Hanover with your talent as a musician, with your solid record in tough courses, and with your wide involvement in school life.

Although Gold Coast's profile is much like Hanover's, its curriculum is somewhat weaker in the social sciences, according to an alumnus who has just come to work in your father's office.

Gold Coast was the most beautiful school you saw last summer, but it is also a little on the small side, and you are looking mostly at larger colleges and universities. Moreover, Gold Coast is rated 5 on cost; it does not offer very much financial aid, and your family will probably qualify for aid when your sister enters college in two years. Besides, Gold Coast has a higher overall score than Hanover, and a low score wins. Hanover is your number one choice.

School	Academic Program	Loca- tion	Size	Extra- curricular Activities	Cost	Level of Difficulty	Total
Hanover	1	2	3	2	4	1	13
Gold Coast	2	1	4	2	5	1	15
Central U.	1	1	2	1	3	2	10
Sunbelt U.	3	2	4	4	2	2	17
Midwestern U.	2	2	2	3	3	3	15
Gateway	2	4	1	2	3	4	16
Atheneum	2	3	1	3	3	4	16
State U.	2	4	4	3	1	5	19
Small College	3	5	4	2	2	5	21

From the schools you have ranked at the second degree of difficulty you choose Central University. It has a total score of 10, whereas Sunbelt University, the other school in this category, has a high score of 17. Central, you will have noted, has the lowest score overall, but it is not your first choice. It should be first according to the rating system, but you have always dreamed of applying to Hanover since you were quite young.

No rating system can adequately express your fervor for Hanover, so it will remain your number one choice!

If you don't make Hanover, and the chances are pretty good that you won't, the rating system tells you that Central University is just as good as Hanover, except for that intangible emotional factor. In addition, your high school has a particularly good relationship with Central, since alumni from your school have done well there. There is no doubt that Central should be your second choice. Its curriculum allows you to construct an area studies major, which is what you want to do; if you pursue international law, you would be able to focus on one particular area of the world, such as Africa or Asia.

Initially you liked Sunbelt University, even though it is somewhat small and does not have any special programs for history majors. Although it is easier to get into than Hanover, your enthusiasm for Sunbelt pales now in the light of the ratings you have given Central. You have also learned that Sunbelt's admissions standards are rising due to an intensive public relations campaign that resulted in a high volume of applications this year. So Sunbelt should be scratched as a number two choice.

Midwestern's case speaks for itself. Although not in the best location, it is an ideal size—around 4,000 students—and its history department is good, surely better than Sunbelt's. Furthermore your scores, grades, and the other elements of your profile definitely put you in the group that Midwestern will accept. Your counselor says: "If you keep your work up to your past standards, you ought to make it." You decide to apply.

Although Atheneum has as many points as Gateway, your father graduated from Gateway in 1970. This fact will greatly enhance your admission chances at Gateway, as will your high school record and SAT scores. Even if your grades decline slightly as you shoulder the increased responsibilities of senior year, you still ought to make Gateway. You have no alumni ties to Atheneum, and you might have a little trouble getting in there. So Gateway clearly becomes your number 4 choice.

As your backup, or safety choice, you select your state university, rather than pick Small College, which is located in a picturesque Midwestern town and that may be in need of students next April. State University is very near home, but your parents have said they would pay for your room and board on campus. So you will be able to live independently at the school. Moreover, close scrutiny of State's catalog reveals that its history department has quite a variety of courses, as well as internships in government offices. You also decide to apply to State because you feel you would receive more of a challenge in a school of its size (5,000 students) than in a smaller liberal arts college in a rural setting. Finally, State University is cheaper by far than your other choices! It therefore meets the standard test of a safety choice: "If all else fails, it is a place where I would be willing to go and do my best."

Apply strategically so you'll have a real choice

Submitting your applications at these schools that you have selected strategically gives you peace of mind. Because they are all within the range of your abilities, you are almost assured of at least three admissions. Consequently you will have a genuine choice among them to make at decision time in April. With the confidence this gives you, you will be able to focus most of your attention on gaining admission to your first and second choices.

You are maneuvering yourself into a position to say to your first- and second-choice schools: "Look, you are one of my two top choices. I am not shopping around; I really want to come." Students often underestimate how much their desire to attend a school can persuade a college to favor them with an offer of admission. When many students have credentials that look alike, the desire of a particular student to come to the college can make a real difference in the minds of the Admissions Committee. After all, if you look at it from the college's point of view you see that they are interested in students who will turn up in September and register as freshmen.

Good candidates who are willing and able to pay for college are harder to find. Colleges also have to compete for students for economic reasons. As the price of college rises some students who in less costly days would have applied to private colleges and universities are now limiting their choices to the cheaper public colleges. The result is that the private colleges and universities have improved their programs, have often increased their financial aid, and have intensified their recruiting efforts.

This "buyer's market" can work to your advantage. If you have one particular school that interests you, be sure to let that school know. Sometimes there are application plans that enable you to do this in a formal way. Let us discuss a few of them.

EARLY DECISION

If you've done all your college research and there is one school in particular where you would really like to be—and you consider yourself a strong candidate for the school—you may be able to apply to it through an early admission plan. Not all colleges and universities have early plans, but many do. Under the simplest and most well-known early program, the Early Decision Plan, students submit their credentials early, usually by November 1 of the senior year, and sign a statement that they will accept the college's offer of admission if tendered. Students then receive word of their status by December 15. If a student is denied early admission, in most cases the colleges will defer final action on their application until March when all regular applications are decided upon.

Early Decision applicants, as a rule, are very qualified students with strong test scores and high grades. The competition for Early Decision is often greater than that for regular admission; if your record is not as strong as the college's profile, don't apply for Early Decision. Rather, focus on improving your record for later application.

Note: *Students applying for Early Decision must be willing to accept the college's financial aid offer, which will be based on the family's financial records for the previous year. (The award is later adjusted for the current year.)*

EARLY ACTION

Some universities have adopted a one-sided version of Early Decision that they call Early Action (originally offered only by Brown, Georgetown, Harvard, and Massachusetts Institute of Technology; Yale returned to Early Decision in 1995-96, after many years as an Early Action school; Princeton is following suit). Under this plan a student need not accept the college's offer of admission but may apply to other schools as well under the deadlines for regular application. Students considering Early Action must bear in mind several important features of this plan:

- ◆ Early Action is very discriminating. If your record is not superior in every way, you should devote your energies to strengthening it and applying at the regular time instead.
- ◆ You can be rejected under Early Action. And many of the students who are rejected under Early Action are ultimately rejected under regular decision in April.
- ◆ No financial aid awards accompany acceptance under Early Action. Awards are adjusted when year-end figures are submitted to the college in February, after the student has been accepted.
- ◆ Candidates who really want to attend a particular school should not regard Early Action as the way to express their interest, because the Early Action schools are so competitive that the candidate's sincere interest in attending is not that important to them.

ROLLING ADMISSIONS

Rolling Admissions bears some resemblance to Early Action, only its calendar is different. This program, offered by many state universities and other schools, allows candidates to submit applications at their convenience up to a certain date, often January 1 or sooner. Students then receive a letter of acceptance or rejection within four weeks of filing their application. Because many rolling admissions schools do not require a deposit until April or May, many ambitious candidates use rolling admissions to gain early acceptance at a school they regard as a backup choice and then concentrate on their top one or two choices for regular admissions. Whatever the motive, students should pay careful attention to published deadlines.

Some caveats about rolling admissions:

- Some institutions use rolling admissions to fill their entire classes, so file your application early in order to gain a place in the freshman class.
- Students using a rolling program for their backup school cannot afford to ignore other deadlines at the institution, such as the deadline for filing financial aid applications and, if accepted, a housing deposit.

LETTING A SCHOOL KNOW THEY'RE #1

If you are not sure which school is your top choice, don't feel pressured to apply early to any of them. If, however, you have made a decision on your first-choice college later, after you've applied, you can write a letter to the dean of admissions of that school in February and indicate your preference. A brief, simple letter is fine (see sample):

---

34 Webster Street
Westchester, New York 10783

Mr. Charles A. Smith
Director of Admissions
Coburn College
Hawthorne, New York 13321

Dear Mr. Smith:

Ever since I first heard about Coburn two years ago while working with an undergraduate who was a fellow camp counselor, I have wanted to come to the school. Recently I completed a thorough investigation of a number of colleges, and I still favor Coburn over the others. The special program for engineering students, the nationally recognized swimming team, and the opportunities for continuing my interests in drama and music all particularly appeal to me.

I just wanted you to know at this point, when you are considering my application, that I really do want to be accepted. If I am, I will definitely come. I know I have much to learn, but I think I have something to contribute, too.

Yours sincerely,

Martha A. Prentice

BE WARY OF THE SHOTGUN APPROACH

Every year there are a number of students who choose to respond to the inconsistencies of the college admissions process by filing a large number of applications in hopes of receiving multiple admissions through sheer luck. This is called the "shotgun approach." What these students do not realize is that in applying to a number of schools with difficult and very similar admissions standards, they may be maximizing their rate of rejection, rather than increasing their odds of acceptance. When you stop and think, schools that are equally difficult to get into will react similarly to candidates whose credentials do not come up to the mark: they will reject them.

Moreover, if you file many applications, you will not have sufficient time to develop an approach tailored to the requirements and the style of each school, to research the colleges sufficiently, and to determine how they might fit your particular academic or extracurricular goals. There's a good chance that any tactical error you make, such as a weak personal essay, will be repeated on all applications because you will probably be submitting the same application everywhere. The risk of rejection increases rather than decreases.

So give yourself the chance to match yourself with the colleges to which you are applying. Consider just what their special merits are and try to develop an edge over other candidates in your category. (The concepts *match* and *edge* are discussed in Chapter 5.)

Filing numerous applications also puts you in the position of not being able to signal your first choice. Because you devote equal and insufficient energy to all your schools, you're not able to focus on the one school you really want to attend. You may wind up with no choice at all!

My advice? Select five or six colleges across a range of difficulty, and stay with them!

MAXIMIZING YOUR ODDS FOR A QUALITY EDUCATION

By the time you come to the end of the selection process, having figured out which colleges you intend to apply to, you also may have come to the realization that the distinctions among the colleges are not that significant and that you could be happy at a number of them. That's a reasonable and proper outcome. By educating yourself about the schools on your list, you have made a number of slight distinctions based on academic program, cost, size, location, and the like; you've evaluated the colleges, physically and philosophically. You have a pretty good idea of what life at each school is like. You have developed a list of schools, all of which are similar and appropriate for you.

When you receive your acceptances and decide which one of the schools you will attend, you will do so with the knowledge that this college or university is the place where you are going to carry out the most important responsibility you have right now: educating yourself. The college will provide the environment in which learning will happen, but you will take the responsibility for making it happen. Jean-Jacques Rousseau once remarked that "It is not the difference in the quality that matters, but the quality of the difference."

You are going to be making that difference during the next four years. Whatever catalogs promise, whatever college ratings say, whatever pictures the guidebooks paint, whatever judgments guidance counselors pronounce, you have the final say about whether your experience will be a productive and successful one. If you have approached your selection of colleges rationally and also relied on your instincts to make judgments about them, then you can be assured you are making sound decisions in selecting the schools to which you will apply.

So relax and be confident about yourself and the process you have followed. The chances that you have selected the right schools are very high.

THREE

Visiting a College

"College visits don't have to be a disaster, but they sometimes are, because people don't think enough about them in advance."

Patricia B. Gildersleeve, College Advisory Service, New Hartford, New York

LAURA RICHARDS' VISIT

Laura Richards did not have any difficulty remembering her first college visit. Just before her graduation from college, four years later, she recalled that hot August day when she and her mother had just turned off the Interstate and began looking at the map in earnest: "We had 18 miles to go to Coburn and we knew that if we didn't lose our way, we might be on time for my 4 p.m. interview."

"I tried to remember what I had read in the college guidebooks, but the stats for Coburn just blurred together with the other small liberal arts colleges I was considering. Plus the fact that when I did remember a fact or two about Coburn, they got tangled up in the route numbers my Mom and I were supposed to be looking for. Then there was my Mom herself. She was starting to panic, because she had not asked for specific enough directions when she called and made my appointment two weeks before.

"Then I began to panic because I realized that I had not taken the time to pick up a copy of my high school transcript, which I thought might assist my interviewer in seeing what I had done in high school.) I had a pretty good record to show, too.) Nor had I talked to a couple of Coburn alumni who lived in my neighborhood. I felt totally unprepared!

"Well, obviously, we got there, and I took over; I headed directly for the receptionist, announced myself, and Mother brought up the rear. However, a few minutes later, when the admission officer came out to greet me, my mother was right there and I wasn't; I was in the ladies' room touching up my makeup. When I emerged, I noticed that my interviewer was dressed casually, and here I was, decked out in a voluminous print dress and high heels. I wish I had thought to wear more comfortable and appropriate clothes.

"We next had to deal with what my mother would do during the interview, and finally my interviewer and I were able to move to his office for a *brief* chat about my interest in Coburn!"

MARTHA PRENTICE'S VISIT

Martha Prentice went to the same high school as Laura Richards and also visited Coburn. But her experience was quite different. "I phoned the admission office and said I was finishing my job as a waitress on the 20th of August and that anytime between the 25th and the 29th of August would be convenient for me," she related. "I asked for the last morning tour and inquired as to whether I could have lunch with some students who were working as interns in the admission office."

"And since I was reasonably sure that I wanted to enter the engineering field, I asked to speak with one of the engineering profs after lunch, and they found one for me! Then I scheduled myself for an interview after that. By the time I got to the interview, I really knew the school and knew what to ask."

LAURA

If Laura Richards had made a few notes and made a similar phone call—and not allowed her mother to do it—she might have spent a more productive August day on the Coburn campus. Instead of arriving at the interview harried and short on information about Coburn, Laura would have had ample time to make a preliminary survey of the college. She would have read the catalog from cover to cover. She would have gleaned the campus newspaper to get a feeling for the main issues on campus. She would have learned from current Coburn students what they thought about the quality of undergraduate life there.

Preparing for Your Campus Visit

Laura's hurried and poorly planned visit to Coburn gives us many clues about what not to do when arranging a campus visit. Here are some things that will make your visit more successful than Laura's:

1. Make sure that you—not your mother or father—contact the school yourself, and ask for directions if necessary.

2. Request and read the catalog and schedule a tour of the campus before going in for an interview.

3. Ask for any special materials that may be pertinent to your interests, such as a list of off-campus internships or college-sponsored music groups. Also ask for a copy of the campus newspaper; it will acquaint you with important issues on campus.

4. Get the names of current undergraduates who live near your home. Call them before your visit to ask them to talk to you about the school: the academic challenges there, the social climate of the campus, the rapport they have with their professors are all good topics to discuss. You'll probably come up with others.

5. Ask for the names of faculty members in your field of interest. Try to make an appointment to see one of them when you are on campus. Most admission offices will be happy to set up a meeting with a faculty member for you; you may even be able to sit in on a class.

And from her conversation with a professor in her field of interest she would have been able to make some assessment of her ability to handle the curriculum at Coburn. Despite her poor planning, her story ended happily: she was accepted at Coburn.

MARTHA

But it was Martha Prentice who got more out of her experience. The admission office told her that a Coburn sophomore named Sarah Chapman lived near her home in Westchester. When she got home, Martha telephoned Sarah at school and had a long talk with her about Coburn. Martha and Sarah liked each other immediately. They found that they had several friends in common and that they were both interested in the sciences.

Sarah was majoring in Coburn's special program in animal behavior and liked the science department. She had played field hockey at her high school and was a member of Coburn's field hockey team. Martha also played field hockey, as well as basketball, and she wanted to find out about women's sports at Coburn. Since Coburn had been coeducational for only ten years, Martha did not believe all the claims the college made in its special pamphlet on women's sports at Coburn.

In the course of their hour-long conversation, Martha was able to get interesting answers to most of her questions. Here's what she asked Sarah:

- What attracted you especially to Coburn? Has it lived up to your expectations? What has surprised you about the school? What has disappointed you?
- Do you know any women who are majoring in engineering? What do they say about the program?
- Have you gotten solid academic and career advice at Coburn? How frequently do you see your faculty adviser? Can you change advisers easily if you need to? Have your teachers and adviser suggested courses and research topics that have helped you proceed toward your graduate work in veterinary school?
- Tell me about life in the dormitories. I know there are all sorts of living arrangements—single-sex, coeducational, the communal kitchen idea—as well as a few off-campus apartments, but what I really want to know is how you like where you live.
- In the same vein, do students seem to care genuinely about one another? Is the social life relaxed yet interesting, or do you feel pressured into going to the football games on Saturday afternoons? What about your other female friends—how do they feel about the climate for women? And the men? Have you met some nice ones?
- Can we talk about sports for a minute? Frankly, I don't believe all that I read in the Coburn catalog about "individualized instruction, spacious and well-equipped facilities," and the "enthusiasm of fellow participants." What has been your experience with the field hockey team at Coburn? Has it been relegated to second place because of Coburn's

prominence in football, a male sport? Can you tell me about the field hockey conference? Does the team play a rigorous schedule? Does it compete in any regional tournaments? Could you tell me about the actual facilities for women—the locker rooms, uniforms, and equipment? Are there female coaches for most of the women's sports?

♦ Finally, since I know I will only be able to play one varsity sport at Coburn and I am interested in both basketball and field hockey, what is your opinion of these two teams and their coaches? Do people enjoy playing these sports on the intramural level as well?

Before Martha knew it, an hour had flown by, and Sarah had to go back to her job as a lab technician for a local veterinarian—a job her zoology instructor had helped her find. This impressed Martha, as did Sarah's enthusiastic answers to most of her questions. Martha looked forward to visiting Coburn and asking some of the same questions of the other Coburn students she'd be having lunch with.

After her talk with Sarah, Martha thought about some questions she wanted to ask the engineering professor she'd be meeting with. She was impressed with the engineering offerings at Coburn. There were only 3,000 students on the campus, yet the engineering department offered four degree options: a Bachelor of Science in Chemical, Civil, Electrical, or Mechanical Engineering; a Bachelor of Science in Engineering (which is a much more general degree program that allowed interdisciplinary work); a five-year program that awarded a Bachelor of Arts or Bachelor of Science in the liberal arts and engineering; and an integrated bachelor's and master's program that led to two degrees at the end of five years. Martha's mental list of questions came together along the following lines:

♦ **The Future.** What advice would you offer someone entering the engineering field today? What specific areas of engineering appear to be crowded? What areas appear to need students? From my own reading I would judge that aerospace is overcrowded and environmental engineering is underpopulated. What would you say?

♦ **Flexibility of Program.** I know that I will enjoy the basic engineering courses in civil and mechanical engineering and the like, but I also want broad liberal arts training. I know I want to study some economics and accounting so that I would be qualified to enter the management field if my engineering specialty ever became outmoded. Given these interests, which one of the four degree programs would you suggest I follow?

- **Faculty Presence.** The Coburn catalog says that the ratio of students to teachers is ten to one; that figure only means something to me when translated into class size. In the engineering department, roughly what percentage of the classes have ten students or fewer? What percentage have a hundred or more? How many instructors does the student have access to in a given lab period? Are there opportunities for individualized tutorial instruction for undergraduates?
- **Faculty Quality.** Could you tell me a little about the engineering faculty? What are some of the honors recently won by members of the department? I assume that many of them do private research. Is student research ever integrated into a professor's own area of specialization?
- **Facilities.** Do you feel that the engineering facilities at Coburn are adequate for training undergraduate engineers? (If the facilities are deficient in one particular area, what special arrangements, if any, have been made for students who are interested in that sector of the engineering field?)
- **Undergraduate Life.** What is your feeling about the undergraduates here at Coburn? Do the faculty and students mix on an informal social basis? Do you enjoy this interaction with students yourself? Do the students appear pleased with the education they are receiving? Is there a tendency for students to conform to the views of their professors or to express their divergent opinions?

When Martha arrived home, she jotted these questions down (leaving room to note their answers after her visit) and placed them in the manila folder she had designated for Coburn. Martha filed these questions away in her Coburn folder. She knew that she would not have time to ask them all. She also thought to herself: "If I don't get answers to all of these, Coburn could still be the right school for me. There are lots of elements of choosing a college, after all." When it came time for her visit, Martha and her mother left early in the morning, with an hour's margin built into their schedule just to be on the safe side. Martha dressed neatly yet casually in clothes that made her feel comfortable rather than formal. When they arrived on the campus at 10:15 a.m., they found they had time to go to the cafeteria for a cup of coffee before Martha went off on the campus tour at 10:45 a.m.

Visiting with Parents

During Martha's interview her mother had arranged to have lunch with a friend who lived nearby. She rejoined Martha at the admission office when the interview was over. However she did take the afternoon tour to have her own look at the school. She also spent some time in the school's art studio since she was a commercial artist by training. Her mother's plans left Martha free to operate on her own. In a conversation with her parents at the beginning of the summer Martha had explained that she wanted to handle her college exploration herself. Her parents had agreed. Not only would it be a learning experience for Martha, but her parents also understood that colleges take their direct relationship with applicants seriously and are inclined to look with disfavor on parents who appear to interfere in the admission process.

Martha and her parents had agreed that one parent would show up at the end of an interview to demonstrate the family's interest in helping her make the right decision about college. At that point, her mother or father could ask questions of the admission officer and answer any questions the officer might have for them.

Martha's Tour

Martha had already drafted her questions for her student tour guide, and she raised those questions during the hour-and-a-half tour and the luncheon with other students that followed. These questions centered on student life and access to facilities. Martha asked about the work load, the teaching, the relationships among students. She also queried the tour guide about the library's hours, the facility of the campuswide computer network, and the attitude toward female athletes. After lunch and her interview, she met with an engineering professor.

Martha also inspected the gym carefully. Having learned from Sarah Chapman of improvements in the women's locker rooms, Martha wanted to see them herself. She asked about the gym's hours. Would she and her friends be able to play an informal game of basketball some evening in the winter? She examined the new $4-million field house, which had eight handball and racquetball courts, four squash courts, a 200-meter running track, wrestling and weight rooms, a dance studio, trainers' suites, and men's and women's locker rooms.

Naturally Martha visited a dormitory to see a student room and check out the living conditions. If she should decide to live in a coeducational dorm, would she be happy with the existing bathroom and shower facilities for men and women? Would there be sufficient privacy? Were there rooms or spaces in dormitories where students who want to study can separate themselves from those who don't?

She also asked about interdormitory athletic competitions and social affairs, about the faculty and graduate student resident adviser program in the dormitories, and about the relationship between Coburn and the residents of the nearby town of Hawthorne. (What specific activities bring students and townspeople together? Are there areas of tension? If so, what is being done to alleviate them?)

Finally, Martha looked carefully at Coburn's theater. She had been interested in acting for quite a while but had never pursued it. Now she wanted to try her hand at it in college. As the tour group moved through the theater, Martha was impressed by both the main hall for major productions and the so-called "black box" for advanced and experimental student and faculty productions. However, Martha was most interested in the small theater downstairs where informal plays and musicals were put on under student or faculty direction. This was one of the facilities that would eventually induce her to apply to Coburn.

THE INTERVIEW THAT WASN'T—LAURA'S

Looking back on the event four years later, Laura Richards laughed about her visit and interview at Coburn: "I emerged from the ladies' room that hot August afternoon and saw a man speaking to my mother in the waiting room. He introduced himself as David Walenski, assistant director of admission. I was somewhat flustered, because he was so young and good looking. If I had arrived earlier, I could have taken a look around the admission office and recognized the fact that many of the people who worked there were not too many years older than I."

"I made the best of it, blushing as he shook my still-damp hand. My mother, who had no real idea of what to do during my interview, asked how she would spend the next half hour. Mr. Walenski took her to a nearby window and pointed out the various buildings on campus she might find worthy of inspection. Five minutes went by; five minutes of his time that could have been put to better use in my interview! As I recall, the interview that followed went something like this":

> *Walenski*: Well, I realize that you have not had a chance to look around the campus, but you must have seen the brochure we sent you. What questions do you have about Coburn?
>
> *Laura*: You're right. I have not had much time to look over the school, but I am interested in engineering and I wondered what programs you have.

Walenski: In engineering we have four programs: the Bachelor of Science in one of the engineering fields—Chemical, Civil, Electrical, or Mechanical. Then we have the Bachelor of Science in Engineering degree, which allows the student to plan his or her own unique program in engineering and to set up an interdisciplinary course of study if he or she so desires. We also have a five-year program in the liberal arts and engineering that leads to a combined Bachelor of Arts and Bachelor of Science degree. Finally we have the integrated bachelor's and master's program for professional students in engineering. These students can begin graduate study in their third year at Coburn and emerge after five years with two degrees in engineering.

Laura: Oh, that's very interesting. I think I would probably be wanting to follow the Bachelor of Science in Engineering program. I do know that I want to take some liberal arts courses, but I am not sure which ones.

Walenski: Well, there are lots of different ways to approach that degree program. You might be interested, for instance, in our winter-term program, which would enable you to pursue during the January term a humanities or social sciences topic that interested you. This is sometimes called the 4-1-4 setup, which you are probably familiar with. On the other hand, if a particular project in engineering happened to attract your attention, you might also want to pursue it in depth during one of your January semesters at Coburn.

Laura: Are there any other special programs like the January one?

Walenski: Yes, we have an off-campus study program in London and other programs in France and in Washington. My college roommate, for instance, was interested in environmental engineering, and he spent the spring semester of his junior year working for a congressional committee that was looking at the illegal disposal of chemical wastes. May I ask what led to your interest in engineering and what kind of preparation you have had in high school?

Laura: Well, I have always done pretty well in math. I got a B+ in the advanced algebra course in my high school, but I have not yet taken calculus. I may take it next year, if I am not able to enroll in a current events course that a lot of seniors take.

Walenski: May I suggest that you do take calculus, because you will need it in engineering. If you do very well, you could perhaps take the Advanced Placement test at the end of your senior year. Then if you qualify you would be able to opt out of the required freshman calculus course for engineers at Coburn.

Laura: Oh, then I may very well do that. Thanks.

Walenski: Have you had any courses in physics or chemistry? Our catalog says that you should have one of each, but I will be honest with you and say that if you have had two semesters of either physics or chemistry and perhaps a little biology, this will strengthen your candidacy for the Engineering Division. The professors who read the files of the engineering candidates like to see a good deal of science in the record.

Laura: Yes, I have had a semester each of physics and chemistry, but I was not planning to go on with either one because of some other courses I wanted to take that, frankly, would make my record look a little stronger than it would if I completed the physics and chemistry sequence.

Walenski: I would suggest that you consider going on with your physics and chemistry sequence this fall. After all, the colleges will only see your work for the fall semester, and if you take the one you feel most competent in during the fall, either physics or chemistry, then your record will not suffer all that much.

Laura: I appreciate that advice. Can you tell me something about the social life on campus? Are there sororities and fraternities?

Walenski: Yes, there are. The catalog says we have twelve national fraternities and seven national sororities, but actually we have even more because some of the fraternities and sororities are local. They exist only at Coburn. As you may know, the college administration took over the fraternity houses for use as dormitories in the late 1960s, so the frats all have offices in the activities building. Many of their social events actually occur in the activities building, although some fraternities have private houses or weekend retreats off campus where their members can congregate.

Laura: What about students who are not in fraternities or sororities? What do they do for amusement?

Walenski: There are all kinds of clubs on campus, from coin-collecting organizations to beer-drinking societies. When I was here I was very active in the backgammon club and we went on several road trips every year and played a twenty-five-match schedule. In addition, lots of the dormitories organize activities on their own during the weekends. In the winter there is an interdormitory competition called the Ice Sculpture Contest, and in the spring most of the dorms enter a raft in the May Day Raft Race on the Onagonda River. I am leaving out the whole intramural sports program, which is another important aspect of student life at Coburn.

Laura: Please tell me a little about the sports program. I like to play basketball and field hockey. Would there be a chance for me to do that here?

Walenski: Yes, indeed. The girls' field hockey team, or should I say women's field hockey team, plays a rigorous thirteen-game schedule in the fall and participates in two tournaments in November. Basketball offers a similar program of games with six neighboring schools in our league, but I would have serious doubts that you could carry on both sports as a freshman at Coburn, especially if you are thinking about engineering. The requirements for labs and review sessions around exam time would make it tough for you to attend all the daily practices. In a varsity sport, as you know, you have to be there every day. Perhaps you would be able to play field hockey in the fall and then play intramural basketball during the winter term.

What other extracurricular activities are you interested in? How about political affairs? Did the list of speakers in the Cooperstein Lecture Series intrigue you at all? It is posted on the bulletin board right outside the admission office.

Laura: I didn't actually get a chance to look at it but, uh, I am interested in hearing about it.

Walenski: Well, last year we had four prominent visitors as Cooperstein lecturers: Jesse Jackson came two years ago and former Representative Dan Rostenkowski from Illinois, last year; Richard Riley, the U.S. Secretary of Education, and Gloria Steinem are scheduled for this year. So we don't avoid controversy when it comes to inviting lecturers to campus. I say "we" because I happen to be on the committee that invites these speakers to the campus.

Laura: That sounds like an interesting group. I would certainly want to attend that series of lectures if I had the time.

Walenski: May I ask what other colleges you are considering applying to next year?

Laura: My list is not final yet, but I am very interested in Coburn. I probably also will look at Washington University in St. Louis, the University of North Carolina at Chapel Hill, Johns Hopkins, and, for my long shot, either Wellesley or Yale.

Walenski: That certainly is a varied list. Did you know that most of the engineering at the University of North Carolina is taught at North Carolina State at Raleigh, although Chapel Hill does have applied science now?

Laura: No, I didn't.

Walenski: And Smith may be a better choice for you than Wellesley. You would have the opportunity to take advantage of its special program in engineering with the University of Massachusetts. Wellesley does have its relationship with MIT, but the commuting back and forth would be something to consider.

Laura: I suppose it would.

Walenski: I probably shouldn't say this, but it would seem to me that Princeton has a better engineering program than Yale does.

Laura: I hadn't thought about that, and my uncle is a Princeton alumnus, too. He would be very happy to have me apply.

Walenski: And he might give you some help as well.

Laura: I suppose he might.

Walenski: Are there any other questions you have about Coburn?

Laura: Not really.

Walenski: Do you see yourself being happy here?

Laura: Yes, I do. The campus is only three hours from my house; it is very beautiful, and I like the idea of being here.

Walenski: What do you mean by that last statement?

Laura: Well, I don't know really, except to say that I have a good feeling about this place. I am sure that the more I get to know about it, the more I will like it.

Walenski: Well, I hope so, and I certainly will be glad to answer any other questions you have, should you decide to apply. Here is my card; just give me a ring anytime. You may be interested in the special pamphlet we have on the engineering program. It is outside on the shelf behind the receptionist's desk. Some of our other specialized literature is there, too. You may have seen it when you came in. There is a pamphlet on women's sports at Coburn and a short history of the school. It was founded by missionaries in the 1840s; in fact, about 5 to 7 percent of our students still go on to divinity school. There is also a pamphlet we call the picturebook. You might want to take that along with you to read on the way home.

"With that, David Walenski stood up, breathed what he thought was an inaudible sigh of relief, smiled, shook my hand once again, and conducted me out of his office. It was almost five o'clock; the last tour had returned to the admission office and dispersed. The secretaries had already left; it was summer and they worked a shortened day."

"Mother and I then drove back to Westchester, nagged by a vague feeling of dissatisfaction about the afternoon we had spent at Coburn."

What Went Wrong with Laura's Visit?

When you look at what went wrong in Laura's hurried interview with David Walenski, you can see a number of flaws. For one thing, she was unprepared. She had not read the Coburn catalog thoroughly; she had not investigated the special programs in which she was interested. For another, she did not take a campus tour before the interview, nor did she speak to students and faculty members who would give her special insight into the academic and social scene at the college.

Moreover, she asked primarily factual questions that did not force her interviewer to provide any critical analysis of the education at Coburn. Laura's questions merely required Walenski to reiterate a great deal of factual information readily available in the school's literature.

Laura also did not find out about Mr. Walenski himself. What was his background? He had gone to Coburn as an undergraduate. Had he liked it? Was that why he returned to work as an admission officer there? What had been his undergraduate experience at Coburn, his relationship with his fellow students, his contact with professors, his experience in seeking a job or graduate school placement?

No, Laura did not do a very good job of researching Coburn before her campus visit, and, in particular, she did not take the maximum advantage of the interview itself. She did not use the interview to find out the answers to a variety of complex questions about Coburn, nor did she present herself in any special or specific way to David Walenski. Walenski was a fairly skilled interviewer. He could have been much more rigorous in questioning Laura about her reasons for applying to Coburn.

GUIDELINES FOR YOUR INTERVIEW

When Martha, on the other hand, had her interview, she tried to keep the following guidelines in mind:

Assert yourself during the interview.
Make sure that your interviewer knows not only who you are, but what you have done in your high school, the courses you have taken, the sports you have played, the extracurricular activities and hobbies that have intrigued you. Be enthusiastic about the activities and the studies that interest you and in which you have done well. Try to convey your enthusiasm in a way that reveals *why* you like a certain thing.

Use the interview process to probe the nature of the educational and social experience at the college. Make your interviewer work.
For example, Coburn has 3,200 students and so is considered a medium-sized school. Martha might have asked what the officer thinks the advantages of a school this size are as compared with those of a small school with 1,500 undergraduates or a large campus, such as Berkeley, with 35,000 students.

Which are the better academic departments at Coburn? Coburn has only been coeducational for ten years. How would the interviewer characterize the status of women or men at Coburn today? Is it a fact of life and no longer an issue, or do further changes have to be made? What is it like to be a student at Coburn? Would someone with your interests, abilities, and background really be happy there?

Ask analytical questions, not factual ones.
For example, Martha might say: "Coburn is sometimes called a rather homogeneous school, with many students from the upper-middle class and from New York State. Is that true?" Ask the interviewer to describe faculty-student relationships at the school. The figures may be impressive, a ten-to-one ratio of students to faculty, but, beyond that, how much do students see faculty members on a one-to-one basis, both academically and socially?

How do students at the school feel about the place? Is there much use of alcohol and drugs on campus? What about antisocial behavior? On the other hand, is there a fair amount of rational behavior and conformity among the students? Does political correctness dictate a conformity to student attitudes? Are students really involved in the decision-making process at the college? Do they sit on major committees?

If you want to pursue engineering, as did Martha, but also want to take courses in the humanities and social sciences, particularly economics, would it be possible for you to take one engineering course, one humanities course, one economics course, and a fourth course of some sort each semester? Or should you consider instead fulfilling your humanities and social science interests in the January term or in an off-campus program?

Find out about your interviewer.
Try to establish some sort of personal relationship with him or her without straining the bounds of good manners or the normal flow of the interview itself. Who is your interviewer? Is he or she a graduate of the school? What did the interviewer like most about the experience there? What was least impressive about the education at the school during your interviewer's student days? Whatever questions you decide to ask, remember that ideally the interviewer should come to see a little of himself or herself in you. In that way you will be remembered.

Make the match between yourself and the college.
In a way, this guideline incorporates all the others. During the interview you should try to show not only your interest in attending the college but also your ability to contribute to it.

Martha Prentice is an example of someone with much to offer. She is an able student who knows in which field she wishes to study. She is a good athlete, and her interest in dramatics may ultimately translate into a skill that will enliven the Coburn community. However, it is up to you to make your strong qualities known.

You can introduce evidence of your academic ability into the interview quite naturally by taking a copy of your high school transcript. This will show the success you have had in the courses you've taken. Many transcripts also include scores on the SAT or ACT Assessment, SAT II, and Advanced Placement tests. A transcript gives the interviewer something to react to, and many interviewers will gladly give a frank assessment of your chances for admission once they have examined your transcript.

To make the match for your extracurricular contribution, you can ask: "How difficult would it be for me to make a varsity team?" You can then direct the discussion toward your abilities as a field hockey and basketball player. You can also prepare an athletic data sheet (discussed in Chapter 5) to show to the coaches. When you ask a question about a certain area, say the theater, you can begin by saying that you have acted in plays and wanted to know. . . . This tells your interviewer of your interest in and willingness to contribute to a particular area of community life. Remember, admission officers are looking for citizens, not just scholars or athletes or musicians.

By asking incisive questions about the role of the undergraduates in student governance and college policymaking, you can show your willingness in helping to change the college for the better. Very often colleges are impressed with candidates who are willing and able to carry out constructive changes on the campus.

TIPS FOR BEING A GOOD INTERVIEWEE

One: Remember that the interview is not designed to stress you unduly.
Rather, it is designed to focus on your credentials both as a person and as a student. Most interviewers will proceed from what you have to say, asking

questions about the points you bring up. This means that you should take the initiative and play a substantial role in the interview. You should try to set the agenda of the interview and control its content.

Two: Prepare for your interview.
Know yourself. Know your subject—the college itself. Remember, you know a lot already. This is an opportunity to show what you know and to learn more.

According to Don Dickason, Vice Provost at Drexel, in "The College Interview: How to Make It Work for You" (Peterson's Guides, 1994), "Less than one out of five students have prepared themselves well for an interview. If you are prepared, you'll be exceptional."

Three: Listen to what is being said.
If the interviewer asks an ambiguous question, don't be afraid to ask for clarification. Or you can break the question down into its several parts and then proceed to answer each of them separately. Treat every question as important, but don't prevent humor from coming in either. Try to see all the implications in a given question—social, academic, psychological, cultural. Then pick the particular elements you want to respond to.

Four: Be honest.
Often, admitting a weakness can be disarming and may help the interviewer relate to you better. After all, he or she is not perfect either. Honesty is often the beginning of a learning experience, so it is a value that colleges appreciate. Nevertheless, honesty should not take the form of an apology; you should not be overly self-critical. In relating facts or incidents that may be slightly embarrassing, remember that college interviewers will be interested not so much in what you did as in what you learned.

Five: Pauses can be refreshing.
All too often first-time interviewees rush ahead with their conversation, in fear that a pause may create the impression that they are ignorant or insecure. Wrong. Consider the following historical example:

> On December 12, 1941, General George C. Marshall, the Chief of Staff, called in Colonel Dwight D. Eisenhower, who had served in the Philippines, and asked him for his on-the-spot opinion of the best strategy to follow in responding to the

disastrous attack on Pearl Harbor five days before. Instead of answering at once, Eisenhower paused and then asked for three hours to consider the matter, promising to return in the afternoon with his written response. Marshall was a bit taken aback, but agreed. As he thought about it, he became very impressed that Eisenhower took his question so seriously and that he wanted to give the most careful answer he could. From then on Marshall took a keen interest in the career of this intelligent young officer who *thought before speaking.*

Eisenhower carried the pause further than a student in a college interview can, but the point is the same. A pause can also be used to ask for clarification. In addition, a pause can be used to regroup your thoughts before pushing on with your line of argument. Very often when you are having a conversational disagreement and are slowly trying to build your own case, a pause can help each of your points to stand out more strongly than if they were rushed together in a lengthy speech.

Six: Look for the telltale signs that it is time to shift your tactics.
You'll most likely see this in the interviewer's body language and eye movements. Fidgeting, clenching or unclenching of hands, crossing and uncrossing of legs, and a faraway look in the eyes are signs that you had better change your tactics quickly. Bring your response to a close. Ask the interviewer a question. Allow a natural pause to take place. Somehow break the stream of conversation so it can go in a more fruitful direction.

Seven: Remember that if eye contact is not maintained all the time, it does not necessarily mean that either of you is bored.
Very often when people are explaining something or venturing their own opinions, they are not quite sure of what they are saying. Thus they tend to look away from the person to whom they are talking. If, on the other hand, the listener in a conversation tends to look away, then the message being sent is often one of boredom or disagreement.

By contrast, when speakers look directly at you, they are frequently confident of what they are saying and are therefore seeking confirmation from you. They are often signaling that they are willing to be interrupted and are eager to hear your thoughts.

Here's the bottom-line rule for the novice interviewee: *Act naturally and keep a healthy degree of eye contact with your interviewer. Be yourself above all else.*

THE INTERVIEW THAT WAS—MARTHA'S

Now it was Martha's turn to tell about her interview with David Walenski at Coburn:

Walenski: Well, how did your tour and lunch with the students go? Did any questions come up that I could answer?

Martha: Yes, I enjoyed the tour and my talk with the students. Both experiences answered many of the questions I had, but I did want to find out from you what you feel to be the advantages for an undergraduate education of a relatively small school like Coburn.

Walenski: I'd say there are two or three distinct advantages to this institution.

First, the size of Coburn is ideal. With 3,200 students, we can put together a class that has variety and quality in a way that a small college with half as many students cannot. So what you have here at Coburn is a heterogeneous student body that is neither too big nor too small. You are going to get to know all sorts of different people here, and you will learn a lot from them, inside the classroom as well as outside.

Second, I think the facilities at Coburn are exceptional. The unlimited access to the library's collection, the spacious playing area provided by the brand-new field house, and the three different types of theaters, not to mention the facilities over at the engineering school, really do impress me even though I'm very used to them now.

Third, I think that your contact with teachers here will be of genuine and lasting value to you. The teachers here are just that—teachers. They like students. They want to spend time with them. If their primary objective were to publish, then they would be at a big university. Basically they come here to teach and to engage in collaborative learning projects with students. You will see a lot of them if you so desire. They are invariably available outside their office hours, and they really want to help the individual student do well enough to get into a good graduate school or land an interesting, responsible job.

Martha: You mention that you are used to the facilities here. How long have you been here, and what has been your experience?

Walenski: I came to Coburn seven years ago as an undergraduate. I had been picked up on a football scholarship. I had never heard of Coburn until one of the leading businessmen in my community of Altoona, Pennsylvania, suggested that I apply. I had done pretty well in high school, and the football coach here took an interest in my case after I sent him some newspaper clippings. At any rate, I came, majored in government, worked for a year and a half in Washington as a result of a job I had during the Washington semester here, and have come back to work in the admission department.

I may go off to graduate school in a year or so, but I'm going to have to wait for my wife to finish her nurse's training at the hospital in Buffalo. But you asked what my experience here had been. I love this place! I came from a small-town background. Neither of my parents went to college. I was very grateful for the scholarship I received. I worked quite hard here and I feel I got something out of it.

I met a lot of different people. One of my roommates was a champion swimmer from Winnetka, Illinois. Another one was a science wizard from Baltimore. I had visited both their homes before I graduated. I also had the opportunity to take a variety of courses, some in fields I never knew existed. I even took that special Japanese history course for nonconcentrators. I also learned the French language (you know you have to meet a language requirement here) and that was a great experience for me. I think that in a big university I would have been lost. I would not have gotten to know so many people. Here I also had the chance to shine in a couple of areas and I met some people who will be my friends for the rest of my life.

Martha: That's a pretty persuasive argument. Many of the things you said are of interest to me. I want to get to know new people. I want to take a variety of courses, but I also want to finish here with a special skill in at least one area. Can you tell me which the strong departments are here and which the weak ones are? Is engineering really that strong?

Walenski: To be honest, I don't think that music is terribly strong here. The department has failed to obtain a couple of grants that would have helped it a good deal, and several of the younger promising teachers have left. However, I think you are in good shape if you pursue engineering with a minor in economics. Several of the engineering professors have had nationally acclaimed articles in the *Journal of Professional Engineers.* Because our engineering facilities are not as extensive as those at, say, a place like the University of Michigan, we do not get all that fancy government money to build a mock-up of a lunar capsule. However, our engineering professors are nationally recognized—at least, several of them are—and I would add that the college's Glickenspiel Award for distinguished teaching has gone to a member of the engineering department in three of the past five years. That's really something.

Martha: I am certainly impressed with that statistic. However, could I shift the subject for a moment? I would like to find out a little something about the social life here. I know it may be hard for you to answer, but what is your impression of the role of women here? Have they been fully integrated? How about the fraternities and sororities? Do they dominate the social life here?

Walenski: I will take the latter question first. Fraternities and sororities exist on a take-it-or-leave-it basis here. About half the students belong to a fraternity or sorority, but since freshmen all have to live together in three dormitories, and since there is not sufficient housing for all fraternity and sorority members in their houses, students do not tend to break off into house cliques. If you do not want to join a sorority, fine. If you don't, you'll probably get invited to many of their parties anyway. I wouldn't worry about fraternity or sorority domination one bit.

Now on the question about the role of women. That is pretty hard for me to answer. We have been coeducational for about ten years. Not quite 50 percent of the undergraduates here are women. Certainly I did not sense any discrimination against them when I was an undergraduate here. Since the competition for admission to Coburn is sharper among women than among men, the women tend to be a little bit brighter, and sometimes even more dynamic, than the men. So they can more than hold their own, even though technically they are in the minority.

I would say quite frankly, though, that the main problem for Coburn in regard to women has been to attract and then to retain competent women faculty members. We still need to make progress in that area. For instance, no woman has won the undergraduate teaching award yet. There just aren't enough of women faculty!

Martha: What is the ratio of female to male faculty members?

Walenski: Actually now it is about 20 percent female, and as you can see this is under half the percentage of women students. So what this all boils down to is that there aren't as many role models, as the sociologists like to say, for the young women here as there are for the young men. But other than that, I would say that women here have a fulfilling experience. There are undergraduate women resident advisers in the dormitories; there are women on the boards of most of the campus organizations—last year the editor of the newspaper was female; and women artists and politicians are featured in the special events that often occur on the campus. Jeane Kirkpatrick, former ambassador to the United Nations and professor at Georgetown University, received an honorary degree here last June, for instance.

Martha: From what you say, I gather that the role of women at Coburn is not a particular issue. What, then, are the social and academic issues that have come up on the campus during the past year?

Walenski: I would say that the role of women is an issue, and one that the school is sensitive about. That there has not been a public outcry about women's rights should not obscure the fact that the administration cares very deeply about according women an equal place on this campus. You can see that from the special pamphlet on women's athletics that was sent to you along with the catalog.

If you looked at the campus newspaper, you probably know that the big issue last year was the investment of Coburn funds in companies doing business in South Africa. Both blacks and whites raised the alarm on that issue.

Martha: I saw that, but what did the school do about it?

Walenski: After a series of articles in the newspaper and interviews with trustees, the treasurer came out with an itemized statement of all of the school's investments. That was in late February. In early March the concerned students and staff, of whom I was one, held a huge rally in front of the administration building. We had megaphones, a sound truck, placards, the whole lot. Faced with our opposition, the trustees agreed to withdraw school funds from companies having a poor track record on integrating their work force in South Africa. It was a great victory.

Martha: It must have been exciting. I have given a lot of thought to this issue, since I may well end up somewhere in the business sector after graduation. But I feel that educational institutions ought to go pretty slowly on this whole question of investment in countries that abridge the civil rights of their citizens.

Walenski: You do?

Martha: Yes, I do. I feel that the maintenance or withdrawal of investments in countries like South Africa is closely related to American foreign policy and not entirely the concern of educational institutions. I think if the President believes that it would be in the American interest to withdraw investments from a country like South Africa, or indeed any of the black African countries, then he and Congress ought to take steps to implement that idea. For individual institutions to be constantly juggling their investments based on their own definition of what is politically desirable may well distract them from their essential purpose of educating undergraduates and result in mixed messages to the country in question.

In terms of our foreign policy, it may well be of greater advantage to the United States to maintain all its investments and then threaten to withdraw them unless certain civil liberties are observed, rather than have individual institutions withdrawing funds in hopes of bringing greater rights to the oppressed inhabitants of those countries. I think we need a more coordinated approach and more leadership from our government, frankly.

Walenski: You do have a point there, and I don't know that I had thought about it in that way before.

Martha: Well (laughing) when I get in, I can change Coburn's position. I have another question that relates to one of my interests. If I were to be admitted to Coburn, just how difficult would it be for me to win a place on the freshman field hockey team? We play pretty good field hockey at Westchester. Last year our team made the state semifinals, but I have heard that Coburn's field hockey team is pretty good too.

Walenski: Yes, it is. Last year the Coburn team went up to the semifinals in the state playoffs and managed to get to the semifinals in the East Coast tournament at Mount Holyoke as well. If you are as good as you say you are and your particular position is not overcrowded with candidates, I think that you could make the freshman team and plan to play about a third of the time. If you hung in there, you would probably make the varsity team the following year when some of the kids drop out because of academic or other interests. I will ask Sharon Cushman, the varsity coach, to drop you a line and give you the team's recent statistics. Sharon is a dynamic lady.

Martha: Thanks. If I am a potential field hockey player, will that enhance my chances of admission?

Walenski: Yes, it will. Every year we try to take a handful of people for each varsity sport. There is no formal rating system or coaches' quota system such as you might have at a state university, but athletics is a concern. We make no secret about that. If Sharon backs you, it will help.

Martha: In that connection, I hope you do not think it too bold of me to ask, but how do I look as a candidate for Coburn? I really am interested in the school, and I have brought along my high school transcript for you to look at if you wish.

Walenski: Well, I can say frankly from our conversation here today that you are a reasonably strong candidate. Let me see what courses you have had in high school. (He looks over the transcript.) This transcript looks pretty strong to me. You have paid attention to the solid courses that we look for: English, a foreign language, mathematics, and the sciences. Do you plan to take a second semester of either physics or chemistry?

Martha: Chemistry is not my best subject, and the physics course is very hard, so I was considering separating them and taking one in each semester of my senior year. I do plan to take physics, which I like very much. Also in the fall I plan to continue with English, to take a course in current events, to begin calculus, and to take the French Advanced Placement course.

Walenski: Except for the current events course, those decisions all make sense to me. I would suggest that in view of your interest in engineering, you take physics in the fall. Then you would be far enough along to take the Subject Test in January and submit that as a part of your application. Thus you would have the Writing Test, French, Mathematics Level II, and Physics Subject Tests. If you got all 600 scores or better, you would look pretty good to us.

Martha: I will consider that suggestion seriously. Is there anything besides grades, scores, and ability to contribute to athletics and extracurricular activities that you and the committee are looking for in an applicant to Coburn?

Walenski: I'd say that we are definitely looking for an intangible quality of dynamism in a candidate. That can come out in a field hockey game, in an aggressive hook shot from the center of the field toward the goalie when there is little time left on the clock. It can come out as a statement, such as "I really don't understand what you are trying to show me, Professor So-and-So; could you go over that again?"

Or it could be a statement made at a student-faculty forum, something similar to what you said to me a moment ago about South African investment policy; for example, "I wonder if it is the responsibility of a small college in central New York State to withdraw its investments from South Africa unilaterally when it perceives that civil rights in that country are being abridged. I wonder if we ought not to heed the advice of the State Department and consult with our fellow institutions before attempting to deal with a social injustice 15,000 miles away."

In short, we are looking for people with vitality, imagination, and a sense of responsibility to themselves and to the community around them. I always remember a line from Alfred North Whitehead. He said, "The task of a university or college is to weld together imagination and experience." The professors here, the libraries, the facilities, they all add up to experience. What we are looking for is a group of students with imagination and a constructive interest in challenging their teachers and this institution as they move through it. If we can compose a class of varied individuals who are bright and spirited, yet aware that institutions and society often change slowly, then we will have done our job.

Martha: Thanks. In my application I'll give some thought to the points you raise.

Walenski: Well, thank you too for coming up today. I think we have to wind up this interview because we have gone overtime. I am very glad to have had the chance to talk with you. I shall look forward to reading your application. In the meantime, if there are any questions that come up, here is my card. Please do not hesitate to get in touch with me.

Martha: Thanks again.

HOW TO USE AN INTERVIEW TO YOUR ADVANTAGE

You know that interviews will vary enormously in their style and content. You can only hope that they proceed as smoothly as the one between

Martha Prentice and David Walenski. Even if they do not, they will probably have a positive impact on your chances of admission. A good interview could swing the balance if your credentials are equal in every other way to another candidate, and if both of you are at the margin of admission.

You should keep in mind, however, that a wonderful interview does not guarantee an admission. A good interview cannot overcome a poor academic record or minimal involvement in extracurricular activities or weak personal recommendations by your teachers or your school. Colleges want to recruit and admit students who have made the most of their educational opportunities, rather than those who only show charm and an ability to converse at the interview.

Nonetheless, as you plan your first college interview, look on it as an excellent opportunity to present your unique personal traits, academic abilities, and special talents to the college. In many instances making the trip to a college campus far from home for an interview is in and of itself a statement of interest and enthusiasm that is not lost on the admission office.

Bear in mind that the interview also serves important ends for the college. It gives the admission office an opportunity to tell prospective students about its strong programs, courses, instructors, and athletic and artistic facilities, hopefully getting them interested in all the school has to offer. Even at competitive colleges, where admission is very selective, the interview is important.

One compassionate admission officer at a very selective college put it well when he said, "I look on the interview as the first and last opportunity a lot of kids will have to make contact with my college. I want the opportunity for it to be as pleasant and as productive as it can be."

Given the opportunity to participate in a college interview, you should show a natural enthusiasm about yourself and your credentials; you should plan to control as much of the content of the interview as seems reasonable; you should listen to your interviewer so that you can give thoughtful responses to questions and discover something about your interviewer as a person; you should be honest about your own failings but not apologetic.

Likewise, you should be honest about your opinions and not tailor your remarks to suit what you think the interviewer wants to hear; you should not fear pauses but use them to your advantage; and finally you should watch for telltale signs in eye movement and body language so that you can shift the conversation if necessary and keep it on a productive course.

Remember, too, that the unexpected can happen. In Martha's conversation with David Walenski, the digression about Coburn's investments in South Africa brought both the interviewer and the interviewee to a new level of understanding. Walenski discovered that the neatly attired upper-middle-class girl from a wealthy suburb of New York City had a mind of her own and wasn't afraid to speak it. In fact, as he said, David Walenski had not thought about the problem of overseas investments in quite that way before.

Martha came to understand that the "climate of free discussion" described in the catalog really did exist at Coburn. She found Walenski's reaction to her statement a reasonable one, and that impressed her.

After Martha left the room, David Walenski jotted down a few notes on Martha's interview report form: "Sensitive, intelligent, mature young woman who knows what she wants but is open to the ideas of others. Reasonable scores, very good grades, probably a contributor to field hockey and may also turn up in student theater productions. I was impressed with this fine young woman. I hope she applies and that we can find a place for her."

Martha's interview had gone well. Her visit to Coburn was a success. So, remember, an interview is a wonderful and necessary opportunity for you. You need to find out important information about a college or university. You also need to develop a judgment about the "feel of the place." You are not just going to college to study! Also, because you are a dynamic and unique individual, the interview affords you the opportunity to express your views and reveal your personal qualities. When you combine your agenda with that of the college's need to find interesting and intelligent students, it is a win–win situation. So make the most of it!

Timing and Testing

The middle school and junior high years are a pivotal time to develop the academic planning, preparation, and motivation needed for higher education.

Eileen R. Matthey, *Counseling for College*, Peterson's Guides, 1995.

Some of you will be surprised to hear that you should begin your college planning in your freshman year of high school. A little college thinking at this early stage will go a long way toward making the selection and admission process as smooth as possible for you later on, in your junior and senior years.

THE FRESHMAN YEAR—BECOMING AWARE

Once the challenge of high school seems manageable and life has settled down to a routine, you should think about what subjects you particularly like, what outside activities give you special pleasure, and what areas of study and vocational skills you might like to explore during the next four years.

Often guidance counselors can help you clarify your thoughts or direct you to courses and programs you might want to pursue but you can also explore on your own. Computer bulletin boards often provide information and ideas for projects or connections to others with similar interests. Sports provides another outlet for energy and skills that may some day help you take a leadership role in the workplace or politics or whatever your chosen field happens to be.

Rebecca Liczko is one high school student I know who's taken time to explore some of her outside interests. She loves helping her mother with her catering business on the weekends and is a whiz at math. She decided to take an optional cooking course in the spring term of her ninth-grade year. She also decided to go to the school's computer center to look at the software that would enable her to help her mother do some simple bookkeeping on the family computer. In making these decisions Rebecca is taking some initiative concerning her future so that she may someday bring together, in a college program, her talent for math and her experience in food preparation. She is keeping her options open but she is also playing to her strengths.

Talk with Older Students

As a ninth grader you may also want to talk to older friends or family members who are in college to find out what it's like. Ask them what they would have done differently if they were just starting high school now—what advice they would give freshmen. Here are some sample responses from a group of college students I recently asked that question:

♦ "I would certainly have gone to see my counselor more. . . ."
♦ "Yeah, and I would have read one of those how-to books."
♦ "I would have gone and looked at a college and tried to picture myself there. I never saw my college until I got there."
♦ "It may sound ridiculous, but the more reading of all that stuff they send you, the better off you are. . . ."
♦ "Yup, there are videos and CD-ROMs the colleges will send you, if you just ask. . . . Sometimes you can even find them right in the library of the counseling center."

Talk with Your Parents

Finally, you should have at least one talk with your parents so that they know that you are interested in going on to college, if indeed you are. Your parents know your strengths very well and may have some ideas about what skills still lie dormant in you. They may have some specific colleges in mind where they think you would be happy. If there happens to be a difference of opinion, perhaps the family could visit certain colleges together during a vacation the following summer. Then you would have a specific example to use as a reference point as you consider other schools.

At some point you will need to talk with your parents about the financial situation regarding your college tuition—a clear understanding of finances is very important.

♦ Have they been planning for the cost of your college education?
♦ How do they plan to deal with the cost of educating other siblings or step siblings?
♦ What can you do to help, not just in a financial way but also in finding out information that your parent(s) may need to know about financing college costs.

Chapter 7 discusses the money side of college—the costs and the many kinds of loans, grants, and awards that may be available to you.

Now that you've had a talk with your parents, with some college students, with your counselor, and you've made some decisions about classes and school activities that will give you a good start toward college, go back to enjoying your freshman year.

THE SOPHOMORE YEAR—SELF-ANALYSIS

The tenth grade is an ideal time to start exploring your interests and your dreams about your future and to begin to focus on a possible career. Start the tenth-grade year with an interview with your guidance counselor. It may be possible for you to use computer-based assessment exercises at your school or one nearby to help you identify your underlying inclinations, talents, and dominant personality traits. You may want to get help from a guidance counselor to find out what you are good at, what kinds of social situations bring out the best in you, and how you approach challenges.

Discussions with your friends and parents already may have helped you get a better understanding of the kind of person you are and what your apparent talents are. Now you want to add to this the formal results of a preference test and an interest inventory. When combined with your personality profile these results will help enormously as you begin to think about your possibilities for the future.

Start Exploring Career Possibilities

When you have the results of these tests you should have a general idea of what fields of work you might want to explore. Next locate the career reference section of the counseling center, where you'll probably find books on a whole host of careers. You may even find computer programs designed to assist students in exploring careers. If your school doesn't have such a program, your guidance counselor may be able to access one for you on a state or national database. *Career Options* from Peterson's is one of them.

Take some time to pore over the books and/or software; get a feel for the careers that interest you; study the qualifications necessary to get started in them and the type of work that's involved; get a feel for the work environment and future job opportunities. You may know a little about some of these careers already, but now it's time to get a bit more serious.

Take Some Tests

During the sophomore year you should also be thinking about the college admission testing process itself. Although a few colleges do not require the standardized entrance tests, most do, so you should plan to take either the PSAT or the Preliminary Act (P-ACT+). Some students also plan to take the SAT I: Reasoning Test, offered by the College Board, or the ACT, offered by American College Testing. Most schools will accept either one. A smaller group of students move on to take the SAT II Subject Tests that are required by some selective colleges and universities.

If you do elect to take either the SAT I or the ACT test, which is offered five or six times a year, schedule your tests when you have completed most of the academic work of the junior year.

The P-ACT+

The P-ACT+ test is offered by American College Testing. This is not a formal practice test for the ACT Assessment but rather a test that helps students become familiar with the testing format, the way questions are put, how test sections appear, and how to work out their answers to questions and fill in the proper spaces on the answer sheet.

The PSAT

The Preliminary Scholastic Assessment Test (PSAT) is given as practice for the SAT in late October. It's also a crucial test for good students because it serves as the qualifying test for the National Merit Scholarships. (Its full name is actually PSAT/NMSQT.) Even if you don't get a scholarship (few do), just being a semifinalist gets you recruited by the best schools—that may offer you money. Guidance counselors can help with registration for the test, and when the results come back, interpret them for individual students. A pamphlet accompanying the test results will also help you interpret your responses and scores.

Choose Classes That Develop Your Skills

As you begin to make the connections between your aptitudes, skills, personality, and your possible career, you should be sure to take any high school courses that will highlight your skills and illuminate those career possibilities for you. Guidance counselors can usually help you identify the courses that suit you best while double checking that you're taking the proper college-preparatory courses as well. If in doubt, if your counselor is too busy to see you, you should take the most demanding program you can handle, including Advanced Placement courses, if they are offered by your school.

Have Another Talk with Your Parents

During your sophomore year you should have a more extensive conversation with your parents than you had last year. Tell them about your plan to take the various tests and replay for them the insights of your guidance counselor. You should also talk again about how your college education will be paid for so that both you and your family can begin to plan for these expenses if you have not done so already.

Get Some College Directories

In addition, you should begin to build up a small library about colleges, concentrating on reference works rather than specific catalogs from individual schools. *Peterson's Guide to Four-Year Colleges* and *The College Handbook*, by the College Board, are both good, comprehensive directories of colleges in the United States.

THE JUNIOR YEAR—SETTING STRATEGY

Everyone knows that the plot thickens in the junior year when the time comes to get serious about college planning. If you didn't complete some of the college-planning tasks earmarked for your sophomore year, get them done in the fall of your junior year. Also begin your testing program, keeping in mind two salient points as you work out your own schedule for test taking:

♦ First, the timing of the tests should be keyed to the courses you are taking. If schools to which you'll be applying require SAT II Subject Test results, then take them in your key subjects soon after you've completed the appropriate courses so that the subjects are fresh in your mind. Take the SAT I or ACT on the other available test days.

♦ Second, do not take the tests too many times in hopes of improving your scores. Your scores will not improve significantly, and the colleges will not necessarily be impressed by several sets of SAT I and SAT II scores. If you are sick on a certain test date and feel you could do better with another opportunity, then of course take the test again. Or if you have taken one of the SAT preparation courses or extensively reviewed the subject matter covered on the SAT II Subject Test since you were first tested, then you should attempt the tests again. Otherwise follow this rule of thumb: *SAT I or ACT twice, SAT II no more than twice, and leave it at that.* There are other things to do on Saturday mornings besides taking tests.

A College-Planning Calendar for Your Junior Year

October—Take the PSAT and, if you have not already done so, read the materials describing the test's content. When you get your results, discuss them with your counselor, who has additional materials to help interpret your scores.

January—Take the SAT I or, if required by the schools you're interested in, the SAT II in subjects you have completed in the first semester of your junior year. For specific information on the SAT II consult the pamphlet "About the Subject Tests," available in your counseling center.

February—Take the ACT Assessment if you think it will be a better indicator of your strengths than the SAT I, or if any of your college choices require it. If you check *Peterson's Guide to Four-Year Colleges* or *The College Handbook*, you'll see that there's only a small number of schools that will only accept the ACT, or neither the ACT nor the SAT I. If you take the ACT, get a pamphlet called *Preparing for the Enhanced ACT Assessment* from your guidance counselor and review the suggestions for the subject-area tests.

March/April—Familiarize yourself with your school's guidance library, both printed and electronic. Consult the College Board's *Index to Majors* or see *Peterson's Guide to Four-Year Colleges,* which has an index to majors by school, to locate the colleges and universities that offer the majors you are interested in pursuing. Incidentally, both Peterson's Guides and the College Board have computer search programs that may be available in either your school or your community library. Peterson's is called the *College Selection Service* and the College Board program is named *College Explorer Plus*. If you have access to Internet or one of the commercial networks, these programs may be available at various Web sites.

If you have chosen to take the ACT and did not take it in February, take it during this period.

In addition, examine the colleges your counselor suggests and those that you have learned about from friends, family, and your own reading. Write for additional materials from the colleges that interest you. During your spring vacation, if you have one, visit a college near your home and take the guided tour. Whenever possible, talk to students who are attending a college.

May—Take the Advanced Placement tests if you are enrolled in advanced courses and your teachers approve. Remember that although the Advanced Placement tests are expensive and take time to properly study for them, many colleges and universities will give you college credit for them if you pass. This means that you can save some tuition fees and you can finish college in less than four years, perhaps even in three. Advanced Placement tests are on the rise; in 1994 over 701,000 tests were taken by high school juniors and seniors around the world.

June—There are now nineteen different SAT II Subject Tests, formerly called Achievement Tests, and it is important to consult the test schedule so that you take SAT II in the subjects you will not be continuing in your senior year. Consult your teachers for advice on whether or not you should take some of these exams and when to take them.

If you do not take any SAT IIs in June, you may want to take the SAT again, but do so only if you feel you can better your first score significantly! June is also another time to take the ACT, if you wish to and have not already done so.

Summer Vacation—Plan to visit and have interviews at the colleges that interest you the most and that are located too far from your home to be visited easily in the fall. (See Chapter 3 for how to make the most of campus visits and interviews.)

THE SENIOR YEAR—ACTIVE ENGAGEMENT

The last year of high school is the time when you need to do your best academically. Outside activities and leadership positions are important, but colleges will definitely want to see a strong record in the senior year, especially if your record in the lower grades leaves a bit to be desired. The senior year also will give you an opportunity to go beyond the preparation requirements of a particular school: to take that course in Probability and Statistics, to pursue a fourth year of a language, or to try something new like art history or music appreciation. Use your good judgment. Consult your college counselor. If necessary, call one of the colleges you intend to apply to and ask an admission officer.

Remember, too, your senior year is a time to extend yourself in other areas, such as leading a sports team or producing a play or exploring an exchange program with another high school abroad. Thinking about your senior year before it happens will help you to make the most of the possibilities it holds.

September/October—This is the season to procure viewbooks, posters, specialized pamphlets (such as those about financial aid or sports programs) from all the schools you're most interested in. Call the schools' 800 number and ask for what you need.

During this two-month period many colleges will send representatives to your high school, or they will set up display tables at college fairs, or they may hold receptions in your area. These occasions are opportunities for you and your family to ask specific questions and get any additional information you need. Attend these meetings to make yourself known to the college representatives. Representatives really do like to meet students and often pass along their impressions to the admissions committee. They also will give you their business cards if you ask.

On weekends plan to visit nearby colleges to which you may apply. Schedule yourself for a campus tour followed by an interview. Keep your college counselor informed of your plans and any new developments, such as honors and awards that have come your way or specific words of encouragement from college coaches or admissions officers. Remember to complete and file applications to state schools with early or rolling admissions deadlines. The increased popularity of the state school option has caused many state universities to fill before their final filing dates, usually in January or February.

This is the time to take the ACT as a senior. It's also the time to pick up an application for the Financial Aid PROFILE if you intend to apply for financial aid. The PROFILE form will be sent to you in the same fashion as the SAT I and SAT II admission tickets are. You and your parents will complete the form in January and send it to the College Scholarship Service as instructed.

November—Take the SAT for the last time—your second or possibly third try. Submit Early Decision or Early Action applications by November 1 to November 15. Begin to fill out your regular college applications as well. Do the easiest first, and continue this process through the Christmas vacation. Allow three to four days for each application. Send off applications to schools with early deadlines first.

December—Most seniors will take their final set of SAT II Subject Tests this month. Distribute teacher recommendation forms to those teachers who have agreed to help you. The ACT is also offered this month. If you did not take it in October, you should do so now.

January—Send off your final college applications by January 1 to January 15, the deadlines for most applications. Submit portfolios, musical tapes, or other supplements to your application later in the month. If you did not complete your testing in December, take the SAT I or SAT II later in the month as well. Remember to make sure your parents complete the PROFILE form this month and submit it as early in February as possible.

February—Submit any special letters of recommendation from coaches or prominent alumni by the first of February. If you have a first-choice college, consider writing to the admissions committee and informing them of your preference.

As colleges make their tentative evaluations of students at this time, they may notify your guidance counselor informally of your chances of admission. Listen to what your counselor has to say. Read between the lines. File additional applications if the horizon darkens.

March—Nothing to do but wait! Try to avoid agonizing. Keep your academic work up to your previous level; improve it if you can. If you are placed on a waiting list later on, your midwinter record will take on great importance.

April—Colleges notify applicants of their decisions. If you are admitted to three or more of the schools to which you applied, you will have tough choices to make. Plan to revisit these schools. Be sure to talk to students this time. If financial aid figures in your decision, ask the colleges that accepted you to explain their offers thoroughly. If your financial circumstances have changed since you first applied, bring documentation with you to the financial aid office and ask for a formal reevaluation of your aid package.

May—Reply to the colleges that accepted you and choose the one you think will be best for you—not one your parents or friends think you ought to attend. If by chance you have been placed on a waiting list, follow the suggestions you'll find in Chapter 9.

TESTS, TESTS, TESTS

Because high school curricula, grading standards, and learning environments vary widely, the SAT or Scholastic Assessment Test "provides a common standard against which students can be compared." The test actually has two parts, the SAT I, which replaces the old SAT (Scholastic Aptitude Test), and the SAT II, which is the new name for the Achievement Tests, now called Subject Tests.

SAT I

This test emphasizes reasoning ability in both the verbal and mathematics areas.

The verbal section contains two 30-minute sections and one 15-minute section. Compared to the old SAT, there is increased emphasis on critical reading, longer reading passages, and some paired reading passages. Vocabulary will be tested in the context of the reading passages. The Test of Standard Written English and the infamous antonym section have been eliminated. There is more time allotted to the verbal section than previously (75 vs. 60 minutes), and there are fewer questions (78 vs. 85).

The math section, likewise, has two 30-minute sections and one 15-minute section. It allows the use of a calculator, but one is not required. In contrast to the old SAT math section, the new version has ten questions that will require students to produce their own response and enter it in special grids on the answer sheet. As with the verbal section, emphasis on data interpretation and application of data to mathematical questions lies at the heart of the test. More time will be given to answer the same number of questions (60 questions in 75 minutes).

Taking the Tests

Because not all of the SAT II Subject Tests are given on each test date, and they are related to the completion of certain courses, you should allow the SAT II Subject Tests you plan to take to set your overall testing schedule. You will still have ample opportunity to take the SAT I on two occasions if you choose to. The normal pattern is for students to take the SAT I for the first time in the spring of their junior year and a second time in November of their senior year.

The subject of taking the SAT I more than once brings up the question of using coaching or preparatory courses to improve scores. Readers of the national press will remember the criticism voiced by a small but vocal group against the College Board and its testing affiliate, the Educational Testing Service. The critics argued that the old SAT has a "code" that could be broken and that intensive SAT preparation courses would ensure improvement in scores. Students considering such courses should bear a few points in mind before plunging wildly ahead:

◆ The new SAT I relies less on memory and more on analytical reasoning than the previous version.

◆ Colleges will have to reset their validity scales for the new SAT I as a predictor of performance. In the meantime, they may choose to rely a bit less on the SAT I in the admission process.

◆ As a part of the test revision process, the scoring system has changed. This *recentering* means that scores for all testers will increase, as the mean for the test rises from the mid-400s to 500.

◆ In addition, most colleges consider the results of SAT I testing in the broader context of the SAT II and, more important, in the context of your high school record. To this they add consideration of your extracurricular involvement, leadership, and personal qualities as illustrated in teacher and school recommendations. So in the end the SAT I is part of a much larger picture.

◆ Then there is the phenomenon of score fluctuation from one test administration to another. This fluctuation is normally 20 to 30 points and is nothing to worry about. If a test preparation service guarantees a 60-point score increase, remember that is really only half that amount. If you do decide to take an SAT prep course, focus on one that will teach you skills and information rather than a technique to "beat the system."

IMPROVING YOUR SCORES ON YOUR OWN

There is much that you can do without outside help to improve your scores:

College Board pamphlets

When signing up for the SAT ask your counselor for a pamphlet called "Taking the SAT I Reasoning Test." It contains a sample test with answers. You can take this practice test, even time yourself, and arrive at a tentative score on your own. Then you can move on to the books like *SAT Success*, *Word Flash*, and *Math Flash*, all from Peterson's, or *10 SATs*, published by the College Board. With these tools, you can study quite successfully on your own.

Computer programs

There are also a few good software packages on the market, such as *Peterson's SAT Success* book with software disk. These programs can be bought for a reasonable price and perhaps shared by families with college-bound students. In selecting a computer program, keep in mind three questions:

1. Is the program designed in such a way that students will know where and why they got wrong answers?
2. Does the program have graphics or sound capabilities and, if so, are they really helpful—or distracting?
3. Are there accompanying materials, such as workbooks, practice tests, and perhaps a manual that complement and expand upon the program itself?

Common sense

Aside from formal preparation, remember that the SAT I is not unrelated to what you may be studying in your mathematics, English, and other classes! Continuing to do well in English, math, and related courses (such as physics and history) will help you improve your SAT performance. Also, the simple process of growing socially and intellectually can improve your test results because this kind of growth is related to the development of thinking skills.

Remember that there is much to be gained from a sensible scheduling of the SAT I and SAT II. You can eliminate much of the anxiety of taking the tests merely by planning ahead for them. And if you schedule the tests so that you've left yourself intervals between them, you'll have time to work on any weak spots the early tests reveal.

Planning for the tests and taking some of them in your junior year will not only be helpful to you, but it will also be helpful to your guidance counselor. She will have a chance to look over your early test scores and gather some preliminary data so that she can give you and your family some advice about taking further tests. She can also give you some preliminary impressions about your chances for success in gaining admission to colleges you are interested in. Test information helps everyone to be realistic and to plan accordingly.

Moreover, if you begin your testing schedule in your junior year, you will have a better idea of how you compare with other college-bound students and perhaps adjust your college choices so you can avoid applying way over your head or beneath your ability. (Check out the college directories and guide books. They normally give average SAT/ACT scores for each college's freshman class, and you can see where you stand relative to other students who have been admitted to that school in past years.) Knowing average test scores at specific schools will help you to distribute your choices over a range of colleges, thus ensuring a number of acceptances at decision time in the spring.

THE SAT II

The SAT II Subject Tests measure your mastery of a particular subject like calculus, English, or American history. There are 15 different tests, and normally a student would not be expected to present more than three for admission to a college or university. *(Remember, some schools do not require the Subject Tests at all! Consult your catalogs to make sure.)*

In planning for your college prep tests remember to schedule the tests to coincide with your courses, and limit the number of times you repeat the tests. Because timing is so important, build your test schedule around your SAT II Subject Tests. Take the SAT I or ACT at sensible intervals, once you have decided where your SAT II Subject Tests will fall.

If you want to take the Mathematics Level IIC exam, for instance, do so soon after you've finished your classes in algebra, solid and coordinate geometry, and trigonometry and functions, and when you can do simple graphing on your calculator—not when you have just begun your study of calculus!

Likewise, you should take the French Subject Test after you've covered all of French grammar, most standard French vocabulary, and the various styles and levels of written French. In other words, you should be able to read French quickly and understand the author's point of view, the feelings of the characters, and the mood or tone of the work. Moreover, you will need to schedule the listening portion of the test in November, for French is one of the five language tests that now has a listening component.

Clearly it would be a mistake to attempt the French Subject Test before you had completed at least two years of intensive study of the subject. Three years would be better.

However, it would also be wrong to defer the French Subject Test until you had reached the Advanced Placement–level course in your high school. By that time you would have gone beyond the critical point for the listening portion of the test. Your memory of the proper grammatical forms might have become clouded by the fact that you had been doing more reading than writing or speaking French.

To come to grips with the SAT II, ask your guidance counselor for a copy of a pamphlet called "Taking the SAT II Subject Tests," published by the Admissions Testing Program. This pamphlet describes the material covered by each test and gives sample questions.

The final decision about whether and when to take a given Subject Test should lie with your teachers. They should know what the content of the Subject Test in their particular subject is and how well the course you are currently taking covers the test material. Many excellent high school courses do not teach specifically for the particular Subject Test, nor should they. An exciting American history course, for example, may be based on extensive reading of primary source documents and focus on social and economic policy. Students in this course could still take the American History Subject Test if they engaged in intensive study of a short textbook on American history before taking this fact-oriented exam.

Often teachers who want to help their students to do well on the SAT II will offer mini-review courses or give advice about specific areas of the subject matter that require further study for success on the Subject Test.

If you take a Subject Test at the proper point in your course of study and get a good score, you should not have to take the test again. If you're thinking about taking the test in, say, French, math, or biology again because you think you can improve your score, take a few minutes to answer the following questions first:

◆ *Are you completing another course in the same subject?* If so, then take the test again. If you took the French Subject Test after three years' study of the language and scored 600, for example, and you are now taking a course requiring you to read certain French playwrights in the original, then you should probably take the Subject Test a second time.

On the other hand, if you have taken the Biology Subject Test once and are currently studying histology, you should probably not take the Biology Subject Test again. Histology is not included on the test; it is too specialized. Unless you have an opportunity for extensive review of basic biology topics during winter or spring vacation, for example, you should probably stand on your original biology score and not jeopardize it by taking the test a second time.

♦ *How will the Subject Test relate to your college major?* If you do plan to select your college major from the same general area as the material covered by the test and you believe that you can improve your score significantly by taking the test again, then try to take it again. An applicant to Princeton, for instance, who obtained a 600 on the Biology Test and who is intent on pursuing the study of microbiology in college should plan on taking that test again.

♦ *Did you get a crazy low score?* If you have achieved a score of 700 on a Subject Test, rejoice and be satisfied with that; do not risk getting a lower score on a second attempt at the test. On the other hand, if you scored below 500 the first time you took a Subject Test, you ought to try to take that test again, even if you are no longer studying that particular discipline. Demanding colleges look askance at scores below 500 and are generally impressed with scores over 700.

If you are really worried about what to do, you can always call the admissions office of the college to which you are seeking admission and ask for advice. Or you can ask the guidance counselor at your high school and then make your decision. In the meantime, study the schedule for the SAT II and try to give yourself adequate time for preparation.

ACT ASSESSMENT TESTS

If you are considering taking the ACT, get a copy of the pamphlet "Preparing for the Enhanced ACT Assessment" from your guidance counselor. In this pamphlet, you will find a detailed description of sample questions, accompanied by an explanation of the correct and incorrect answers. The pamphlet also gives you strategies and activities useful in preparing for the test.

The ACT itself is given five times a year: in October, December, February, April, and June. And it's divided into four sections: English,

Reading, Mathematics, and Science Reasoning. It also has a career-interest inventory section that is quite helpful.

The English portion of the test contains 75 items to be completed in 45 minutes—there are subscores in usage/mechanics and rhetorical skills. The first score shows how well you understand the mechanics of punctuation, grammar, and sentence structure; the latter shows your knowledge of organization, style, and appropriateness of expression.

The reading test has 40 questions to be completed in 35 minutes. It tests how well you apply your skills of reasoning and referring to a broad range of texts in such areas as prose fiction, humanities, social sciences, and the natural sciences.

The mathematics test is a 60-item, 60-minute test that assesses your level of understanding in elementary algebra, intermediate algebra, plane geometry, and trigonometry. The mathematics section measures quantitative reasoning rather than memorization of formulas, special techniques, or computational skill. Each item in the mathematics section of the test poses a problem, suggests several alternative solutions, and offers the choice of *none of the above.*

The science reasoning test is a 40-item, 35-minute test that measures your ability to interpret, analyze, evaluate, reason with, and solve problems posed by scientific facts. Since this section of the test touches on concepts in biology, physical sciences, chemistry, and physics, it develops a picture of your ability to:

- ♦ understand data presented in graphs, tables, and charts;
- ♦ focus on the interpretation of experimental results in *research summaries*; and
- ♦ deal with conflicting viewpoints that arise from different hypotheses.

REGISTERING FOR TESTS

Registering for the ACT, SAT I or SAT II does not have to be complicated, although some students make it so. Most high school counseling centers have registration forms for the tests; envelopes addressed to the Admissions Testing Program in Princeton, New Jersey; and copies of a pamphlet called "The Registration Bulletin," which very often also contains the registration form and envelope. The ACT Assessment application comes in a self-addressed envelope; if your counseling center does not have one, call 319-337-1270 and request an application.

Test Options for Students with Disabilities

Students with learning or other disabilities can choose one of two options for taking the SAT I and SAT II. Plan A calls for special accommodations for students "with documented visual, hearing, physical, or learning disabilities. . . ." If you have such a disability you can request special editions of the SAT appropriate to your needs. With Plan B, if you require extended time and have a documented disability, you may obtain permission from the testing service and then arrange to take their tests at your home school at times arranged with your counselor. Inquiries about these plans can be obtained from SAT Services for Students with Disabilities, P.O. Box 6226, Princeton, N.J. 08541-6226.

DEALING WITH TEST ANXIETY

With registration details out of the way, you can now turn your attention to the matter of preparing yourself for the SAT, ACT, or SAT II. A month or so before the test, ask yourself the following three questions:

◆ How do I really feel about taking tests? If the answer is that you are generally relaxed and successful in a test situation, then the questioning can end there. If not, then move on to the next questions.
◆ How might I rehearse for the test I plan to take?
◆ What special skills will I need to employ in the test situation itself?

A group of students assembled in Princeton, New Jersey, spoke candidly about their first reactions to the college admissions tests:

◆ "Well, I feel fine about tests until I encounter the first question I can't answer. Then I just tighten up, have trouble concentrating, and get stuck, and it's all over! I worry that I'll never get anywhere in life."
◆ "When it comes to tests, I am the kind of person who gets hypnotized by the clock. I watch the minutes tick away and become more and more tense until I can't work anymore. I consequently never finish tests on time and always leave them with a sense of deep frustration."

- "I have worked hard and concentrated in my high school classes, but I have disappointed myself and others on standardized tests. I just wish people would stop asking me my scores and start to appreciate me for the person I really am."
- "In test situations I just can't focus on the test! I keep thinking how much fun I am going to have next Saturday afternoon as center on the girls' basketball team at the state championships in Springfield. I never study enough beforehand."

These comments all relate to various forms of test anxiety, and it is important to deal with their sources first. Here are four common ones:

1. concerns about self-image (illustrated by the second example);
2. concerns over how others will treat you if you do poorly (illustrated by the third example);
3. concerns about future security (the first example); and
4. concerns about not being prepared for the test (the third example).

(James H. Divine and David W. Kylen, *How to Beat Test Anxiety.* Woodbury, N.Y.: Barron's Press, 1979, p. 12)

If you have concerns about test anxiety, try taking them up with your guidance counselor. If that proves awkward or impossible, sit down by yourself and try to list, in order of their importance, the sources of your test anxiety. Then make a list of appropriate responses to each source of anxiety. Here are some examples:

Response: If you are concerned about your future security, remember the example of your grandmother, who, although she never did well on tests, somehow rose through the ranks of the local bank before retiring with a nice pension.

Response: If you clutch on exams, remember your first head-first dive into a swimming pool. How did you approach that feat of bravery—by relaxing and talking to yourself, right? Follow a similar approach to tests.

Response: If the clock intimidates you, say to yourself, "I will not be able to answer all the questions perhaps, but I am going to cover as many as I can. I will jump over the difficult ones and not make wild guesses. I will try to get to the end if I can." Preparing for the Enhanced ACT suggests practicing with a kitchen timer in order to keep yourself within the limits required by a test.

Response: "Difficult questions make me panic. I can't make the fine distinctions when given four or five possible answers to a question." An appropriate strategy would be to skip the difficult questions. Remember that wrong answers cost you only a quarter of a point on the SAT I and don't count at all on the ACT.

Response: If you have trouble making distinctions on multiple choice tests, go through each section of the test with all deliberate speed, then return to the questions that puzzle you. After crossing out responses that are obviously wrong, translate into your own words the answers you cannot choose between, then select the one that best responds to the question. Try not to read too much into the various choices; don't make them more complicated than they really are.

A Group Approach to Test Anxiety

Sometimes counseling centers will offer group counseling sessions to help students with test anxieties that go something like this:

Students are asked to share their experiences (and counselors may share theirs). These experiences are listed on a blackboard and members of the group then brainstorm and suggest remedial techniques for each of the problems on the list. These *remedies*, or responses, are recorded in a second column on the blackboard. The counselor/leader ensures that the recommended techniques are directly related to the individual student's problem and that they are realistic and can actually be carried out by that student.

Next the group conducts a rehearsal of the test situation itself. This exercise enables students to identify how they react in a test situation and to eliminate inefficient and counterproductive behavior. The group first appoints an observer and then proceeds with a short sample test. At the end of the test, the observer describes each person's behavior. For example, "Dave appeared stone-faced and stared into the middle distance a lot"; "Joan bit her nails and her pencil unmercifully"; "Tom kept crossing and uncrossing his legs, then scrunched up in the chair and perspired a lot, especially after looking at the clock."

Now each student's behavior is entered in a third column on the blackboard. The group then gives specific suggestions for ways to change each person's behavior, noting those suggestions in a fourth column. What results in this last column is an individual recommendation for each student and an overall model for an intelligent examination strategy.

If you become involved in a group session such as this, transfer the words in each column to four separate index cards. For the behavior noted in the preceding paragraph, the fourth column for Dave reads: "Dave should keep head and neck flexible, focus on the test paper, look up only occasionally." For Joan: "Joan should keep her hands as still as possible and perhaps chew gum, if permitted, to avoid mutilating her pencils and distracting herself." Tom should "sit in a more relaxed, upright position and look at the clock only when he has come to the end of a section."

Columns two and four of the model yield the proper combination of mental strategy and physical behavior that students need as they cope with their anxiety about taking tests. Supplementing these skills with a few simple muscle-relaxing techniques will further enhance their ability to cope successfully with the tests that lie before them.

Simple Relaxation Exercises

John Emery of the Human Resources Institute in California has suggested the following muscle-relaxing exercises for people approaching anxious moments in their lives:

1. Settle back in your chair and relax. Take a few deep breaths and begin to let yourself go.
2. Now extend both arms straight out and clench your fists more and more tightly as you count slowly to five. Then relax and let your arms drop. Concentrate on the differences you perceive between the tension phase and the relaxation phase.
3. Focus on your forearms. Extend your arms as above, and push out on a slow five-count as before. Relax again. Do the same for your biceps, flexing your arms toward your body and then relaxing after five seconds.
4. Concentrate on your forehead. Wrinkle your brow, hard, on a five-count. Relax.
5. Close your eyes tightly as you count to five. Then relax slowly.
6. Do the same for your neck and shoulders, sitting up rigidly, then relaxing. For each exercise, conclude by contemplating the difference between the tense feeling and the relaxed feeling that follows it.
7. Do the same for your stomach muscles. Then let them relax, and try to spread this relaxation throughout your entire body.
8. Now move to your thighs. Straighten out your legs and turn your toes up toward your face on a five-count and relax.

9. Relax your calf muscles a similar way, turning your toes away and down as hard as you can as you count to five. Then relax again. Repeat, turning your toes up.

10. Finally, in a relaxed position, close your eyes and review your exercises, trying to *spread that relaxed feeling* outward from each particular muscle group throughout your whole body.

(John R. Emery, *Systematic Desensitization: Reducing Test Anxiety*, in John D. Krumholtz and Carl E. Thoresen, eds. *Behavioral Counseling/ Case and Techniques*. New York: Holt, Rinehart, and Winston, Inc., 1969, pp. 270-272)

Rewarding Yourself for "Good Behavior"

Test anxiety can also be approached by inventing a simple game called Rewarding yourself for good behavior.

♦ Dave, who blanks out and stares into the middle distance during tests might promise himself a solid ten-minute break after taking a mock test if, and only if, he does not look up and blank out for ten minutes while taking the practice test.

♦ Joan might reward herself by having something decent to eat if, and only if, she is able to abstain from chewing her pencil while taking a practice test.

♦ Tom could decide to limit his clock-watching to two time checks per test section and reinforce this behavior by promising to buy himself a dazzling shirt he recently admired in a shop downtown if, and only if, he succeeds in controlling his behavior in a practice test.

Alternatively, you could consider denying yourself a particular reward if you cannot come up to the standard you have set. Whatever your decision, the important idea to bear in mind is that you must discover and then employ your own techniques for combating test anxiety. The more individual and reasonable the reward or punishment system is for you, the more effective it will be.

THE REAL THING: TAKING THE TESTS

With your anxiety reduced through awareness of what your test problems are and the techniques you need to master them, you are ready to go to the test center on a given Saturday morning. Some further reminders:

♦ Take your ticket of admission with you to the test center. Make sure that you have entered any corrections on the second sheet of the test ticket before going to the examination room.

♦ Take two or three sharpened No. 2 pencils with you. Make sure they all have adequate erasers.

♦ Take at least one photo identification card with you, such as a driver's license or a student identification card issued by your school. If you don't have either of these documents, ask your guidance counselor for advice. He or she may be proctoring the examination and thus will be able to supply visual identification.

♦ Plan to arrive early—at least 15 minutes before the scheduled time. If you are unfamiliar with the test center, plan to be there 30 minutes before the test. You may find that only one door to the test center is open that Saturday morning, or you may have to walk through an unfamiliar neighborhood to reach the test center. Allow time for such contingencies. Call in advance and ask directions. While you are at it, ask the name of the person to whom you should report. This is especially important if you are walking into the test without prior registration.

At the Test Center

Once you arrive at the test center and pass through the registration line, you will be assigned to a particular test room. If you are taking the SAT I or II and have read the pamphlet "Taking the SAT I" you already know what to expect. (See description of test above, on page 81.) If you are taking the ACT, you know that there are four sections—two for 35 minutes each, one for 45 minutes, and one for 60 minutes, for a total of 2 3/4 hours. As with the SAT I and the SAT II, there is at least a half hour of instructions involved in each test.

As the test instructions are being read, or earlier if you have time, review your muscle-relaxing exercises. Then go over in your mind the detrimental behaviors that you have discovered in yourself through group discussions or your own private reflection. Accentuate the positive as you bring these thoughts to mind. Think of what you will reward yourself with if you successfully manage your behavior: that delicious sundae, that colorful shirt, or the party invitation you told yourself you would accept if, and only if, you could find the courage to skip over the hard questions and finish each test section.

Walk-in or Standby Registration

Walk-in or standby registration for the SAT I or SAT II Subject Tests is a last resort, to be used when you forget to register in advance. (The ACT does not allow walk-in/standby registration.) Students in this predicament should follow these steps:

1. Get a copy of "The Registration Bulletin" from your school's counseling office. Fill out the test registration form before going to the test center.

2. Write a check for the test fees you may incur. All the fees are listed on the back cover of "The Registration Bulletin." The check should be made out to the Admissions Testing Program. Cash will not be accepted.

3. Contact the test center in advance. Although test monitors will not know how many spaces are likely to open up, there may be special directions for standby candidates.

4. Take photo identification with you to the test center.

5. Arrive at least 45 minutes early. Standby registration is not guaranteed, and often walk-ins are accepted on a first-come, first-served basis.

Work Carefully

When it's time to start the test, work slowly and methodically. Every ten questions, check to see that you are blackening an answer space that corresponds to the number of the question you are answering. Some sections will have more spaces on the answer sheet than there are questions. Do not let that disturb you.

The No. 2 pencils that you have brought along are sufficiently soft to blacken each space thoroughly. If you want to change an answer, be sure to erase your first response thoroughly. Otherwise the computer will record two responses for the question, and you won't get any credit for your answer.

Use the test booklet for any scratch work you may need to do. On the SAT I test, scratch work is not scored by the testing services. By no means should you think that scratch work is appropriate only for the mathematics problems. As you read through a long passage in a reading comprehension section, you may want to underline the main idea or put a question mark in the margin of a paragraph that puzzles you. You will undoubtedly be asked about the author's point of view or the tone of the passage, so if you run across a phrase or sentence that reveals either or both of these, mark it accordingly.

Answering Questions

Remember that on the SAT I you neither gain nor lose points for questions that you do not answer, so do not hesitate to withhold a response if you are unsure. Remember, too, as a rule of thumb, that if you omit 20 percent of the questions and give correct answers to all of the remaining 80 percent, you will score 700 on the test.

The rule for guessing at an answer: it's reasonable to guess when you know that two of the suggested answers are wrong. Random guessing is unlikely to increase your score.

On the ACT, wrong answers do not count but it still makes sense on both tests to answer the easy questions first and then return to the more difficult ones. Both carry the same credit. Do not guess wildly just so you can answer every question.

When the test is finally over, make sure that there are no extraneous marks on the answer sheet. Double-check to be sure that the answer sheet has the same number as your test booklet. If it does not, inform the examination proctor. Collect your pencils, and you're off, hopefully, to enjoy the reward you have earned by your calm and sensible approach to the exam.

INTERPRETING YOUR SCORES

SAT I

In about five weeks after you take the SAT I, you will receive the results of your exam on a sheet called *Student Score Report*. Now you, your parents, and your college counselor need to interpret the results on the Report and revise your college choices if necessary. By scrutinizing the test report form, you will be able to see what areas you need to work on before you take the SAT again, if indeed you decide to retake it.

You see that your verbal score is 640. Whew! Not too bad! Then you notice that score is broken down into percentiles for reading and vocabulary in the summary section below. Your raw score for reading comprehension is 75. Looking at the percentile breakdown below, you see you are in the 83rd percentile of college-bound seniors. Eighty-three percent of the students who took the test scored lower than you. That is quite a few, when you think about it. You recall that the average verbal SAT for State College is 550, and the reading comprehension raw score averages around 65. You see that your hard work in English and your outside reading program have paid off.

You then note that your vocabulary score is in the 70th percentile for college-bound seniors, so you can relax a bit. Studying the list of words that you have laboriously compiled in the back of your English notebook for a year and a half has paid off. A brief glance up to the right of the report reveals that while your 640 verbal score places you in the 83rd percentile overall nationally, it only puts you in the 75th percentile among your state's college-bound students.

These figures tell you that admission to a competitive college within your particular state (which has a large number of high scoring students) will depend on doing better on the SAT next time. You resolve to study "Taking the SAT I" again and to consider obtaining a computer program to help you sharpen your comprehension skills and improve your vocabulary. You also decide to speak to your English teacher to see if she has any books to recommend for a reading program that parallels your other efforts. You might also ask your social science and science teacher to suggest authors and documents, since the SAT I includes passages from this area as well. By acquainting yourself with a variety of styles and points of view, you will be able to improve both your vocabulary and comprehension scores.

Now your math score; it's 600. Hmmm, good but not great. This places you in the 75th percentile of your national high school class. In other words, 25 percent of all students taking this test did better than you. You recall that one of the competitive colleges you are considering has a mean math SAT score range of 570–630, and you note that within your state your math score places you in the middle of the college-bound high school seniors (50th percentile). However, you are in only the 75th percentile for college-bound high school seniors. This means that you ought to brush up on your mathematics skills also before taking the SAT again. Because you are now taking trigonometry and functions and are well beyond the level of the mathematics aptitude portion of the SAT, you should review the mathematics section of "Taking the SAT" and a book published by the

College Board called *Real SATs*. Peterson's *SAT Success* is also very helpful, as is Peterson's *Panic Plan for the SAT*.

Set aside 30–45 minutes a day to review one of these books. It can make a real difference next time you take the SAT I. You will undoubtedly join the 65 percent of students who, according to the College Board, improve their scores the second time around.

SAT II Subject Tests

Let's assume now that you have taken a set of Subject Tests and that you have your score report before you. The report gives the results of your testing on three Subject Tests: Writing, Mathematics Level I, and American History and Social Science. You can interpret these results just as you interpreted the results of the SAT. The results of the Writing Test are important because it contained a 20-minute writing sample in addition to the multiple-choice section. There are subscores for both, ranging from 20 to 80. The writing score represents your ability to express yourself clearly and shows how you compare to the nation's college-bound students. The multiple choice subscore will do the same for your ability to recognize faults in usage and structure.

The writing sample portion of the Writing Test replaces the Test of Standard Written English (TSWE) that used to be a part of the SAT and was relied on by some colleges for placement of students in freshman writing composition courses. So some colleges and universities may require that students take the Writing Test and send their writing samples to them. However, they will have to have the student's permission to do so. (Order forms for this procedure will be included with your Score Report.) If your Writing Test score does not meet your expectations, seek the advice of your English teacher and your guidance counselor. Normally a little practice with short, topical essay writing will improve your test scores here.

Say your score for Mathematics Level I is 610—not too good. In the columns to the right of the score you see that among the college-bound you are in the 75th percentile. Suppose that the mean score for students entering three of the five colleges you are interested in is 650. You may have made honors grades in math for the past three years, but you have not done as well as your competition at three of your schools.

Perhaps you did not review the material sufficiently and should now go over it again in order to score higher on your next try.

Perhaps you have gone too far beyond the material of the Mathematics Level I test and should have taken Mathematics Level IIC (with calculator) instead. Although it is a harder test and the standard deviation measurement is higher, the mean score is also 123 points higher too! Better prepared students tend to take this test and score higher than students taking the Mathematics I test.

Even so, you should talk to your mathematics instructor for advice on what you should do next—prepare for the Level I again or reach for the Level IIC. Economics and potential science majors should seriously consider moving on to the Math Level IIC and holding back their score on the Math Level I (see Score Choice procedure, below).

Fortunately, your American History and Social Science test score of 700 is another matter entirely. It places you in the 85th percentile of the college-bound group taking the test—very good by national standards and, indeed, by the standards of virtually all the colleges in which you are interested. As you do not plan to major in American history in college, this score will not help you in the admissions process all that much. But it still looks good, and it gives you a hint of where some of your abilities lie. In other words, once you are in college, it might be a good idea for you to consider taking some history courses as part of your program.

The Subject Tests often tell you where your competence lies and can be useful in suggesting future paths you might follow. Your interest in economics might lead you into a career as an economic historian. Budding scientists may veer someday toward the law or politics. One can never tell.

The American College Test (ACT)

In interpreting your ACT results you need to consider a number of different scores. The composite score is an average of the four subtest scores, on a scale from 1 to 36. Each of the four subtests is scored on a 1 to 36 scale as well. A score of 18 will be the mean score for the nationally representative sample of students who take the test. There are also seven subscores on the ACT. These are displayed on the test evaluation report you receive. The subscore scale runs from 1 to 18, with a mean score of 9 for the national sample. On the official test report form, you will also find the percentage of students who received the same or a lower score, for both your home state and in the nation at large.

Using these scores and percentages, you'll be able to ascertain how well you are developing a variety of academic skills and performing in major content areas. By consulting with your guidance counselor and teachers, you can work on techniques for improvement. High scores in certain subject areas may suggest a good chance of success in particular college

The Score Choice Option

Score Choice is an optional service introduced in 1993. It allows you to request that the Admissions Testing Program hold back your SAT II Subject Test scores until you have had a chance to review them. Once you see how well you did, you can then decide to release a given score into your official record, which is then sent on to the colleges, or hold it back. Exercising this option gives you an opportunity to take Subject Tests in the early years of high school and not be penalized by a possible low score before you can take tests again after further course work. The Score Choice Option applies to Subject Tests only, and once a score is released, it cannot be withdrawn.

majors, and high skill ratings may suggest success in particular careers. Low scores may indicate that you need to concentrate on improving some skills before moving on to college.

As with the SAT I and SAT II, colleges that use the ACT Assessment will give some indication of ACT composite or even subtest score averages or ranges in their school profiles. Colleges are generally impressed with the predictive validity of the ACT. In a current example given in "Using Your ACT Results," 78 percent of the students whose ACT scores placed them in the top 20 percent of their class did in fact have an A or B record during their first term of college, although there are many low-scoring students who beat the odds.

Once you have analyzed your scores on the SAT, SAT II, or the ACT, you are ready to go on to the next step in the testing process: congratulating yourself on your high test scores and reviewing your weak subject areas and making plans to retake those tests at the next appropriate opportunity.

FIVE

The Application Makes a Difference

The application is a golden opportunity that some kids overlook

William T. Conley, Dean of Admission, Case Western Reserve University

College candidates today have many opportunities for productive oral discussions about college, with their friends, with teachers, even with alumni of particular schools in which they are interested, but most students don't place enough emphasis on their written communication with colleges and universities. Remember that the most important opportunity for you to present yourself to a particular college comes in the admission packet. It's called the college application.

Here is your opportunity to control the dialog so that you can make the points you feel are your strongest and submit the evidence you feel is the most persuasive. In general, through your application you have an opportunity to *control* the conversation with the colleges to which you are applying.

The comments below will give you some idea of the importance colleges place on students' self-presentation on the application. Comments of this sort are commonly recorded on the jacket of an applicant's folder; these particular remarks are the actual final judgments of the admission officers at a fine small college in New England.

♦ "Nope. Despite A's, summer courses at the Wharton School, and nifty scores, the raves aren't uniform. The *person* is missing in the essay and in the extracurricular activities (War Games and Model UN). May be brilliant and precocious but he is also narrow and limited in his outlook on life.''

♦ "Wait List maybe. Proctor (student leader in dormitory), math team, varsity water polo, and New England champion swimmer. Termed "diligent, shy, responsible'' by school. Essays show ambition and drive but lack the depth or perspective we usually see. A caring kid who takes his job as proctor seriously. At least he is other-directed, and community minded, even if the essay is flat and nonreflective. A good person.''

♦ "Admit this kid! Art, hockey, lacrosse, guitar; a favorite of the counselor, who likes her warmth, integrity, and creativity. Perceptive essays show she is a strong person who would make maximum use of the opportunities here. Still growing personally and academically, but impressive application all the same.''

These perceptive admission officers are not only looking for candidates who are academically talented; they are also seeking candidates who have in their application shown themselves to be potentially strong contributors to their community.

TAKE STOCK OF YOURSELF FIRST

Before you even begin to fill out an application you should review your academic and extracurricular interests, your thoughts about possible careers, and your personal values. Then you should think about how these three elements can be related to one another and presented as a coherent whole. You should pay particular attention to your activities in high school and how they might illustrate your unique qualities. Also, if you have spent a good deal of your high school years working at a part-time job out in the real world, you may have insights into that world that will impress members of the admission committee.

Once you have visited campuses, had interviews, viewed college videos, and read school literature, you may begin to see how you would fit into the institutions to which you're applying, both academically and socially. As you fill out your applications you can relate your interests and background to the academic and extracurricular opportunities at each college. Some of the connections may be subtle or even tenuous, so don't overdo it. Just keep in mind the strengths and interests you have and, where possible, relate them to those of each school.

HOW THE COMPETITIVE PROCESS WORKS

If you're applying to one or more of the selective colleges, be they public and/or private, know at the outset that you'll be competing against other candidates with similar interests and abilities, not against the whole applicant pool. Therefore, you should feel comfortable in subtly identifying yourself as a member of one of the five admission groups discussed below. This is part of *making the match*. Then try to distinguish yourself from the other candidates in your particular group. This is called *developing the edge*. If you are an athlete, for instance, you should feel free to expound on how playing your particular sport has helped you learn to be a leader.

Neither of these two tasks is easy, yet the concepts of *match* and *edge* will help you as you shape your applications. The identification of admission categories was first described by Richard Moll, former director of admission at the University of California, Santa Cruz, and now a widely respected consultant to colleges and universities. These categories or groups accurately describe how many admission officers think about candidates. As they try to put together a class of students each year, they try to attract as diverse and talented a collection of individuals as they can.

Thinking in the broad categories of scholars, people with special talents, students who have family connections to the institution, special groups who bring social diversity, and all-arounders helps admission officers approach their annual task of putting together a class.

Although the theory of admission constituencies is more visible in the admission behavior of selective colleges and universities, it is also useful for a general understanding of the college admission process as a whole. Less selective colleges and the state universities also have their constituencies: in-state, out-of-state, multicultural students, athletes, and scholars.

1. The Scholar Category

Since the business of higher education is scholarship, it logically follows that colleges and universities place a priority on scholarship in selecting students. One indication of the importance of academic strength to colleges is the recent expansion of merit scholarship programs across the country. Today over 60 percent of America's colleges and universities seek to attract talented students by offering them financial inducements. This shows the significance that colleges attach to demonstrated academic ability.

Every college wants to attract the best students it can find. Professors want able, creative, and, in some cases, unorthodox minds in their classrooms. So they tell admission directors to deliver *scholars*. Hypothetically these students have SAT scores averaging 700 or ACT results of 30 or higher, three Advanced Placement tests with a score of 5 on each, and National Merit Scholarship Qualifying Test scores of 210 or better.

These candidates might not be very lovable; they may be prickly people who seem to know all there is to know about computers or Indians or Shakespeare or cytology. Yet they are the kind of students who will animate college classrooms. They will ask the tough questions of professors. They will spend long hours in the library or laboratory researching a minor point, and they will be elected to Phi Beta Kappa and probably win a traveling fellowship after graduation. They may even go on for a Ph.D. They are the scholars.

Such students may not have contributed as much to activities outside their narrow field of expertise as others. They probably will not root vigorously for the football team or the field hockey team. Their major contribution has been and will be to the intellectual energy of their college or university, and that is why they will do well in the admission process.

If you feel that you fall into this category of highly able candidates, you should not draw back from identifying yourself as a *scholar* applicant, particularly in the topic you choose for your personal essay. (Some of the sample essays later on in this chapter will show you the kinds of topics you will want to address in your applications.)

2. The Special Talent Category

Every college and university needs students with special skills. Where would the radio station be without freshmen who know something about broadcasting or the maintenance of electronic equipment? Where would the football team be without depth in its line—three tight ends, eight guards, and a couple of good centers? The admission office of every college must ensure that all the varied activities of undergraduate life will have students able to sustain them.

The smaller the college, the more important this special talent category is apt to be. If Coburn College cannot find three female divers to admit to each freshman class and thereby ensure that the swimming team has at least one good new diver each year, the whole women's diving program will be threatened, and the league championship reported annually in *Sports Illustrated* is in jeopardy.

If you have a special talent, make sure your counselor knows about it. Ask the admission officers at the schools you're most interested in about their needs for such talent; then, whenever possible, match your talent with those needs. A few years ago, the director of admission at a small selective college had little reluctance in revealing what special skills his school needed that year. He told an inquiring high school counselor, "We just have to find a hockey goalie since our backup goalie is going to spend his junior year abroad. And we desperately need an oboist, too. Have you got either?"

If you have a special talent, you must realize that although the number of other applicants with whom you may be competing is small, the competition is nevertheless intense.

"Having a special talent is no guarantee, however," says a first-year student at Princeton and goalie for the women's lacrosse team. You can have good test scores and have worked very hard in high school to be in the top tenth of your class and still not be a shoo-in.

The college that seeks an oboist may have among its 4,500 applicants only three candidates who play the instrument, but all three may play it well. If you think you can play the oboe well enough to win a place in the college orchestra, shape your application so that it draws attention to your musical talents. You should also make a tape of your playing and send or take it to the director of the college's orchestra. If the orchestra director likes it, then you can—and should—ask for his or her help in gaining admission.

Similarly, athletes should prepare athletic data sheets (see page 149) and establish contact with college coaches. Like music directors, coaches are assembling their teams, and using videos, comments from high school coaches, and their own observations of play to rank their candidates in terms of their potential. Candidates will probably be able to find out those rankings and estimate their chances of admission into schools looking for such talent.

Special talent candidates need not worry as much as other students about weaknesses in their scholastic record. If a college is looking for an oboist and a good one applies, even the most selective will tend to de-emphasize her C's in mathematics and a 550 score on the Biology Subject Test. The basketball player who is involved in his sport three hours a day and on weekends is not expected to have quite as high an academic average as other candidates. The strong match between the college's need and the student's talent will frequently overcome other admission factors.

Even though a candidate has a special talent, he or she may not want to *package* his or her candidacy in the same way for all the colleges applied to. There are two reasons for developing this two-track approach:

First, the competition may be too intense at some schools, and representing yourself as an outstanding member of a particular group may still not be enough to survive the competition. However, if you show your talent but also express broad interest and capability, then you might be a stronger candidate at that very school.

Second, the student may want to secure admission on a regular basis so that he or she can then choose whether to continue with his or her special talent. The oboist may want to take a rest from formal playing. The basketball player, who has been competing successfully for six years, may want some time away from the sport, perhaps to write a sports column for the student newspaper. Take time to consider what is best for you.

3. Family Category: Legacy or Leverage

An applicant who falls into the family category usually has alumni connections with that school. Since the alumni of private colleges and universities provide essential financial support, admission offices are eager to respond to candidates who are the children of alumni/ae. They cannot always admit them as their parents would like, but they do try to treat them in a fair and friendly manner.

Occasionally the family category can be interpreted to include groups other than alumni. It can mean, for instance, that the school has a special interest in candidates from a particular region. Harvard, for example, has always considered the Greater Boston area as a kind of extension of its own community of Cambridge and so looks with favor on applicants from that area. The history of Oberlin is tied in with the special history of Ohio, and, quite naturally, Ohio students fare well in the admission process there.

The family category can also embrace what are called *development cases*, which are candidates from families with potential for large donations to the school. These students have an advantage, as do candidates from important political families or whose parents are in leadership positions in higher education.

Most applications have questions about the connections of the applicant with the college. They ask where parents and other family members went to school or give you a place to state any relationship with the school that you might have. If this question is missing, then be sure to tell the college that a parent or grandparent, for instance, graduated from the college in a succinct sentence or two.

Take care not to rely on your legacy

Bear in mind that the more difficult the admission standards of the college, the closer the alumni tie will have to be in order to influence the admission committee. Having a great-aunt who went to Wellesley or the University of Michigan will not impress admission committees at those competitive schools very much. The very selective schools such as the Ivy League ones will only be influenced by the tie to an alumni parent, sibling, or close relative, such as an uncle, aunt, or grandparent. At these institutions about 40 percent of the *legacies* are admitted, and that is considerably better than the overall average for acceptances. Obviously, however, a large number do not make it.

Note: *The message here is that you should not assume that your alumni connections will assure you a place at your college of choice, and the more select the school, the more you will need other factors in your favor: scholarship, special talent, all-arounder, or being from a multicultural group.*

In many admission offices each category is looked at separately after the general review of all candidates. So the hockey goalie who is the son of a prominent alumnus may wish to emphasize his talents as a goalie in hopes of being admitted in the athletic round of decisions. Then, if that fails, he has a second chance to gain admission in the alumni round.

4. All-Around Candidate Category

The all-around constituency is the toughest of all to delineate because most applicants, like most people in the world, fall into this category. That said, colleges still need lots of all-around kids. These are the people who come to campus with a strong interest in challenging themselves academically, who want to make a contribution to the college community, who will value the college experience of the people they will meet, and who will become proud and successful graduates.

Although all-around candidates may never be scholars or sink the season's decisive three pointer, they realize the importance of a good education to a fulfilling life. They may also have definite career aspirations and know what major they wish to pursue in college, and thus will set an example for other students who are less definite about their academic focus and career plans. Or these candidates may not be at all certain about their career but want to explore the college's curriculum and sample its intern or overseas programs. Whatever the case, all-around kids typically bring liveliness and stability to their colleges and are valued highly by admission committees.

These all-around candidates also realize the importance of extracurricular activities in an academic community. They have usually played an active role in their high school community, and they want to make an extracurricular contribution of some kind to their college. They may not be sure just what form that contribution will take, but they will do something—open a snack bar in their dormitory or host prominent visitors to the campus—something.

These candidates also offer promise as loyal alumni of the institution. They are good people who want to do well in school and beyond. Many will appreciate the education they receive and, as graduates, will become enthusiastic alumni and bring favorable notice to their school by virtue of their integrity, competence, and enthusiasm.

If you're one of these all-around students, don't be discouraged by the large numbers of other all-arounders in the candidate pool. Even though the rate of admission for all-arounders is lower than for the other groups, you'll make up the vast majority of the freshman class! What you need to do when you apply is to pay special attention to developing your own unique qualities as a student, school citizen, and a person. This exercise will be your individual *edge* and help ensure admission to the college of your choice.

5. Special Groups

Since the 1960s, colleges and universities in the United States have responded to the social and economic disadvantages of certain groups of Americans by admitting qualified candidates from these special groups. In addition institutions have sought to respond to the globalization of our economy and communications network by recruiting students from around the world.

The special groups that colleges and universities seek are often defined in racial terms: African American, Asian American, Native American, and Hispanic American. Special group designations also include women, other ethnic Americans from disadvantaged backgrounds, and international students.

Recruitment of special groups is a task that all schools take very seriously. They see their task as anticipating the social and ethnic makeup of the society of the twenty-first century and finding and educating the leaders of that society now. Most institutions have appointed one or more admission staff members whose main responsibility is the recruitment and evaluation of these special students. They may be members of the sought-after groups themselves.

As happens within other constituencies, applicants who are members of a special group must compete with members of their own group in the admission process: African Americans with African Americans, Asian Americans with other Asian Americans, and so on. Even so, these candidates should remember that they still have a competitive advantage because they are sought after by the institution. Sometimes at less competitive colleges who may not have the resources to recruit widely for special group candidates, these candidates may have a significant advantage over others in the admission process. Then the question for the multicultural or international or female candidate becomes: "How diverse and dynamic will this particular college be for me?" At the very selective colleges, however, competition among special-group students for admission can be as intense as that in any category. The question of how well you will fit in and succeed remains the same, however.

In applying as a special-group candidate, don't exploit your special status for the admission committee. But don't obscure it, either. Think honestly about what your cultural or other special status means to you and how you want your education to illuminate your cultural past as well as your integrated future. Does your cultural background, for instance, influence your potential for contributing to the college you wish to attend?

One African American student handled this rather well in writing his application essay about an academic experience that had deeply influenced him:

> The academic experience that has meant the most to me has been reading the book *Bury My Heart at Wounded Knee*. This book has affected my outlook on the oppressed Indian nation of the United States and of the great injustice it has borne. This book stirred my emotions, and I related to the injustices that are quite often inherent in being a member of an oppressed group. Being black myself, I can truly relate to the plight of the American Indians and understand their reactions to their oppressors.

My good fortune in being chosen to attend the special summer school set up by my state's governor allowed me to meet people from a variety of social and economic backgrounds. The experience has given me a new perspective on life, and it will enhance all future personal relationships that I may have.

DEVELOPING AN EDGE

When college candidates determine the constituency to which they belong and present their own personality, academic interests, and extracurricular accomplishments to the admissions office as a member of that particular group, they succeed in "making the match" between themselves and the school.

You might react to this statement by saying that candidates with average scores and grades will have no chance of admission if they follow this route. Or you may object on the grounds that such a conforming approach robs candidates of their individuality. Such reactions overlook the second dimension of the application process, namely, "developing an edge" or an advantage within a certain category so that the application reveals the candidate's uniqueness as a person and as a potential contributor to the life of the college community.

Normally candidates develop their *edge* in their essays, and here it is important for the candidate and the family to be honest in the presentation to the colleges. Admission officers can tell when students have gotten too much help on their essay or are striking an insincere pose.

I remember a moment when, after completing a strong oral recommendation for a boy I knew and respected, I was told by a seasoned admission officer that the student's application had sounded a "bit hollow and had a false note." His essays were "contrived and self-serving," the admission officer said. "I didn't get the feeling that he believed what he was saying or that he really liked anything."

While trying to tell the college what he thought it wanted to hear, this applicant masked himself. He had probably been afraid that he would sound a little trite or uninteresting if he described himself in a plain and simple way, so instead he constructed a more elaborate, false identity in his application, and the perceptive admission officer saw through it.

Thus, a candidate who was in all other respects an excellent student and a fine person, with a scintillating sense of humor, was not admitted to the college he desperately wanted to attend.

Guidelines for Developing Your Own Edge

Rule #1: As an applicant you must not only "know yourself"; you must also "be yourself."
This is the first rule to follow in developing an edge. Look at this forthright statement from a college candidate:

> My goal is to become as educated a person as possible. I certainly plan to become a productive addition to society through some profession, but I believe in the sovereignty of my spirit, and its enlightenment is my ultimate goal. Everything is *grist for the mill* for me: the hard-rock guitar or the fine blend of 10,000 maniacs at a rock concert or the full-voiced choral music of Handel. I enjoy reading Shakespeare and Doonesbury, going to the Matisse show at the Museum of Modern Art, and delivering a good cross-check during a spirited ice hockey game.

The candidate shows himself honestly and forcefully in this passage. He sets himself off from other candidates by his vivid and varied examples and by his honesty about himself. He has developed his *edge.*

Rule #2: Set yourself off from the other members of the group by letting the college know of your talents.
If you fall into the scholar category, tell the college what it meant to you to build your own telescope or to put together a clavichord. If you are sincere, your natural enthusiasm will effectively convey your intellectual interests and illuminate your accomplishment in the process. One boy wrote about a special project he was doing on the poetry of T. S. Eliot:

> Investigating Eliot's early works, the reader sees a growth and budding of Eliot's faith from the self-doubt and questioning of *The Hollow Men* to the cogent, assured speeches of Thomas à Becket in *Murder in the Cathedral.* To me, this progression of thought is not merely an impotent intellectual inquiry. It has found a parallel in my own life and that of countless others. Eliot's search for a plausible personal definition of God and the meaning of the lives we live is important to me. I have many questions: Who is God? How does He affect our lives? What is

immortality? Eliot has helped me formulate some tentative answers to those questions and shape my own odyssey.

If you are an excellent swimmer and thus fall into the athlete category, you should describe your accomplishments fully in your application. Tell how you have participated in the local YMCA program and that you entered the AAU competition in the summer, winning your event. Submit your times in a few events to document your case. In addition, you should suggest seriousness about academic matters as well. One champion female swimmer wrote at the end of her application:

> Even though I love swimming immensely and spend two hours a day at practice, I do it primarily as a diversion from the arduous routine that my heavy course load imposes on me. From swimming, I have learned the value of self-discipline and of practice and how to win and lose with graciousness. But I have tried to transfer these insights to the pursuit of my chosen career, veterinary medicine. I think I have made good progress at Wheelock High School and that I can continue to excel as a swimmer and as a student at Coburn.

Rule #3: Show a desire to contribute to the college community.
This element is especially important for family, all-around, and special-group applicants. One son of an alumnus described on his application how he encouraged his music teacher to begin drilling the school marching band so that they could perform at the fall football games and elicit stronger support for the team. In an essay entitled "The Spirit of '95," he wrote:

> This endeavor added new spirit and life not only to the varsity team but to the student body. They cheered the team on to five consecutive victories. At the last game, nearly every student was there! For me the development of spirit in the student body is the best thing that can happen to a school. It makes for a close and friendly relationship among the students. It even attracted faculty to some of the games. I hope that there will be a similar opportunity for me at college, for I really think there is nothing finer than a whole community of different individuals working together toward a common goal.

The daughter of another graduate responded to the question about her significant extracurricular activities:

> Hoping to combine my desire to help the school community with some personal development, I became actively engaged in class activities and student government. As class president, I organized various activities that, with student participation, have raised money to support worthy causes: Greenpeace, relief for victims of the famine and civil war in central Africa, and Hot Meals to help our local homeless. Candy sales, pancake festivals, fairs, dances, prize money from a statewide school spirit contest, and other activities have brought into our school treasury over $3,000. These funds will also be used to reduce graduation expenses for some of the needy members of my class in my large urban high school.

A minority woman applying to a large university talked about what participating in religious activity had meant to her:

> Every Saturday I go to Branch. During the meeting we sing, we pray, we study God's teachings, and we have fun. Sometimes we go swimming or ice-skating or Christmas caroling and meet with other groups so that we can share our faith with non-Christians. I hope that there is a group like this at Hanover College. It has meant a lot to me, and I believe that religion can help bring a community together.

Rule #4: Present yourself as slightly unconventional within one of the constituent categories.
Such an approach takes delicacy and good sense, so proceed with caution. Here is part of an essay that did *not* work because it presented too rough an edge to the college. The candidate was not admitted:

> People often call me eccentric, and you know what? They're right. I like to be different. I once wore the same suit jacket for a whole month just to see if any of my teachers would notice. I once did not study at all for a Latin exam, just to see if I could pull it all together on the test. And I got a C. My friend studied until 2 a.m., he told me, and he got only a B–. I watched

the Bears play the Colts until the same time and only got a slightly lower grade. I didn't do this, though, just to "beat the system." I did it, rather, to set a challenge for myself, to see if I would crumble under the pressure of not having studied for the exam.

Another thing I like to do is impress adults in conversation. I know quite a bit about politics and I frequently make political predictions to see how adults react to them. Sometimes what I say is pretty outrageous, yet the adults always take me seriously and try to make sense out of what I am saying. I get a kick out of watching them try to formulate a serious response to my outlandish statements.

On the other hand, the following essay enhanced another candidate's chances for admission because it made him different but still reasonable:

Quite frankly, I have encountered some difficulty at Wimset High School because of the restrictions of the school's curriculum and the demands of the coaches—I play football and lacrosse. Sports have cut into my genuine desire to be by myself to read and paint. I find myself torn between the school's demands that I achieve success in traditional ways and my own interests, which extend beyond the walls of worthy Wimset. That makes me a little eccentric, I guess. But I have been artistic since I was young, and I have not been as productive in this area as I would like to be. So I intend to continue with this interest in college if I can.

Some people regard me as being a little aloof or pompous. This is because I once gave a little speech to our art class. One day we had no teacher, and everyone was throwing things around or doing nothing, and someone proposed that we go to the corner store for a snack. I told them that they could do as they liked, but that I did not regard the art class as a "creative playtime period." I wanted to finish a particular painting. That brought a lot of catcalls, but the painting did take second prize in the student art show, so I am not sorry for what I said. I think one can balance studies, sports, and the creative arts, and I hope I can do this successfully in college.

The maturity of outlook and the honesty of this essay gave the candidate an edge that caused him to be accepted at all the colleges to which he applied. He honestly believed himself to be different but he was able to see his own uniqueness as an individual in the context of a society that made legitimate demands on him. His ability to strike a balance among his various talents, while developing his mastery of them, makes him an ideal prospect. Discerning admission officers saw that this young man would make a contribution to his college community and that he would not be afraid to question its prevailing values. He could help his college to change and improve. He had a very special edge indeed.

Peccadilloes Can Spell Trouble

Two simple rules can eliminate much of the harm that applicants bring on themselves when they approach a college application hastily:

First, before you fill out the application, write your responses in pencil on a separate sheet of paper or type them on your word processor. Then look them over to see if they literally fit in the space provided and are appropriate to the question asked. This reduces the likelihood of messiness and minor errors on the form itself. You may want to photocopy your application and fill each blank on the copy first, then use that copy to fill out the original application.

Second, always move from the simple to the complex. Fill out your easiest application first; then tackle the ones that ask more detailed and sophisticated questions.

College applicants often ask, "Do you type your responses or write them in longhand?" If you can type, then by all means type in the blanks of your application. And unless specifically requested not to, use a typewriter or word processor to write the long essay. If you have neat handwriting and do not type, then answer the long essay question in your own hand. If not, try to find someone to type in the short answers for you, since these will be entered by data entry people who have many applications to record.

THE ELECTRONIC APPLICATION

Electronic applications are becoming a more and more common option at colleges across the country. The schools that use them will request that you complete theirs in one of four ways:

The Final Responsibility Lies with You

Because you are in total control of your applications and your parents and counselors will probably not see them, responsibility for neatness and clarity of expression lies solely with you.

♦ Plan for enough time to fill out and review the application. Three or four hours is not too much time to spend on an application with an extensive essay and a series of other detailed questions.
♦ Make sure that you have all the routine information neatly entered. Your parents' education (graduate degrees and occupations, for instance) can be relevant to admission.
♦ Take care to proofread for neatness and clarity of expression, organization, and "look."
♦ Have someone else give the application a brief review before sending it off. Colleges rightly expect applications to be completed solely by the student, but this does not mean that you cannot have a parent or a trusted friend review your application before you send it. Ask the reviewer if the essay sections make sense, and if they know you well, if they think you've left out anything important about yourself.
♦ Keep copies of everything—including your cancelled check for the application fee.

1. **Hard, or paper, copy**. You complete the application on the disk that the college sends you. Then you print it out and send the paper copy back to the college or university.
2. **Disk copy**. You complete the application on the disk that the college sends you. Then you print out a paper copy for yourself and send the disk back to the college or university, which in turn prints out the application and works from a paper copy.
3. **Database-enhanced disk.** This is the same operation that you carried out in number two, but now the college or university *reads* the application directly into its database and makes its decision by referring to your file in that database. In this mode you would connect to the college by the Internet or by one of the commercial networks, such as CompuServe or America Online.

4. **Interactive disk format**. Here again you complete the application on the disk that the college sends you. Then you connect to the school via a modem, and the application is *read* directly into the college's database.

Electronic applications are available from four different sources:

1. **Colleges and universities themselves.** Check the college's literature or call its 800 number to find out if it has electronic applications available.
2. **Private companies who have developed applications for groups of colleges.** These companies will contact students through direct mail and may have made arrangements with the guidance office of your high school. Students then complete a generic application—with the different responses required by particular schools—which the company sends electronically to the colleges. These companies also forward school recommendations and transcripts as a part of their service.
3. **Electronic bulletin boards.** Colleges and universities are now making their applications available electronically on the various national on-line services: CompuServe, Dialog, Dow Jones, America Online, and Prodigy. Peterson's Home Page on the World Wide Web has The Common Application (see #4).
4. **The Common Application.** This application is accepted by a large number of colleges and universities. It is available in most high school guidance offices and electronically.

ANSWERING THE APPLICATION QUESTIONS

Clearly, electronic applications are the wave of the future, but until then many students will still be completing their applications in their own handwriting or on a typewriter or word processor. Here are some pointers for doing a good job with them:

♦ **Be legible.** If you do fill out your applications by hand, use black or blue-black ink. Strive for maximum legibility—which is very helpful at 12 midnight when the tired admission officer may come to your application. Be smart. Put yourself in the admission officer's position. Avoid doing anything that would make his or her job harder or longer. Remember, always put your name on any extra sheets your essay may require.

♦ **Be consistent.** When completing the factual sections of the application—those that ask for personal information—always write your name in the same way (which should conform, incidentally, to the way you gave your name on the SAT or ACT). If you do not customarily use your middle name in full, give it only where it is expressly called for, and use your initial otherwise. Nicknames are off limits too, unless requested. Likewise, give your parents' names and titles as they appear in their formal correspondence.

Normally your home will be your mailing address, unless you are at a boarding school.

♦ **Be precise.** Give the number, street, apartment number, zip code, and any other details that may be necessary to ensure that communications to you from colleges do not go astray. Be precise about your parents' employment as well.

In the section that calls for information about your school, enter the six-digit school code number of the Admissions Testing Program/ American College Testing Program. Give the name of your guidance counselor. If the application asks for your principal's name and makes no mention of your guidance counselor, also give the guidance counselor's name. Find out your most recent rank in class and enter it in the appropriate space. Some schools will rank by actual number, some by a weighted system, others by a decile system, and others still, not at all. In the last instance you would write: "Atlantic High School (your school's name) does not rank."

In the section asking you to specify a major, you may be surprised by the number of choices, especially if you do not know what your major will be. On applications that permit you to do so, rank your interests rather than checking the response boxes for "general liberal arts program" or "undecided." If, on the other hand, you wish to combine economics and French in preparation for graduate work in international business, then you should append a footnote saying that. You can also address the topic of your college major in the personal essay portion of the application. In designating a major, you should try to match yourself with the specific programs offered by the college.

♦ **Be clear.** Many students are confused and annoyed by the amount of space given on the application to the section asking for a list of extracurricular activities. They see their own situation as "different" from that being sought by the colleges, and they struggle with how to be clear about what it is they do when they are not studying. The format of the application should not stand in the way of this process of presenting the "real" you.

EXTRACURRICULAR ACTIVITIES

Before you begin this portion of the application, list, on a sheet of scrap paper, those organizations or causes that have meant something to you and that you have contributed to in your high school years. Remember, if you have worked at a job for extensive periods of time, that you will need to be clear about the impact of the job on your outlook and experience. In either a job or an extracurricular activity, highlight the positions of leadership or responsibility that you have attained. Here is a sample list:

Chess Club
3 hr./wk., three years
First Board, District Winner, 1995

Basketball
12 hr./wk., four years, played forward
Captain, was named *City Chronicle* "Player of the Week"

Sales Clerk
women's clothing, Saturdays and vacations and full-time one summer

Assistant manager
supervised shipping, display changes, and verification of employee hours

In presenting your extracurricular activities/work to the colleges, you want to show:

- the amount of time per week you devoted to them;
- skills that you acquired;
- the number of years you have been involved in them;
- special awards or honors you have attained in pursuit of them; and
- leadership experience/or positions of responsibility you have gained while participating in them.

You also want to be sure to include your voluntary community activities, such as working with the elderly or the homeless. If there is insufficient space for these activities on the application, or the question is not asked, prepare a separate sheet for this information and send it along with the application. (See also Chapter 6.)

On many applications work experience can be presented in a similar fashion as extracurricular activities.

Many students worry that they are not involved in enough activities at school or that they are too young to have had much work experience. Remember that a small number of activities or jobs is not necessarily a bar to admission to a selective college, particularly if you're an academically gifted student or if your extracurricular activities are limited because financial hardship compels you to work after school.

Activities vary from student to student

In general, colleges understand that students differ widely in their extracurricular activities. What can give you an edge is your depth of commitment to a particular activity. The chess player who works after school so she can earn enough to travel to the national championships in Des Moines and the young man from a rural background who stays home weekends to care for his Rhode Island Red chickens (which consistently win regional 4-H championships) are both candidates who are far more interesting than students with a large number of traditional activities that have not challenged them very much.

Recently a counselor described an unusual combination of extracurricular interests he encountered in a college candidate:

> I met a young woman whose great love, after her pet pigeon, was Russian cooking. She was gifted academically; she avoided athletics. She spent the bulk of her time amassing Russian recipes and cooking for her friends. After a year or so, her Russian instructor suggested that she publish a cookbook of her favorite recipes in Russian and English. The young woman managed to accomplish this during her junior and senior years in high school. She described it thoroughly on her college applications and submitted a copy of her book with each one. She was admitted to most of her top choices. Her edge was this single accomplishment—the only extracurricular activity listed on her application!

Leadership

While other characteristics are certainly important, one's leadership ability is often what sets one candidate off from another in the selective college admission process. After all, college admission officers are trying to identify and attract the leaders of the next generation to their colleges.

"We seek candidates who demonstrate a willingness to take an interest in others," says Harvard's catalog, "who place themselves in situations that call for personal initiative and leadership."

When filling out your college applications, review your activities at school, in the community, and during the summer, and focus on those in which you've used your leadership skills. It may sound trite to say that you were an assistant cabin leader in a summer camp or that you led your volleyball team to the state finals, but it is in situations such as these that you develop skills in managing people and often an appreciation for ethical issues involved in organizational behavior.

When you graduate from college and venture forth into society, it will not be enough for you to be armed only with the mastery of a particular subject such as mathematics or French. You will also need to know how to influence people to do things. So whatever your extracurricular activity, it is quality, not quantity, that matters.

A seasoned observer of the college admission process recently stated: "The biggest single mistake that applicants to selective colleges make is thinking that being very active will impress college admission officers, when actually a long list of activities may suggest some weakness, indecision, or lack of commitment." (Christopher T. B. Murphy, Associate Director of Admission, Yale College.)

Indicate what you like to do, describe your activities thoroughly, and leave it at that. Remember that leading in one activity is more important than following in several—that the depth of your commitments are invariably more important than their breadth.

ESSAYS: ANSWERING THE PERENNIAL QUESTIONS

Now that you have dealt with all the questions requiring brief responses, you are ready to go on to those that call for longer answers—the essay questions. These questions are of two types: those that require a specific response and those that are open-ended, allowing you some latitude in your response. Notice the variation in the sample essay questions below:

- "Provide a brief essay about your activities, interests, achievements, and talents. The goal of the essay is to help us to get to know you as an individual. Point out your strengths, and explain any inconsistencies in your record. You might comment on your experiences at school, in the community, or at work." *University of Michigan*
- "Describe a humorous experience." *Johns Hopkins University*
- "On the following page, . . . please write a brief essay of 200–500 words. You may choose ANY topic about which you would like to write: your family, friends, or another person who has had an impact on you; the unusual circumstances in your life; the best or worst features of your secondary school; a recent development in your community; a scientific or other problem which you would like to solve; travel or living experiences in other countries; a question we should have asked in our application; a discussion of ethical issues which interest you or pose a challenge to you. Any subject of *direct personal importance* is a good choice." *Harvard and Radcliffe Colleges*
- "The application essay allows you to provide information about your academic achievements and unique attributes and experiences that is extremely valuable in the admission and scholarship evaluation processes. For admission purposes the University is seeking information that will distinguish you from other applicants in terms of your goals, aspirations, and achievements. You should discuss these areas in your essay, as well as what is important to you and the reasons why, your main academic interest and why you chose it, and your educational and career objectives. Please also write about your life experiences that have influenced your intellectual and personal growth." *University of California at Berkeley*
- "If you had to formulate the perfect admission question, what would it be and how would you answer it?" *Dartmouth College*
- "Please select one of the following: (1) Briefly describe how Ripon College can help you to achieve your academic and personal goals, or (2) What experience or event has had a significant impact on your life?" *Ripon College*

What Colleges Are Looking For

In evaluating the written responses to these varied topics, colleges look for evidence of your writing ability, motivation, creativity, self-discipline, character, and capacity for growth. Be candid in your essay, because what admission officers are really looking for is the human being behind all those grades, test scores, and stellar accomplishments. No reasonable admission officer expects an essay to describe a perfect person, brilliant scholar, and champion athlete. The reader might be suspicious of such a presentation—and should be.

Consider this response to an essay question that asked the applicant to imagine interviewing a famous historical figure:

> I would want to invite Theodore Roosevelt to dinner, because of all the people in history I know of I have the most empathy for and interest in him. I was initially impressed with the fact that, even though he was born to wealth and prominence, Roosevelt had to overcome many hardships of his own. His struggle to strengthen his body is well known, but people often don't remember that T.R.'s first wife and his mother both died on the same day, and his son Quentin was killed in World War I. Those experiences strengthened Theodore Roosevelt in a different way. They gave him a compassion for others. I would like Roosevelt's advice on how to express human compassion in the hard and cynical world of politics today. How would he balance American interests against the fundamentalism and nationalism in the Middle East, for instance?
>
> I would also be fascinated to talk with Theodore Roosevelt, the intellectual. He wrote about history, he loved the natural world, and he was a keen student of politics. Where would he draw the line between the interests of big business and the need to protect the environment? As the person behind the conservation of government lands for the use of the general public, would he despoil those Wyoming hills he loved so well in order to mine the coal beneath them? Would he dam the Penobscot in northern Maine? What about the destruction of the South American rain forests? Is there a 1990s version of "dollar diplomacy" that might apply?

There are many questions of this sort that I would like to ask Mr. Roosevelt at our dinner. But I would also hope that he would do some talking on his own. I would want to hear his high-pitched voice and great laugh. He was a great raconteur, and I would want to hear his version of some of the legends that surrounded him. What was his reason for walking through the White House lily pond with the Japanese ambassador? Why did he bring a horse into the White House?

I also would want to find out Mr. Roosevelt's reactions to the famous people of his day: Admiral Mahan, Elihu Root, George Washington Carver, Jane Addams, Kaiser Wilhelm, and—dare I mention him?—Woodrow Wilson.

Whatever happened and whatever T.R. said, I hope I would come away from the dinner with some new ideas of my own about how to achieve change in the American political, social, and economic system. For Teddy Roosevelt, above all else, was a "Conservative as Liberal," that is, he sought to change America within the existing framework as he understood it. Because he was so resourceful in doing this, because he managed to do it with humor and style, he has always intrigued me. Even though he has been dead over seventy years, he is still relevant. It would be fascinating to spend an evening with him.

This essay, written by a young woman applying to an Ivy League college, is somewhat uneven, but it does show writing ability. It also reveals her capacity to think critically and her motivation to ask intellectual questions of her subject. She wants to know about ecology, world politics, and history. The essay does not convey much creativity, but you have to give her some credit for her subject! Creativity can be addressed in the free, personal essay or in other parts of the application. So can self-discipline. Capacity for intellectual growth is forcefully suggested here, however. The questions asked of Mr. Roosevelt have a strong intellectual thrust. The writer is open-minded. She does not prejudge any of the answers that Roosevelt might give.

Fortunately, this young woman's interest in Roosevelt stems naturally from her proficiency in American history and a research paper she did on him in her junior year. She is currently taking a course in world politics and doing well.

Make All "Optional" Essays Mandatory

On some applications you'll be given an opportunity to write an optional essay of a more personal nature. The request may come with words similar to these: "To help us understand you better, take this opportunity to express your interests, your background, and your aspirations. . . ."

You may be tempted to skip this essay and the additional effort and time it will require. Don't! Write all optional essays; most of the other students competing with you for acceptance undoubtedly will. The application is the only opportunity you'll have before the admission committee.

At the same time you do not want to cram your application with too much information or write a long essay. Keep in mind that your application will probably receive 20–30 minutes of consideration at a selective college: 15 minutes for the first reader, 10 minutes for the second, and five minutes in front of the committee. So don't bore people!

The essay reveals more than a little of the author's character, too. The author shows sensitivity to others. She is concerned about world peace. She cares about the environment. She has a capacity to appreciate and value other people. The admission officer who reviewed this application saw the writer as being especially well suited for a special subdivision of the college's curriculum called the College of Social Studies. So this essay provided match as well as an evaluation of the candidate's academic and personal qualities.

Analyzing Two Sample Essays

Here are two more essays selected from applications to two colleges. Each college asked the applicants to respond to the statement: "Describe a significant, educational experience in your life." Read through each essay, evaluating each for evidence of writing ability, motivation, creativity, self-discipline, character, and capacity for growth. (Hint: One is particularly good, and one is deficient.)

A Home Away from Home

The experience that has moved and taught me most was the experience of going on assignment to a shelter for runaways as a cub reporter (with an assumed name and identity) for *Philadelphia* magazine. During my four days there, I came to learn a lot about the runaways, and I found that I learned from them as well. I learned about one of the real values of life, about people taking care of each other. Despite the fact that these were disadvantaged kids, or maybe because they were disadvantaged, there was a level of camaraderie and genuine concern among them that I had never experienced before. About half the kids at the shelter were black, half white, but it seemed that racism could not exist there because the people were bound together by their struggle to survive.

These kids didn't have what so many of us take for granted—love, support, and the security of food and a warm bed every night. But there was a quality in the way they spoke and acted with each other that I admired and hoped to remember when I left them.

Though I stayed at the shelter for only four days, I came away with both a new sense of the plight of runaway kids and a new sense of hope. "They seemed at first like a strong group of oddly matched but invincible musketeers," I wrote. But, in fact, they were not invincible. They were very vulnerable.

I learned that when a person under eighteen leaves home, even an intolerable home, he becomes a "status offender." He is then a ward of the state, at the mercy of the courts. The "detention," or incarceration, of these kids has become a common occurrence.

Some of the kids I became friends with had been raped or knifed in the youth study centers the courts placed them in; many had been handcuffed and had slept in jails after running away from an insane, alcoholic, sexually abusive, or violent parent. Most had been robbed of their dignity, their self-respect, their very humanity, by the system designed to protect them.

Early on a Thursday morning I walked with Darwin, a boy from the shelter, to Family Court at Eighteenth and Vine streets, where virtually all of Philadelphia's runaways end up. We sat in

Courtroom C, waiting to find out where the courts would put him since his parents no longer wanted him. After we had waited for an hour and a half, Darwin was called in to see the judge alone. A few minutes later he was half-pulled, half-led out by a sheriff, handcuffed to another boy. Although he had done nothing more criminal than run away from an intolerable home, Darwin had become a "custody case," another number in the courtroom files, another kid for the state to put away.

In my article I tried to re-create the pain of this experience, and also its wonder and beauty. Then I tried to instill in my readers not only a sense of my rage but a rage of their own—so that perhaps they will respond, in powerful numbers, so that some small part of the system will change.—*Tania Lewis*

The Pioneer in the World of Ideas

Long ago I wanted to be a fireman, a policeman, or something equally dashing. I have changed since then, I suppose, and my sights aren't set so high. I would be satisfied with being a college professor or a lawyer. However, I must still have some trace of my early romanticism because I daydream every now and then of being James Bond and foiling Dr. No, or Michael Jordan and scoring the winning basket as the buzzer sounds, or soaring above the earth as an astronaut. I think, though, that if I really could choose a great adventure, I would go into the future and help explore space.

The most exciting possibility for me will be the landing on Mars. I'll be too old before they get around to the rest of the solar system, and I'll be dead before mankind is ready to take on the galaxies. For my great adventure, I think I would like to be the first person to stand on the surface of Mars. I think that would satisfy my desire for adventure for quite a while. If I don't get to Mars, I'd like to be a pioneer of some sort; I'd like to do something or discover some idea or challenge that has never been done before. Because most of the physical frontiers on Earth have been stormed, Mount Everest, the South Pole, a solo Atlantic flight, I am left with the world of ideas. Though in some ways a second choice, it is the best possible opportunity for me, and I think the world of ideas will satisfy my desire for adventure for some time to come.—*Alton O. Rozwenc*

The First Essay Has the Edge

These two essays have merit, but, in terms of providing insights into the candidate, clearly the first essay has the edge. It gave the student who wrote it an edge, too. This essay not only reveals the candidate's ability to write clearly and even movingly of her experience but also shows her motivation to deal with a social problem by using her journalistic skills. There is a degree of creativity here, too, not only in the essayist's rhetorical approach to the reader—note the irony in the sentence suggesting that we take love, support, and the security of food and a warm bed for granted—but also in her point about "the wonder and beauty" of the young children who somehow are surviving this devastating experience. The last paragraph gives a sense of her character, too.

The essay also suggests the student's capacity for growth. Elsewhere in her application she said that she wanted to major in sociology or psychology. This fact, coupled with her comment that lots of people will have to respond in their various ways in order to rectify the situation, shows that she realizes the complexity of the runaway problem and the need for the proper education of the people who deal with them. The author certainly shows a capacity for growth in her desire to see the system change and her commitment to help that change occur.

It is now clear that the second essay lacks considerable force, but let's not gang up on the writer. He does show motivation, even if it is generalized—he wants to be a "pioneer of some sort," but he is not focused along academic lines.

Self-discipline, at least in an intellectual sense, does not appear to be this student's strong point either. He does show some ability to communicate and has the intelligence to understand that ideas often provide vicarious possibilities for exploration. His last paragraph is opaque, however. He needs to develop his thought further. He might have talked about how he planned to use his imagination creatively to "explore the universe of books" in college.

If only he had said that he wanted to explore the curriculum of this fine college, or that he liked the idea of being a pioneer in combining different types of ideas, for example, the biological and historical. Moreover, the remark, "I am left with the world of ideas," creates the impression that he regards the world of academe as being in some way subordinate to the real world of action. While in one sense it may be, the world of ideas can always inform and orchestrate the world of action. Had the writer of the second essay even glimpsed this relationship and articulated it in his essay, he would have shown a greater capacity for personal and academic growth. Moreover, he has given no indication of his values or character. He seems like a nice person—a reasonable sort—but even so, the admission officers wondered where he would fit. There's no match to this essay, much less edge.

MISTAKES NOT TO MAKE

Here are some things to remember in filling out your application and particularly in planning and executing your long essay answers:

♦ Don't seek too much help from your parents, friends, or teachers. It will show—to your detriment.

♦ Asking a friend or parent to suggest a topic for an open-ended essay is quite different from having that person correct grammar and imagery. The former is permissible; the latter is not. You must stand on your own in presenting yourself to colleges.

♦ Do the mechanical work on the application yourself on a typewriter or word processor. By no means allow your mother's or father's secretary to type the application.

♦ If you make a mistake, erase it, or if you misspell a word and forget to plug in Spell Check, so be it. Move on. No one is perfect, and as long as the essay gives an indication that it was done with thought and care, the readers will not count a couple of typos against you. On the contrary, a "sanitized" essay that looks too professional, without an error—or an original thought—could weigh against you.

♦ Pay careful attention to the instructions on the application. Some colleges want all responses written on the application itself; others are more flexible, in which case you can run over suggested word limits and include extra pages.

♦ Follow the instructions. Don't take liberties. If you have visited the college and have asked about application policies, then you can judge whether to take some liberties with the instructions on the application.

♦ Do not use the same essays for all the colleges to which you apply. To do so is to jeopardize your "match." Because each college is different, the responses you give, even to similar questions, should be slightly different. If you have a basic essay that reflects the criteria of ability, motivation, creativity, self-discipline, character, and growth, then you can tailor it to suit the programs and personalities of the various schools to which you apply.

♦ As you work on your applications, moving, as suggested earlier, from the simple to the complex and from your least to most demanding one, you will necessarily increase the sophistication and breadth of your essays in the process. Thus, by the time you reach your last and most difficult college, which is probably the one you want most to attend, you will produce your best effort.

♦ Often colleges will include a supplemental sheet on which you can provide additional information or comments. It would be unwise to assume that this sheet can be ignored.

♦ Don't overlook the optional questions. The supplemental sheet can be used in the event that you receive an additional honor—let us say you are named a National Merit Finalist or are elected to the National Honor Society—or forget to mention community activities, then think about it later.

♦ If you do happen to have something special to say to the college either after you have filed your application or in the event that the college provides no form for additional information, then you should write to your interviewer or the director of admission.

♦ Don't hesitate to write a letter or make a phone call to ensure that supplemental information or level of interest is registered with the college. Let us assume, for instance, that over the course of the fall and winter, one college becomes your favorite. You should not hesitate to communicate that fact to the school. Your letter need not be long. In it merely state that you like the school very much, believe you could contribute [perhaps an example here would help], and would accept an offer of admission if one is made. Make sure to inform your guidance counselor in the event that he or she is in contact with the school for any reason. You never know what the effect of such a letter might be.

THE FINAL PARTS OF THE APPLICATION

You have finished your part of the application, but all is not quite over yet. Various other sections of the application have to be distributed to the appropriate people.

The secondary school report

This form should be given to your guidance counselor after you have filled in your name and address, your school's Admissions Testing Program and/or ACT school code number, and the name of the guidance counselor.

Normally this report will be sent in with those of the other students applying to a particular college, so you should not jump up and down if you receive a card from the college saying that the secondary school report has not been received. High schools often have later deadlines than students. Try to give the guidance office at least three weeks to process your application and secondary school report form.

The midyear school report

Give this form to your guidance counselor, again after you have filled in the portion asking for name and address, Admissions Testing Program/ACT school code number, and name of the guidance counselor. This report is sent in at midyear, after the secondary school report form, and allows you to update your record.

Teacher recommendation

These forms go to the teachers you have chosen. Remember to complete the top portion first. Somewhere on the teacher recommendation form the student is given the option of waiving the right to see the report once admitted to the college. Unless it deeply bothers you to surrender this right, sign the waiver, and give your teachers the maximum opportunity to say what they think about you. For teacher reports to have credibility, they must be complete and honest. Some teachers, knowing that students will later examine the reports, will be constrained on their recommendations. They may fall back on clichés or unsupported conclusions that will not be particularly persuasive to the admission officer reading them. Don't take that chance; waive your rights.

You should also give your teachers stamped, addressed envelopes so that they can send their recommendations to the colleges. Ask them to keep a copy of their comments, in case you call on them again to write another recommendation.

Financial aid forms

Fill out the Financial Aid PROFILE if it's required by the schools to which you're applying. Parents will receive the Registration Form in September/ October. This form will list the colleges that require the PROFILE. This is how students and parents learn if the schools they're applying to require the PROFILE. After they complete and mail the Registration Form (listing their schools), then they receive the PROFILE by return mail. Also, the Free Application for Federal Student Aid (FAFSA) should be completed if you are applying for any government-sponsored financial aid (grants, loans, work-study). You should discuss your responses with your parent or guardian so that all the information you give on the forms corresponds to that on the Financial Aid PROFILE of the College Scholarship Service or the Family Financial Statement of American College Testing. (See Chapter 7 for a full description of this procedure.) The Financial Aid PROFILE has now replaced the Financial Aid Form.

KEEPING TRACK OF YOUR APPLICATIONS

Having dealt with the matter of supplementary material, you are now finished with your applications. You have generated a lot of paper, to say the least, and now you need a way to keep track of it. Begin by preparing a folder for each of the colleges to which you have applied and put the papers in chronological order with your application on top. Use the cover of the folder for the chart described below.

If you elect to store your college application information on the computer, again make a folder for each school and then name each document you put in. Be sure to copy everything onto backup disks, in case anything happens to your computer. You can do this on your computer or in paper form.

Make a chart that will help you keep track of all the information you will be sending, and receiving, from each of your colleges. On the left-hand side of the folder jacket, begin the chart (see pages 132-133), by listing in the first vertical column each of the parts of the application, the application fee, and a space for "Other." In the second column, record the date you received each part of the application; in the third, the date you sent it to the college or gave it to a teacher or guidance counselor; in the fourth, the date the college acknowledged receiving the document; and, in the last, a space for subsequent actions. Leave a column at the extreme right for "other" events that may need recording.

Now protect yourself by making a photocopy of each completed application. Before you make the copy, attach your check for the application fee to a page that has some space so you will have a copy of the

KEEPING TRACK: Coburn College

Form/Item	Date Received	Date Sent (Name)	College Acknowledgment of Receipt	Photocopy Made	Subsequent Actions
Preliminary Application	15 Oct.	20 Oct.	15 Nov.	No	
Personal Part of Application	1 Dec.	20 Dec.	15 Jan.	Yes	
Secondary School Report/High School Transcript	1 Dec.	15 Jan. (Guidance Office)	15 Feb. "No"	No	High school transcript not received; another copy sent 1 March
Teacher Recommendation (I)	1 Dec.	10 Dec. (Mr. Brown)	15 Feb.	Yes	
Teacher Recommendation (II)	1 Dec.	10 Dec. (Ms. McPhee)	15 Feb. "No"	Yes	Coburn did not receive Ms. McPhee's report; she sent another 17 Feb.
Peer or Other Outside Reference	1 Dec.	10 Dec. (Coach Allright)	15 Feb.	Yes	Allright called Coburn track coach for me on 18 Feb.
Supplementary Material: Athletic Data Sheet		28 Dec.	15 Feb.	Yes	
Financial Aid Statement	1 Dec.	10 Jan.	15 Feb.	Yes	
Application Fee		20 Dec.	15 Feb.	Yes	
Other Mr. Knowles (summer employer)		15 Jan.		No	Sent to Wm. Hawkins, vice president of Coburn (Knowles' ex-roommate)

KEEPING TRACK: State University

Form/Item	Date Received	Date Sent (Name)	University Acknowledgment of Receipt	Photocopy Made	Subsequent Actions
Application Booklet	15 Sept.	15 Oct.	15 Nov.	Yes	
ACT/SAT Scores	6 June	6 June		Yes	
Secondary School Report/High School Transcript	15 Sept.	1 Oct.	15 Nov.	No	
Alumnus/a Reference		1 Oct. (Judge Hoffman)			
Supplementary Material: Athletic Data Sheet		1 Oct.		Yes	Coach Allright called State University coach for me on 10 Oct.
Application Fee		1 Oct.	15 Nov.	Yes	Notification of admission by 1 Feb. or earlier

check as well. And be sure that you or your parents hold on to the cancelled check when it's sent back to you, in case confusion arises.

Double Checking with the Four Cs

As you bring your application to a close and review the various documents that make up your admission folder, ask yourself if you have met the criteria that we shall call the four Cs: clarity, candor, completeness, and contribution:

- Have you said everything as *clearly* as possible?
- Have you been *candid* about yourself, your strong points and your weak points?
- Have you been *complete* in your responses to the questions on the application, even though some of them may have seemed vague or repetitious?
- Have you attempted to show that you can make a *contribution* to each particular school?

♦ Have you not only shown your match but also *demonstrated your edge?*

Simply said, do you feel good about what you have said and the way you have said it? If so, you have probably done well in this, the most difficult part of the college admission process.

Quite apart from whether you are admitted to the colleges to which you have applied, you have already learned a lot. You have studied the colleges and learned how to ask analytical questions about them. You have sharpened vital organizational and management skills. In the process you have learned a good deal about yourself. This knowledge will endure regardless of how the colleges eventually act on your applications. Rejoice in your new skills and self-awareness as you face the anxious days of waiting that lie ahead.

SIX

Constructing a Powerful Application

Students often think that if they do everything right, the application does not matter all that much. That's not true.

Teresa M. Lahti, Dean of Admissions, Kalamazoo College

Mounting a successful college candidacy depends not only on how well you do what you do but also on how well you present it to your selected colleges. The types of courses you take in high school, your grades, what your guidance counselor says about you, your teachers' recommendations, and finally the special talents and strengths demonstrated in the supplementary materials you submit on your own behalf are all important parts of your presentation.

And each of these areas has to connect with one another, to *fit together*, in the jargon of the admissions office, for your application to achieve its goal—getting the admissions committee to accept you. Each component of your application folder—grades, scores, recommendations from the school and from teachers, should provide different kinds of information, but there must be common themes running through all these components in order for the application to be truly persuasive. For example, if you have excellent test scores, you must also have equally impressive high school grades that were obtained in your school's most advanced courses. Moreover, your talents must be confirmed by what the guidance counselor and the teachers say about you and by what you say about yourself in the application.

Because there are a lot of strong applicants out there, you will have to make sure that your particular talents are presented in the special way they deserve. For your teachers and counselor to say merely that you have a fine mind and are a good person is not enough. There must be proof, in the examples used and in the strength of the descriptive language, so that you can be distinguished from other intelligent and well-qualified candidates also applying to the college.

Remember that college admissions committees are constructing their next freshman class when they read applications. They are seeking diversity of background, training, and opinion. At the same time they do not want to create a discordant community on campus. They want a dynamic student body, composed of people who are sensitive to each other's differences and who want to build a strong community. They also want students who will be able to have some fun too. So, in addition to whatever strength you are putting first in your application—academic talent, artistry, athletic potential—you need to consider other important traits admissions officers will also be looking for.

Sensitivity to others may be one. A sense of humor is also highly valued, as are personal integrity and creativity. Whatever your particular combination of talents and traits, make sure that that combination is apparent in your application, preferably not just once, but again and again. If evidence of such qualities forms a pattern, then your folder is said to *fit together nicely*, and the college has a complete and credible picture of you.

As you think about the application, reflect a little on the values you identified in the exercises in Chapter 1. You should try to integrate those values into your approach to your application and to demonstrate them to the people who'll be writing your recommendations. This is a time for real honesty with yourself.

If you work hard because you like academic studies (rather than because good grades impress others and may get you into a *good* school), then you should convey that fact to your counselors and to your recommending teachers. If you have a particular passion, be it for rock music or blank verse, then it is time to let other people know about it. If you feel you might have done better in a particular course had you not spent so much time doing volunteer work, then you should be sure that the teacher in that course knows what the facts are. You can present a convincing picture if your recommendations all speak of hard work and genuine social commitment and the school record shows consistently high—but not always top—performance.

YOUR HIGH SCHOOL RECORD

The foundation of any college candidacy is the high school record. When admissions officers read your school transcript, they are looking for two things:

1. how well you perform with the talents you have, and
2. how well you have used the educational opportunities available at your high school.

Your goal should be to achieve both breadth and depth in your high school courses. Make maximum use of your high school's curriculum, keeping in mind that it is not the quality of your high school that matters most but rather the quality of the work you accomplish at that school. Go as far as possible in your particular area of interest, be it the classics or music or mathematics. If your high school does not offer sufficient instruction in your field of interest, you might want to pursue that interest at a local junior college or night school.

THE STRONG TRANSCRIPT

The model program of Anne Marie Gregory on page 139 shows a series of course decisions that have been wisely made. No college admissions officer could fail to be impressed by what Anne has done with her time at White Falls High School. She has taken English each year and has established her competence by scoring well on the Subject Test in writing and the new Subject Test in literature. She hopes to repeat that fine performance on the Advanced Placement test in English at the end of her senior year. Note that Anne has pursued math to the Advanced Placement level and will take an exam in that field in the spring of her senior year.

Anne's choice of science courses makes sense, too. Beginning with biology, she went on to chemistry and then to physics, in which she has taken the Subject Test. Science is Anne's favorite subject, and she has managed to take all the upper-level science courses at White Falls High.

Anne has slowly built up her command of French, too. Although it is not her best subject, she has taken it every year, and her score on the Subject Test in French with Listening Test is commendable.

Finally, Anne has taken solid courses in social studies during her four years of high school. A full year of American history at the Advanced

Placement level and an urban political history course have made it possible for her to take the Advanced Placement test at the end of her junior year. Her score of 4 is very good and will undoubtedly qualify her for placement or credit when she gets to college in the fall.

Perhaps not as obvious as the decisions that led Anne toward her strong record in math, English, and science are the decisions that have led her to experiment in a variety of other areas. She has taken half-courses in elementary drawing and painting and in concert band. She has also taken summer courses in computer and now knows how to manage Microsoft Word, Windows, and even do some basic things on Excel. These skills will undoubtedly help her in getting summer jobs and perhaps even jobs on campus during school, if she needs the money. Notice also that Anne has resisted the temptation to take full courses in these areas, although doing so might have improved her grade point average.

Should You Avoid Peripheral Courses?

If you, unlike Anne, have real ability in art, should you avoid courses in art just because colleges sometimes view them as less than solid? Of course not. In fact, some colleges flatly say that they want candidates to have had exposure to the arts. As long as art courses, or other courses that might be termed *peripheral*, are balanced by attention to the five basic liberal arts areas—English, mathematics, history, science, and languages—then you will be in good shape.

Remember that expertise in art or music, arc welding, the flute, acting, or whatever should be documented in the comments teachers or counselors are asked to make and in the supplemental material you might choose to submit. Selective colleges are usually interested in students with expertise in specialized areas only when it is accompanied by a strong and broad high school record.

THE WEAK TRANSCRIPT

Unlike Anne, many students don't take the time to organize a strong high school program for themselves. Some of their classic errors can be seen in Giselle Ramboult's transcript on page 140. If you take a good look at her transcript, you'll see that she has chosen her courses with an eye to easing her high school work load so that she could keep up an active social life. Giselle made several mistakes that she could easily have avoided. With some better planning she could have been a stronger college candidate.

THE STRONG TRANSCRIPT

White Falls High School

Name:	Gregory, Anne Marie
Soc. Sec.:	#001-23-1480
Sex:	Female
Parents/Legal Guardian:	William and Carole Gregory
	14 Mill Crest Road
Address:	White Falls, Pennsylvania 15820

High School Curriculum	Mark	Credit	
Grade 9			
English (review grammar and expository writing)	A−	1	Class rank: 10/450
Math (algebra II)	B+	1	
Science (biology)	B+	1	SAT I:
Language (French I)	C	1	V590—M640 (jr. yr.)
History (modern China and Japan)	B	1	V640—M690 (sr. yr.)
Physical Education	Pass		SAT II Subject Tests:
			American History—690
			English Composition—700
			French—690
			Physics—700
Grade 10			
English (themes, poetry, and the novel)	B+	1	
Math (geometry)	B+	1	
Chemistry	A−	1	
Language (French II)	B−	1	
Economics Theory and Practice	B	1	
Music (trombone lessons)	Pass	1/2	
Physical Education	Pass		
Grade 11			
English (analysis and exposition)	A−	1	Summer term:
Math (functions, precalculus)	A−	1	Typing
Physics*	B	1	Data Processing
Language (French III)	B	1	
U.S. History*	B+	1	Advanced Placement Test:
Art (elementary drawing and painting)	Pass	1/2	U.S. History 4
Grade 12 ** †			
English (literary analysis)*	A−		
Math (advanced calculus)	A−		
Advanced Physics*	B		
Language (French IV)	B		
Urban Political History	B+		
Music (concert band)	Pass	1/2	

*Advanced Placement or honors course.

**Marks are for first semester only.

†Advanced Placement tests in English literature and calculus will be taken in senior year.

THE WEAK TRANSCRIPT

White Falls High School

Name:	Ramboult, Giselle Denise
Soc. Sec.:	#001-32-5909
Sex:	Female
Parents/Legal Guardian:	David and Linda Ramboult
	15C Town Hill Apartments
Address:	White Falls, Pennsylvania 15820

High School Curriculum	Mark	Credit	
Grade 9			
English	A	1	Class rank: 4/450
Math (prealgebra)	A	1	
Art	A	1	SAT I:
World Problems	A	1	V550—M600 (jr. yr.)
Speech	A—	1	V600—M650 (sr. yr.)
Wood Shop	A—	1	
Physical Education	Pass		SAT II Subject Tests:
			English Composition—550
			Math Level I—630
			Math Level II—630
Grade 10			
English Composition	B+	1	
Math (statistics)	B+	1	
Language Arts	A—	1	
Drafting	A—	1	
Typing	B	1	
Physical Education	Pass		
Music Lessons	Pass	1/2	
Grade 11			
English (style)	A—	1	Summer term:
Business Math	A—	1	Elementary Chemistry—B
American History	A—	1	
Geography	A	1	
Drama	B	1	
Music Lessons	Pass	1/2	
Physical Education	Pass		
Grade 12*			
Communication Skills	A	1	
Cultures of the World	A—	1	
Anatomy	B+	1	
Photography	A	1	
Concert Band	A	1	
Physical Education	Pass		

* Marks are for first semester only.

❖

Giselle's transcript gives the impression that she selected easy courses rather than challenging ones. Any college admissions officers who reads the course descriptions will see that Giselle has not challenged herself. Giselle chose a music or art course in her program each year, instead of taking more substantive courses like history and languages. She should have made sure that she got in three years of French and at least two history or social science courses.

While Giselle has made use of the variety in her high school's curriculum, she did not pursue any of her electives with much commitment. She sampled art, drafting, drama, photography, and concert band, but she didn't study any one of them at length. If she were genuinely interested in art, for instance, she could have focused on painting, taking courses in watercolors, oils, or other media. She could then have prepared a portfolio for examination by the admissions officers and art departments of the schools to which she applied. If her interest lay in art history, she could have taken courses that would have prepared her for the Advanced Placement test in art history. The same would hold true for music or drama.

It is not the courses themselves that have undercut Giselle's chances for admission to a selective college; it is the lack of depth in any one field that has hurt her chances for admission to a selective college. Her studies show breadth but not depth. Many of Giselle's courses fall into the category of *gases*; her grounding in the liberal arts appears to be less than solid. Around the committee table, college admissions officers will say that Giselle is not sufficiently prepared to undertake the demanding work at their institution.

There is no question that Giselle has done well in the courses she has taken. She ranks fourth in a class of 450 (whereas Anne Gregory, pursuing a solid and more challenging program, only ranks tenth, using the high schools' unweighted system). Still, Giselle has shortchanged her college preparation. She has taken no foreign language and has paid little attention to the sciences. The only history course she had is the required one in American history, and colleges like to see broader and deeper preparation in the social sciences. When it comes to Subject Tests, many colleges require three different ones, and Giselle has only math and writing.

Giselle has not taken any Advanced Placement tests, which, although not required, still have a positive impact on college admissions officers.

ACADEMIC PREPARATION

What our look at Anne's and Giselle's transcripts has shown us is that there is a basic core of courses that all college-bound high school students should complete as a part of their college preparation. Now let us look at the catalogs of two selective universities and two selective colleges (Harvard/Radcliffe and Princeton, and Bowdoin and Oberlin) to see what core of courses they all recommend high school students follow:

- four years of English with an *intensive* emphasis on writing
- four years of mathematics, *preferably including an introduction to calculus*
- three *or four* years of laboratory science
- two *or three* years of history or social science, usually including one on the United States, plus a non-Western course
- three or more years of *the same* foreign language
- one year of course work in the fine arts is often recommended

In addition to covering the academic bases outlined above, "you should read widely on your own and try to become familiar with computers and word processing," to quote one of the schools above. As a college candidate you should realize that the educated mind is continually in the process of expansion and change and does not rest when a course is completed or a paper is done. Colleges and universities are looking for students who are genuinely engaged in the process of assimilating knowledge from a variety of disciplines and experiences and applying it to the challenges they are meeting in their classrooms and in the world beyond those classrooms.

COURSE CONTENT

As I hope I've made clear by now, your high school course selection is an important factor in developing your candidacy for college. But if you are applying for admission to some of the more selective schools, you cannot assume that your enrollment in the most challenging courses in your high school will assure you admission. You also have to be sure that the colleges to which you're applying know about the content of those courses: the books you read, the exercises, labs you worked on, and the final projects/papers you were asked to complete.

So you should make it a priority to ask your guidance counselor for a copy of your high school transcript and any explanatory materials that will be sent along with it to your colleges. Often high schools have a *Profile Sheet* that gives the average performance levels for their college-bound students on such measures as the SAT I and the SAT II Subject Tests. The profile may describe the honors and grading systems as well.

Find out if your high school sends along course descriptions, and then make a common sense judgment as to which of your courses might need a special explanation. Clearly eleventh-grade Advanced Placement English does not, but a joint humanities/history course, with an internship in the senior year, might require some explanation, especially if there is no description of the course on the transcript or on the profile.

Making Up Your Own Course Description

When Anne Marie Gregory found out that her high school did not have a course description sheet, she decided to write her own. She went to a school pamphlet describing the courses taught at White Falls High School and from it developed the following summary:

Anne Marie Gregory:
Course Work at White Falls High School

English Program   The ninth-grade course in English concentrates on a review of elementary grammar and focuses on instruction in basic writing skills. The course also deals with the various ways in which people interact, as revealed in dramatic scenes that students write, read, and perform.

In the tenth grade students examine various themes in novels, stories, and poetry and discuss how to develop themes in their own writing.

By the eleventh grade students are ready for critical analysis of literature. They also prepare a long biographical essay in the spring term, based on direct observation and an in-depth interview.

The study of technique and style occupies students in their senior course in English. Here they discuss the relation of form and idea in literature, exploring it in their own writing. (My class will utilize the Advanced Placement reading list and take the Advanced Placement exam in May.)

Mathematics The normal sequence for the college-bound student begins with an introduction to algebra in the ninth grade. Polynomials and linear and fractional equations, as well as computation of algebraic expressions, are stressed. Exposure to the computer and the language of BASIC are introduced in the spring term.

In the tenth grade the student turns to a combination of algebra and geometry: linear and quadratic equations in graph form, the geometry of area and volume, and the trigonometry of right and oblique triangles.

Elementary functions, exponents, logarithms, series, limits, and probability are taken up in the spring term. Some students may go on to precalculus this term, which I did.

In the senior year a student normally takes differential and integral calculus followed by the Advanced Placement syllabus in the spring term and prepares for the Calculus BC level examination, which I plan to do.

Science Biology—covering plant and animal systems, cell structure, and elementary anatomy and physiology—normally begins the science curriculum.

Students go on to take the chemistry and physics sequence in the next two years. The chemistry course covers bonding, energy relationships, chemical reactions, modern theories of molecular structure, and a description of specific chemical families and can lead to the SAT II Subject Test for able students. The physics course begins with a study of the basic laws of conservation and the kinetic theory of gases. It goes through electromagnetism and field physics, with a detailed study of the atomic model. Like chemistry, it prepares students for the SAT II Subject Test.

Next, some students go on to advanced physics, which corresponds to a first-year college course, or to advanced chemistry, which is at a similar level.

Foreign Languages The foreign language curriculum attempts to develop the basic skills of reading, writing, and speaking a language, as well as an appreciation of a foreign culture. By the end of the second year, students have mastered grammatical skills and simple conversation and begin reading the literature in a serious way. This continues intensively in the third year of the language, called: "The Humanistic Tradition in French Literature." In that year we studied such authors as Montaigne, Moliére, Voltaire, Gide, and Camus.

Social Studies The only requirement in social studies at White Falls is one year of U.S. history. However, students can include a social science course in their programs every year.

They begin with the history of modern China and Japan in the ninth grade. The China portion of the course begins with an examination of the ancient values of Chinese civilization, then jumps to the impact of Western imperialism on China in the eighteenth and nineteenth centuries. The Japan portion of the course begins with an examination of traditional Japanese society, then moves to a discussion of the impact of industrialization and Japan's subsequent experiences with totalitarianism, democracy, and world leadership.

The economics course that many tenth graders take explores the classical theories of Smith, Ricardo, and Keynes, then examines three modern industrial models: the United States, the USSR, and Japan. The spring term is devoted to an analysis of world trade (NAFTA), inflation in the United States, and the impact of social programs on taxation and government planning.

The advanced U.S. history course is designed to prepare students for the Advanced Placement exam; it covers the political, economic, and social history of the U.S. on an intensive basis. The course also tries to develop effective research and writing skills through a series of short research papers.

The senior course in urban history focuses on the development of one European city—Paris—and two American cities—New York and Chicago. In particular, the course examines how people sought to arrange their political, social, and economic lives during the period between 1850 and 1960 as they wrestled with the problems of low wages, poor living conditions, racism, and violence brought on by industrialization.

Art Although White Falls has no art requirement, I took the elementary art course, which focused on line drawings, water colors, and oils. In the spring term the course introduced some color theory, spatial organization, and a few of the major historical styles of painting. Although it was only a half-course, my art class was still rigorous. When combined with my music lessons and concert band class, I have had several years of arts.

Anne produced this informal course description on her computer so that she could send a copy to each of the colleges to which she applied.

EXTRACURRICULAR ACTIVITIES

Having written up her curriculum, Anne turned to a brief explanation of her outside activities. One college application had only two lines for activities, so Anne referred the reader to a separate sheet of paper on which she wrote:

Activity	Length of Involvement	Hours per Week	Offices, Honors
School newspaper (*The Clarion*)	3 years	4	staff, columnist, sports writer
Yearbook (*Pantagraph*)	2 years	2	staff writer, photo layout
Track team (winter and spring)	2 years	4	two varsity letters (high jump), cocaptain
Hospital work	3 years	2	volunteer
Underground paper (*The Bell*)	1 year	2	founder, editor
Music	8 years	1	orchestra, stage band

Whenever a college's application did not allow her to expand on her extracurricular activities, Anne attached this sheet. Since college admissions officers are interested in finding students who have the ability to influence and lead other people, Anne tried on her extracurricular sheet to present all the activities in which she demonstrated leadership potential. She did this in the fourth column of her activities sheet. She also expounded on her leadership skills in the essay portion of an application or, where more appropriate, in response to the frequently asked question "What activity has meant the most to you in high school and why?"

SPECIAL TALENTS AND ABILITIES

Whether or not to submit supplementary information about your special talents can be a difficult decision. If all candidates for admission to college sent in tapes, portfolios, or homemade pies, the selection process would take forever and admissions offices would have to rent warehouses to store everything. In considering whether or not to send in supplementary materials, ask yourself if any of the following applies to you:

- Is there an outstanding accomplishment or a feature of my personality that is not touched on in my application?
- Has my college counselor or a coach or teacher advised me to submit the results of my work in a particular field?
- Have I been encouraged by a representative of the college to submit supplementary information?

If you've answered yes to any of these questions, then you should consider submitting the additional information. You may, for example, want to send along a tape of your tuba solo at a recent concert, or copies of your poems that won prizes in a regional competition, or an athletic data sheet showing your times in swimming or track (see sample).

Whatever you submit, it is important that you observe a few simple rules of thumb:

- Keep it short, sweet, and to the point. Don't have twenty minutes of your tuba tape devoted to the entire orchestra's music. Edit it so that your solo is the focus of the tape.
- Seek the advice of your coach, teacher, or guidance counselor before sending anything, and show it to one of them before you put it in the mail.

- Send evidence, not testimony. That is to say, send examples of your own work, not rave reviews by the experts. This allows the college to evaluate your talents for itself without being influenced by what others may have said.
- Mail your supplementary information to the director of admissions or to the admissions officer who interviewed you and ask that person to direct it to the proper person for evaluation.
- Keep copies of everything, because most colleges will not send back your portfolio or supplementary material.

In some instances it may be a good idea to send two copies of your supplementary information, one to the admissions office and one to the appropriate evaluator at the college. If you do this, ask each of them to communicate with the other about their reactions to your materials. Athletic data sheets, for instance, can easily be sent both to coaches and to the admissions office.

Whatever you do, avoid a public relations campaign. Several rave reviews of a single piece of work will make your folder thicker and your chances slimmer. Professionally printed personal brochures with pictures will only put off a college. Use your head. Put yourself in the position of the college admissions officers who may have to read hundreds of applications between the end of January and the beginning of March. Don't give them anything to read that is not worth their time. Submit your best work in as concise a form as possible.

A Sample Athletic Data Sheet

When Anne Gregory's cousin, Rob Rhinehardt, applied to college two years ago, he prepared a data sheet for his swimming skills and sent it to both the admissions office and the swimming coach of each school to which he applied. Because he was at boarding school, he listed both his home and school addresses at the top of the page and then went on to indicate his times and his awards.

Rob Rhinehardt's athletic data sheet stands out for a number of reasons. It presents specific details. It shows the development of his skills over a three-year period, and it gives the name of his coach so that the information can be verified. It is short, sweet, and to the point.

ROBERT H. RHINEHARDT
Athletic Data Sheet

Home:	37 Dunbarton Drive Ash Forest, Illinois 60333	**School:**	Atlantic Academy Box 566 Mansfield, Connecticut
Phone:	352-882-4605	**Phone:**	223-778-8027
Height:	6'2"	**Coach:**	Bill Storms 14 River Street Mansfield, Connecticut 06099
Weight:	180 lb.		
Phone:	223-778-4208		

I have just begun my tenth year of swimming. The first six were with the Ash Forest YMCA, an AAU team. The last three have been mainly at Atlantic Academy.

Times (all flat start)
Short Course

	50 yd.	100 yd.	200 yd.
Free	22.9	49.2	1:49.9
Back	27.5	59.7	—
Breast	28.5	1:01.8 (New England Prep record)	2:19.0
Fly	25.3	—	—
IM (intermediate medley)	—	—	2:02.0 (school record)

The breaststroke time (1:01.8) placed me fourteenth among prep school swimmers in the nation, and thus I made Prep School All-American. I also anchored a 3:17.9 free relay, which broke the school record, with a split time of 49.2. The relay time missed All-American Honorable Mention by less than two tenths of a second.

Progression of times and places in
New England Prep School Championships

	1987	Place	1988	Place	1989	Place
200 IM	2:07.4	7th	2:05.2	4th	2:02.2	4th
500 Free	5:14.0	9th	—	—	—	—
100 Free (relay)	52.0	4th	—	—	49.2	2nd
50 Back (relay)	—	—	27.8	4th	—	—
100 Breast	—	—	1:04.0	4th	1:02.2*	2nd

* Set New England record in trials.

Preparing Your Own Data Sheet

Not everyone applying to college has the noteworthy swimming skills of Rob Rhinehardt or the well-balanced extracurricular activities of his cousin, Anne, but candidates can still present their skills convincingly on a single piece of paper. Rob's and Anne's examples yield several suggestions for the skilled artist or musician who seeks to present his or her unique talents to college admissions officers:

1. **Show depth rather than scope.** If you are an artist, prepare a portfolio that emphasizes your ability to look at the same object or theme in a variety of ways. Present a series of sketches of the same farmhouse from different vantage points, at different times of the day. If you are a musician, you can submit a tape of yourself playing three classical pieces on the piano. Try to show that you can do one thing well and that you have brought your artistic or musical skills to a high level of perfection in a particular area.

2. **Make variety a subordinate theme.** If you have worked in a variety of media, you may want to present one or two paintings or a photograph of one of your experiments with collage or sculpture in addition to your sketches of the farmhouse. As a musician, you may want to tape a short jazz piano selection in addition to your three classical pieces.

   The important point to bear in mind is that you should put your best foot forward. If colleges are going to accept you on the basis of your talent, then you have to convince them that you could, for instance, fill a niche in their music or art program. Every freshman class needs its excellent pianists and its talented pen-and-ink artists. Do not give the impression of being a dabbler by spreading yourself too thin.

3. **Explain your work.** Write a narrative to go along with your sketches. Introduce your musical tape with an explanation of what you are trying to achieve in your performances. Demonstrate to the viewer or listener that you are articulate about what you are doing and that you have a capacity for self-criticism and an awareness of where you are headed with your particular skill. You don't need to brag; just state your case and let the listener or viewer decide how good you are.

   Bear in mind too that even if you are not as skilled as some other applicant, that does not necessarily mean you will be denied admission to the college. All schools need students who are genuinely interested in the arts, even though they may not be gifted as artists. How will colleges be able to fill courses in music theory or the history of Renaissance painting if they do not have some of these people in their freshman classes? Schools need athletes and they need students keen on studying the obscure sciences, too. So don't be reluctant to identify who you are and what you do that's different.

4. **Document your case.** A portfolio or a musical tape should be accompanied by a recommendation from your art teacher or music instructor, who ideally has heard or seen what you are presenting to the colleges. Encourage your instructor to comment directly on your work. Remind the writer of your recommendation to state his or her own credentials as well as to make a judgment about your work and suggest how far you can be expected to carry your talents in college and beyond.

Who Gets Your Supplementary Material?

Whatever your special expertise, you should ask the admissions office where and to whom you should send your data sheet, portfolio, or tape. Many admissions officers like to have a look at these materials before forwarding them to the athletic, art, or music department for evaluation, in which case you would first submit your materials to the admissions office itself. If, however, your materials are to be sent directly to an instructor in a particular department, you should request that the instructor's evaluation be sent to the admissions officer with whom you have had an interview or some previous contact by mail or phone. This is called completing the loop, and you often have to describe that loop to the various individuals involved.

HELP FROM YOUR COUNSELOR

Many high school students fail to appreciate the important role counselors can play in the college admissions process. Don't be one of them. Indeed, your counselor may always appear to be busy, monitoring attendance, scheduling courses, counseling families, and in some cases teaching and coaching as well as helping students with college and career placement.

As a student aspiring to admission to a selective college, you have to find a way to cut through this and gain access to your counselor. You need to get to know her and then enlist her advice and aid in carrying out college plans. Once you have your counselor's attention, you will find that she may know college admissions officers and how to make the best use of the college admissions system.

To make the most of your time with your counselor, follow these guidelines:

♦ **When you do go in for a scheduled visit, have your questions written down** on an index card so you can refer to them during the conversation.

♦ **Ask the guidance secretary the routine questions** like how to request ACT information, how to get additional copies of College Board scores, or what the status of your transcripts and recommendations is. Guidance secretaries can be an important source of information for you. Do not underestimate their value! If your counselor does not schedule you for an interview automatically, ask for one directly.

♦ **Try to accomplish something in between interviews,** e.g., visiting several colleges, taking more tests, or improving your grade point average. Remember you are seeking advice, and when the facts change, the advice will change. Guidance counselors are busy people, so accomplish as much as you can on your own, and then seek their advice about the next steps you should take.

♦ **Use the interview session to tell the counselor something that could not be learned elsewhere.** Your counselor does not need to know that you are the news editor of the school newspaper; that is probably written down on some form he or she will read before writing a recommendation for you. But your counselor may be interested in knowing that when it came to a political struggle for control of the newspaper, your editorial work was found to be too liberal, so you were not given a high post after three years of distinguished work. He or she might also be interested to learn that you were one of the two students picked by your French teacher to attend a national conference and participate in a panel discussion.

♦ **Find a way to let your counselor know about any extraordinary challenges you or your family has faced or is going through right now.** Your counselor may also be interested in your family background and may be reluctant to ask. You do not have to tell every last detail; you should protect your privacy. A general statement, however, will help your counselor put your accomplishments in perspective.

YOUR SCHOOL'S RECOMMENDATION

As you talk to your counselor, bear in mind that his or her major obligation to you is to write an original descriptive essay about you for the colleges. This is the school's recommendation, a document often running 500 words or more, which, if written convincingly and candidly, can go a long way in helping you get into your first-choice college.

What Colleges Ask Counselors

Let's look at the questions colleges ask high school counselors to answer in their school recommendations.

Academic How would you evaluate the applicant's general academic performance? To what extent has the candidate made use of his or her intellectual potential and of the educational opportunities available?

Extracurricular What is the quality of the applicant's participation in extracurricular, community, or work activities? Please characterize the applicant's leadership capability.

Personal How would you and others describe the applicant in personal terms, including any special strengths or problems?

Other Are there any special circumstances, background information, or other factors (positive or negative) that may be relevant? Would you care to make any additional comments, for example, elaborate on the reasons for your checks on the General Ratings page? Do you wish to compare the applicant with other students from your school who have gone to this college?

These questions show you how specific the colleges expect counselors to be in their reports. Many counselors have too many other responsibilities to begin to provide the level of detail the colleges request. Here is how you can help your counselor make your recommendation as full and as persuasive as possible.

How You Can Help with Your Recommendation

When you're thinking about how to present yourself—your accomplishments and dreams—to the college counselor, remember that a college recommendation will most always be positive. Generally speaking, the language is supportive, and criticisms, if any, are left out of recommendations, both oral and written. So it is important for you to be positive in your approach to what you say and what you suggest that your counselor say. Here are some suggestions:

Academic Make sure that your counselor knows the exact level of the courses you are taking. When discussing your math class, refer to it by name, AP Calculus, not by the number, Math 509. Make sure, too, that your counselor knows about any academic work you have done outside the school, at a local community college or art school, for example. It is not enough to send a transcript of that work to the guidance office since it can easily get lost or overlooked. Inform your counselor directly about such work and let him or her know about your academic abilities. Offer to submit an example of your work for your file. If that is a bit too much, all your counselor has to say is "No thanks."

Extracurricular Make sure your counselor knows about any leadership positions you have attained inside or outside of school and how much time each week you devote to your extracurricular activities. If you are an athlete and have prepared an athletic data sheet, give a copy to your counselor so that he or she can become familiar with your skills and make the school's recommendation reinforce what your coaches are saying about you. Likewise, if you have to work at a job because of your economic circumstances, inform your counselor, and make sure that your application itself is clear on this point as well.

Personal All college candidates have to hold fast to their identities during a process that seems to suggest that certain traits and personalities are desirable to colleges while others are not. Although college admissions people really do strive for variety among the students they admit, it is sometimes hard to discern that when you are a candidate. Here, for example, are the personal qualities Wesleyan University looks for: "evidence of honesty, fairness, compassion, altruism, leadership . . . young men and women with a genuine sense of responsibility and consideration for others . . . [with] a capacity for commitment to society. . . ."

Your counselor and your college need some idea of what kind of person you are: where you are on your own life agenda, how you feel about yourself and your work. So try to be both natural and honest with your counselor when you describe yourself.

Other Sometimes there are special circumstances in your family or in your own life that counselors need to know. You are probably the best judge of whether an incident or situation should be related to a counselor or not. If you are on the fence, discuss the matter with your parents or a valued friend. Certainly anything that might explain a slump in your high school record, a period of time away from school, or the lack of an extensive extracurricular activities list should be explained to your counselor. Discuss these special circumstances with your counselor so he or she can factor such information into your recommendation. In that way circumstances beyond your control will not be held against you during the college admissions process.

LOBBYING FOR ADMISSION

Once you're satisfied that your counselor knows enough about you, then it is time to move on to the next phase—your lobbying effort. During the fall of your senior year, you and your counselor have gotten to know each other. You have set the overall strategy for getting into a college that's right for you. In December your counselor completes the school recommendation, and in January and February colleges are considering your applications. This is when you and your counselor need to coordinate your efforts and set the tactics to implement your strategy. Ask your counselor how to approach the colleges in order to bring subtle pressure on them to accept you. Here are some steps to take:

1. **Often the counselor can best apply this subtle pressure in the form of a fact-finding phone call to the college admissions office.** The purpose of the call is to ensure that your folder is complete, to furnish any new information about you that may have come to light, and to ascertain how you look in terms of the competition for admission. Understand that your counselor cannot call all of your schools for you, and maybe not any of them. Some counselors simply have too many duties and counselees. Still it is worth finding out whether your counselor will do a little lobbying for you, especially at your top school. If the counselor does call, then you will at least get some assurance that your file is complete and that all recent information has been received. You may gain some idea of your chances of admission, too.

2. **Another way to enhance your admission to a college you really want to attend is to write that school a first-choice letter.** Ask your counselor whether this would be a good idea for your particular first choice and what such a letter should say. Once all your visits are made and applications filed, you may come to the conclusion that one particular school is your distinct first choice. If so you can write a short letter to the Director of Admission at that school, saying that it is your first choice and that you will come if accepted. Since colleges are conscious of their yield statistics—how many students accept their offers of admission—first-choice letters sometimes can make a difference for candidates on the margin of admission.

3. **During the lobbying season, you may also want to discuss with your counselor any special connections you may have developed with a particular college.** Parents are sometimes involved in these

discussions because they have friends or other contacts at specific colleges. Students should encourage their parents to talk first with their counselor, so that all efforts can be coordinated and that overkill—going too far with these subtle forms of pressure—can be avoided.

4. **Finally, if the news from a given college is not favorable and your counselor feels that you are probably not going to be admitted, you should ask for advice on which of your second-choice colleges to approach and how.** Here again, the advice and assistance of a counselor can be invaluable.

When you hear from your colleges—usually in April—and have choices to make, you should again seek the advice of your counselor, who has been actively engaged in your quest right from the beginning. Ideally your counselor will know you and the schools to which you have been admitted and may have a different opinion from you as to which is the best match. Counselors also know how to interpret financial aid offers, and you may need some advice in that area as well. Remember that counselors are not just trying to help students gain admission to college; they also want them to succeed there.

ENLISTING HELP FROM TEACHERS

One of the most undervalued documents in an applicant's admissions folder is the recommendation written by a teacher. Teacher recommendations can make all the difference in an admissions decision, especially when the teacher knows the candidate well, knows his or her subject well, can write eloquently about the student, and is familiar with the college to which the student is applying. Although you cannot do much to affect the last three factors, you can help with the first—your teacher's knowledge of you. Consider the following method for approaching teachers to write college recommendations for you:

1. **Ask teachers if they would write recommendations for you early, before they are besieged with similar requests from your classmates.** If they answer yes, make an appointment to discuss your college plans with them. Before the meeting, consider what you feel is important about you as a person and a student. Make a list of your values, your strengths, and your accomplishments; then circle those that this

particular teacher may be able to highlight. Think about how you can help your teacher describe you as vividly as possible.

2. **When you have filled out the top part of the teacher recommendation forms from the various colleges, prepare a properly addressed envelope for each one—with a stamp!**

3. **Next, make copies of your extracurricular activities and highlight any information that is relevant to a particular instructor's subject.** For instance, if the subject is history, then you may want to note that you have traveled to a particular historical site in Europe or the United States or participated in a political campaign.

4. **When meeting with the teacher, begin by briefly reviewing your college plans, in particular, the subjects you want to study as an undergraduate.** You will probably be asking for recommendations from teachers whose subjects you intend to pursue in college. If you are not sure of what your major will be, say so. Don't worry. You have probably done well in the teacher's course; you like both the subject and the instructor. That will be basis enough for a strong recommendation.

5. **Now, briefly describe to your teacher what the rest of your life at school and at home is like.** Give the teacher a context for the recommendation. Although a teacher is only required to make judgments about students' academic competence, some colleges ask for fuller descriptions. So point out on your extracurricular sheet that you play two varsity sports, work one day each weekend, and are president of the debating team. At the very least, these activities demonstrate that you know how to use your limited study time efficiently. As your conversation moves along, keep in mind the specific questions that teachers are commonly asked to address in their recommendations.

What Colleges Ask Teachers

These questions have been taken from the teachers' sections of actual applications:

♦ Comment on the quality and nature of the applicant's academic work. What intellectual qualities and abilities does the student have?

♦ What extracurricular contributions has the applicant made to the school and community? Assess the student's talent, dedication, and leadership in the areas with which you are familiar.

♦ Tell us about the applicant's personal qualities, particularly in regard to integrity, values, and relationships with other students.

♦ What are the first three words that come to mind in describing this applicant? (This is a very important line of instruction. You might want to think of what words you would use and what words you would like others to use. Keep these words in mind as you conduct your conversation with your recommenders.)

♦ Do you have any additional comments that might be relevant; for example, a comparison to former students from your school who have attended our university?

Your Follow-Up with Teachers

After the meeting is over and your teacher has written your recommendation, you should be sure to convey your thanks. In addition to the thank-you note itself, remember to show your appreciation to teachers by keeping them informed of the colleges' decisions. Too often students assume that teachers know what happens to their applications. In fact, they have no formal way of finding out what happened to you. Involving them in the results of your application process is a way of saying thanks and may also result in further bits of friendly counsel and advice.

ENLISTING HELP FROM COACHES AND SPECIAL INSTRUCTORS

If you have a special talent in an area like music, art, and sports, you will have read the section earlier on how to prepare tapes, portfolios, athletic data sheets, and the like. In addition to working closely with your mentor in preparing these special materials, you should enlist his or her support in the recommendation process. Frequently a coach or special instructor can make a telephone call to his or her counterpart on the college side and request that a student be considered favorably. A mentor or special instructor can also write a short recommendation to accompany your work, explaining its quality and highlighting the unique contribution that you can make to the college.

Help Them to Help You

And you can facilitate this process by asking for an honest assessment of your work from your instructor or coach: "Will I be able to make a contribution to a Division I soccer team? Is it reasonable for me to hope that I can play my instrument in the orchestra or sing in the glee club at Coburn

College?'' If the answer is yes, then ask what role your coach or instructor can play in helping you to gain admission.

As with your teachers and guidance counselors, provide your special instructors and coaches with some background about your academic abilities and your other extracurricular interests and accomplishments so that these can be mentioned, where appropriate, in a conversation or letter. You don't have to be quite as specific or lengthy as you will be with academic recommenders; just give the flavor of your life outside their particular area.

Remember, too, that occasionally, in the crush of applications at a college admissions office, students' tapes or athletic data sheets get overlooked. Ask your guidance counselor to check to see that your file—including these items—is complete. Or, better yet, put your own acknowledgment card in with your portfolio. If you get the impression from your counselor or any other source that your special talents are not being factored into the decision-making process, ask your coach or special instructor to call the admissions office directly to plead your case. Usually this will not be necessary, but you should be prepared to do so, in case it is.

YOU, THE CONCERTMASTER

In many ways your role in the application process is like that of the concertmaster in an orchestra. When the conductor is temporarily called away, the concertmaster, who traditionally plays an instrument in the string section in front, is summoned to the podium to lead. When called forward to conduct, the concertmaster sets the tempo, brings all the instruments in at the right moment, and reads ahead in the score to make sure everyone does his or her part.

Like the concertmaster, you are first a musician playing an instrument in the orchestra—in reality, filling out college applications. But when that primary responsibility is completed and those applications are sent off, your role changes. Like the concertmaster, you become the conductor, coordinating the contributions of others to make sure that guidance counselors, teachers, coaches, and special instructors all play their respective parts. If they do so in harmony, then the performance goes ahead smoothly and you're rewarded with applause, in the form of well-deserved letters of acceptance.

SEVEN

Financing Your College Education

Think strategically, and act precisely: those are the two ways to make the most of the dollars you will spend on your child's college education.

Howard J. Thomas, Director of Financial Aid, Oberlin College

PLANNING AHEAD FOR COLLEGE COSTS

The birth of a child fills parents and relatives with wonder and amazement. There are so many possibilities for the child, and the parents want to enhance those possibilities in every way that they can. Few decisions will be more important to those parents than the one to invest in that child's education.

Yet no parent can be unaware of the tremendous controversy about the price of higher education raging in this country today. Ever since World War II and the G.I. bill, the federal government has extended its support of student financial aid. An initial commitment of $700 million a year has risen to an annual education budget of $16 billion a year.

In recent years Congress has substantially reduced funds for education in the face of the federal budget deficit. The watchword has become *cutback*. The financial burden of college education now falls more squarely on families and students than ever before. The salad days of the Great Society are gone for good. The Contract for America calls for a *pay-as-you-go* approach.

The price of higher education has leveled off somewhat in recent years, but it is still high. Moreover, experts predict that the cost of a college education will double in twelve years—which means that a 6-year-old child today will face a $250,000 bill for four years at a private liberal arts college that today costs roughly $100,000. Public universities will probably cost a little bit less, but not much, given the limited state tax dollars that are available. In addition Congress is now considering eliminating the subsidy in the federal loan program, which would mean that students would have to begin paying interest on their loans while still in college. This would add 20 percent to the amount they would have to borrow. Congress is also contemplating withdrawal from the College Work-Study program, which would mean that many colleges would have to spend more of their funds for student employment, and perhaps pass those costs on directly to their students. Thus, the present conservative reaction against higher education adds further impetus to the need for parents and students to plan for college costs. The key to that planning for financing college costs is to begin early and save regularly.

Plan Early—If You Have the Advance Time

Let us assume you can earn an average annual return of 11 percent in a growth mutual fund. To save enough for your child's education, you will need to invest $4411.08 per year or about $367.59 per month for eighteen years. A less adventurous investment at 7 percent annually means a yearly investment on the parent's account of $6924.72 per year or $577.06 per month.* These are formidable figures but they can be reduced somewhat by investing more heavily at the beginning of the time period and then relying on the assistance of compound interest to carry some of the educational expense later on. For instance if you were able to put $5000 away when your child was born, that $5000 would generate $32,718 in eighteen years at 11 percent and $16,900 at the 7 percent rate. The following chart is useful because it displays an average increase of 6 percent in college costs and projects parallel increases in family income.

Stocks versus Bonds

When considering the best vehicle for investing for a child's education, the experts generally agree that investment in stocks is wise even though stocks tend to fluctuate in value. Over the long run, stocks have produced higher

---

* These figures do not allow for income taxes nor do they reflect the fact that at age 18 the parents would not need to have the entire $250,000 in hand. They would only need funds for the first year.

THE COST OF A COLLEGE EDUCATION

Assuming a 6 percent annual increase in today's average college expenses of $8562 for a public institution and $17,846 for a private one, here's what four years of schooling, including room, board, tuition, fees, books, transportation, and personal expenses, will cost in your child's first year of college:

	Year Entering College							
	1996	1997	1998	1999	2000	2001	2002	2003
Child's age today	16	15	14	13	12	11	10	9
Years until college	2	3	4	5	6	7	8	9
Public university	$44,610	$47,287	$50,124	$53,131	$56,319	$59,698	$63,289	$67,077
Private university	$92,982	$98,561	$104,474	$110,749	$117,388	$124,431	$131,897	$139,010

To keep those amounts in perspective, here's a projection of what today's average household income of $53,617 will be, according to Woods and Poole Economics of Washington.

Average income	$60,958	$63,764	$66,760	$69,760	$73,248	$76,759	$80,514	$84,450

	Year entering college							
	2004	2005	2006	2007	2008	2009	2010	2011
Child's age today	8	7	6	5	4	3	2	newborn
Years until college	10	11	12	13	14	15	16	17
Public university	$71,102	$75,368	$79,890	$84,683	$89,764	$95,150	$100,859	$106,911
Private university	$148,199	$157,091	$166,516	$176,507	$187,098	$198,324	$210,233	$222,836

To keep those amounts in perspective, here's a projection of what today's average household income of $53,617 will be, according to Woods and Poole Economics of Washington.

Average income	$88,662	$93,082	$97,814	$102,784	$108,107	$113,704	$119,702	$126,014

Sources: Massachusetts Educational Financing Authority, Massachusetts Association of Student Financial Aid Administrators, Woods and Poole, Inc.

Note: These figures do not allow for income taxes, nor do they reflect the fact that at age 18 the parents would not need to have the entire $250,000 in hand. They would only need funds for the first year, and then the rest for each of the subsequent three years.

rates of return than other investment vehicles. The box below compares the returns from stocks versus bonds, for the past sixty years. The results are quite striking. A dollar invested in 1925 would have grown to $727, sixty-six times greater than if that dollar had been invested in Treasury Bills.

Income Taxes

In building up an investment for your child's college education, your first concern ought to be minimizing income taxes. You must adjust both the timing and choice of assets you give to your child to take full advantage of the tax laws. The table below shows the tax rates of different income ranges for children age 14 and over:

Income Tax

$0	– $22,000	15 percent
$22,001	– $53,500	28 percent
$53,501	– $115,000	31 percent
$115,001	– $250,000	36 percent
$250,001 and over		39.6 percent

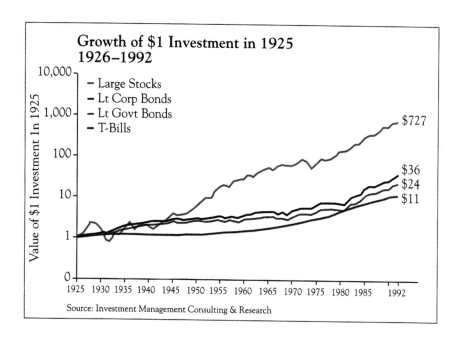

Growth of $1 Investment in 1925
1926–1992

Source: Investment Management Consulting & Research

For children under the age of 14, the first $1200 of unearned income is taxed at what is effectively a 7.5 percent interest rate. Income beyond $1200 is taxed at the parents' tax rate. Therefore, investors will want to have at least $1200 of investment of income earned at the child's tax rate before incurring any taxes on their own.

At age 14, with college only three to four years away, the child's tax picture changes. Until the age of 14, a child can earn up to $22,000 and be taxed at only 15 percent. After that point the child is taxed at the parents' rate. Financial planners advise families in this category to begin the transition from high growth investments to fixed income investments when the child reaches age 14. This maneuver will provide a steady and predictable income stream for paying college bills.

Other Investments

There are other kinds of investment vehicles that have tax advantages for paying for college in the next century. The *Series EE Savings Bond* is one

---

Two Myths About Financial Aid

It's even more important than ever to start saving for college early and not rely on financial aid for help, for these reasons:

Myth 1: Money will always be there for worthy students. Colleges and universities today are already beginning to award financial aid based more on merit than on need. In other words, if a student can enhance the school's quality or diversity goals in some particular way, then financial aid in the form of an outright grant is forthcoming. If a student is deemed not to have a special talent or outstanding academic abilities, then financial aid increasingly takes the form of loans, which must be repaid. In some cases applicants receive an acceptance letter but little or no financial aid; the full, demonstrated need of the student and the family are not met—a practice known as gapping.

Myth 2: Students will be able to work their way through college or go to school on a part-time basis and pay for their degree. Studies show that the rising costs of college in the next century as well as the dwindling supply of financial aid make it highly unlikely that students will be able to afford to support themselves as well as pay for their tuition and fees.

---

such vehicle. Investors can now earn 5.25 percent and not incur income tax if they stipulate that the bond is to be used for educational purposes when they purchase it. When the bonds come due they are tax-free, provided a number of conditions are met. Those conditions are that the bond must be in the parents' name and not the child's, and the parents' gross income cannot exceed $68,250. The tax is graduated for couples earning between $68,250 and $98,250. There are similar parameters for single parents as well.

Life insurance offers another vehicle for setting aside money for college. Life insurance forces you to save regularly, and if you die, the proceeds from the insurance will cover the costs of your child's education. In addition, the earnings within most insurance programs build up on a tax-deferred basis. Life insurance is a protection against the unexpected death of a parent and should be incorporated into your college savings plan. The amount of the policy should enable your child to pay for his or her college education; a term insurance policy best meets that end.

Custodial Accounts

For some parents the thought of setting up a college savings plan that essentially gives the assets to the child after he or she reaches the age of majority (18 or 21) offers too much risk. In this instance you may want to set up trust funds to give yourself some control over your child's assets. You can open a no-fee custodial account at a bank or brokerage house under the Uniform Transfers to Minors Act or in some states under the Uniform Gifts to Minors Act. These acts allow you to transfer a broad range of property to your child: cash, securities, life insurance, and real estate. Each parent may give the child up to $10,000 a year. UTMAs and UGMAs are arrangements wherein the child is restricted by the trust instrument from spending the funds until he or she reaches majority. During that time the parent can control the composition of the trust and the allocation of its revenues. However, remember at the age of majority the assets of the account flow directly to your child. In establishing a custodial arrangement, it is important to appoint a trustworthy and financially astute relative or friend as successor custodian so that if you die, the custodian can spend the money for the benefit of the child while at the same time looking out for the welfare of the investments, which will be considered part of the child's estate.

In considering custodial accounts parents should also remember that they cannot take the money back for any reason—the gift is irrevocable— and that they cannot borrow against the funds, either.

SHORTENING THE COLLEGE EXPERIENCE

In planning for college expenses you and your child may want to consider the strategy of shortening the college experience to three years instead of four. This can be accomplished in either of two ways.

The most familiar route is to take *Advanced Placement courses and AP tests* in high school. In the United States today, students take over 350,000 Advanced Placement tests in order to qualify for about 1,200 accelerated degree programs. At these schools students' AP tests allow them to move through their collegiate experience in three years rather than the traditional four. By taking the most challenging academic program offered in most high schools, students become eligible for the Advanced Placement program and for courses offered to high school students at local colleges and universities.

The International Baccalaureate is another route to advancement in college curricula and a shorter college experience. The IB is a much respected, rigorous curriculum in all of the traditional subjects; it is currently offered in 250 high schools across the country. Like the Advanced Placement Program, successful completion of the various subject area tests at the end of the program leads to the granting of advanced standing in many colleges and early completion of the degree.

The savings of three-year degree programs are impressive. In today's figures at a highly selective and high-cost college, the family saves $25,000 on what would have otherwise been a $100,000 investment. Then assuming the student enters the workforce a year early and earns $15,000 after living expenses (of $10,000), the saving mounts to $40,000. Likewise at a state institution costing $60,000—or $15,000 a year today—the saving becomes $15,000, plus another $15,000 earned in the fourth year, for a total savings of $30,000. This amounts to a savings of nearly one half the projected cost of a college education.

In considering these savings, you should be aware that an intense three-year college experience will be different from the usual four-year one and that it will not be for everyone, regardless of the savings. However, more families are considering this option, especially when graduate or professional schools are being considered after college.

TIPS FOR FINANCIAL PLANNING

♦ **Keep it simple!** Avoid being clever. If you are going to give your child a gift, do so without attaching strings. Contingencies lead the IRS to disallow the gift and tax it at your higher rate. Don't give your children property that you expect to appreciate rapidly. If you give your child stock valued at $10,000 that you expect to increase to $50,000 by the time he/she attends college, then he/she will have to pay capital gains tax on that entire amount.

♦ **Look for scholarships.** Keep your eyes and ears open for changes in collegiate scholarship and financial aid programs. In the event that you will be applying for financial aid, keep careful records of income taxes, appraisals for mortgages, and any special outlays such as those for medical bills. When looking for scholarship funds, remember to check with local business and community associations such as the Chamber of Commerce, Rotary, Kiwanis, and Veterans of Foreign Wars. Many colleges will give credit for outside scholarship funds and reduce loan obligations accordingly.

♦ **Invest strategically.** You should plan to invest aggressively until the child is 14; after that, pursue a conservative strategy to protect your gains.

♦ **Consult with experts.** If you do not have the time or the expertise to develop your own college investment plan, contact a financial planning professional. Saving for college should be a part of your overall plan for thinking ahead toward retirement and making sure that you meet your various commitments along the way.

SOME ENCOURAGING SIGNS

As students and families try to plan for colleges, they can take some comfort in the sincere commitment of the nation's private colleges to try to meet students' financial need. Through innovative loans, grants, support programs, and Work-Study arrangements, not to mention cost-cutting—in areas such as new facilities and faculty salaries—many of the nation's private colleges have increased their financial aid budgets to meet the growing need of their students.

State governments have also assisted private colleges and universities through loan-funding programs and tuition-prepayment plans. Financial institutions have entered the expanding realm of education financing as well. The confluence of public interest and private capital has led to some novel approaches to financing higher education costs.

The National Service Corps, or AmeriCorps, established by President Clinton in the fall of 1994, presents yet another option for containing college costs. Students who are willing to serve in government-approved social improvement projects for only nominal wages are allowed to reduce the payments on their education loans and to extend the payback period. "Every year of service will bring the student an $8000 living allowance and $4725 to be used toward tuition or education loans." AmeriCorps hopes to enlist 20,000 students in 1994–95 and eventually 100,000 in the following year.*

Remember, too, that many private industries and colleges and universities have teamed up to organize internship programs that guarantee students a reasonable wage to support themselves while in college as well as train them to enter a particular field. The end result of many of these programs is that these private schools cost no more to attend than public institutions that are subsidized by the government taxpayers.

On a more general level, the financial stringency of the past decade has instilled in Americans a sense of resilience and an understanding of what tough decisions and trade-offs are involved in the decision to seek a college education. Americans are beginning to accept the fact that college costs are high because the value is high. College graduates have more choices of career and more flexibility in meeting the needs of a changing global economy. Americans now realize that attending college means making short-term sacrifices for long-term gains. This new realism has manifested itself among many college officials, teachers, and government leaders. At the same time it has tended to overlook the families and students at the low end of the social and economic spectrum with virtually no resources for meeting college costs. These students are still at a disadvantage.

THE FINANCIAL AID SYSTEM

In the past twenty years, you may have noticed, the nature of college financial aid has changed greatly. Federal, state, and private programs have expanded considerably, and more students have been able to get assistance

---

* *College Bound*, Vol 8, No. 10, June 1994, page 4.

than ever before. However, the process of applying for aid has become more complex and time-consuming as the availability of funds has leveled off in recent years. What this means to parents and students is that you will need to consider not only the quality of the college or university's academic and extracurricular program but the school's capacity to deliver sufficient financial aid. Further, students and families need to understand that the burden of financing the bulk of a student's education has shifted in the last decade from the college and the federal government back to the student and the family.

The wise college candidate who needs financial aid should therefore apply to a range of colleges to ensure that there are financial options as well as admission options at decision time in April. A sensible college list might include:

♦ **first-choice**—the one the candidate most wants to attend regardless of cost
♦ **second choice**—a college that has slightly less difficult entrance requirements and has a good reputation for making reasonable financial aid offers, according to its literature and the experience of your college counselor
♦ **third choice**—a college where the candidate's chances of admission are at least fifty-fifty and whose literature states that it attempts to meet the financial need of all accepted candidates
♦ **fourth choice**—a college that offers essentially the same conditions for financial aid as the third but there is a much better chance of admission
♦ **fifth choice**—in most cases this will be the state university

Extremely needy candidates should select a sixth college—one that has either a cooperative education program or is near home so that living at home and commuting will help reduce college costs.

TERMS AND THEIR ABBREVIATIONS

Before beginning the research necessary to make these financial decisions, familiarize yourself with the strange language of the financial aid world. The simple initials and terms in the following list describe a whole range of programs, some of which everyone applying for financial aid will encounter at one time or another:

CSS/College Scholarship Service

The CSS is the processing organization of the College Board. The mailing address is Box 6300, Princeton, NJ 08541, phone 609-771-7725.

The Financial Aid PROFILE

The PROFILE is one of the two basic applications you will fill out for financial aid (the FAFSA is the other). Applying for the PROFILE is just like applying for the SAT. Pick up an application form in your high school guidance office. Fill it out, send it in, and you'll be sent the PROFILE by mail in a couple of weeks. The PROFILE form requires information from the previous tax year and for the current tax year, so it is best to complete it in January, but you don't have to! You can complete the form at any time, then update it later at no cost.

Once you and your family have completed the PROFILE you send it to CSS, which acts as a clearinghouse for colleges and universities. The completed form should be sent to the CSS (Box 6930, Princeton, NJ 08541-6930).

When CSS receives the PROFILE, it applies its formulas to parental and student income and assets and makes adjustments for taxes, living costs, and unusual expenses. It then sends the form on to the colleges and universities the student has designated. What the schools receive from CSS is an estimated Family Contribution (FC)—the amount of money CSS believes that a student and his or her family can be expected to contribute toward the student's college education. This information is sent to you and your parents and to the colleges and universities you have chosen to receive it.

College Work-Study Program (CWS)

This federally financed program provides opportunities for students who receive financial aid to work on campus or to work for tax-exempt employers nearby. Normally students receive the minimum wage to begin with. The federal government pays for most of the student's wages; the employer pays the rest. A College Work-Study expectation is part of virtually all financial aid packages. A CWS experience, in addition to supporting expenses:

♦ can add both breadth and depth to a student's education through the contacts made with other students and the nonacademic challenges to be figured out and mastered;

- can be a valuable asset when looking for a job after college;
- allows students to meet new people, interact, and become involved with the nonacademic part of campus life.

Financial aid awards are often predicated partially on the student taking a CWS job and earning a certain amount toward the payment of college fees and expenses. CWS should not be confused with cooperative education programs run by many colleges to provide students with practical work experience in their major field of study.

Free Application for Federal Student Aid (FAFSA)

The FAFSA was instituted in 1992 as a means of simplifying the application process for federal grants and loans. The FAFSA is available in high school guidance offices, libraries, and public agencies. The FAFSA, which asks fewer detailed questions than the PROFILE, should be completed by the end of January and should be sent to the federal processor (the address is on the envelope that is included with the form). The federal processor's office verifies the information on the form and makes a determination of the student's eligibility for federal aid programs. The toll-free number for questions about FAFSA is 800-433-3243.

Grant Aid

This term is used to describe that portion of a student's scholarship that does not have to be earned or repaid but consists of outright gifts by the institution to the individual. Because some schools have more money to give away and others have different ways of computing financial aid packages, grant amounts may vary from school to school. So when you receive your financial aid awards, one institution's offer may be more attractive to you than another's.

Pell Grant

Some needy students will qualify for this federally supported grant program. Eligibility is established on the FAFSA, and the amount of the grant in 1995 is $2300 per year. The federal government sets the amount of the Pell Grant in its annual budget each year. Like other grants the Pell Grant does not have to be repaid.

Merit Scholarship

The National Merit Scholarship and the National Achievement Scholarships are based on merit; they are awarded to students on the basis of excellence in a particular area. The grants of scholarship dollars are not based on a student's need as is the other money given in the financial aid package. Merit scholarships may be awarded by colleges themselves and also by outside agencies. Sometimes there is a special competition and or application involved. The National Merit Scholarship competition (see below) is one example. In an era of slow growth in the number of qualified students moving on to college, merit scholarships are becoming increasingly important to colleges as a method of attracting students who help the institution meet its goals of quality and diversity. A recent survey found that 85 percent of private four-year colleges and 90 percent of public four-year colleges offer merit scholarships without regard to financial need.

The scores received on the PSAT (Preliminary Scholastic Assessment Test) that eleventh (and some tenth) graders take in the fall, along with supplemental information, high school record, and recommendation, determine the selection of semifinalists and ultimately the finalists for these scholarships.

Winners will normally receive a $500 stipend if they are not eligible for financial aid and $2000 if they are; some will be eligible for higher corporate awards if they have an affiliation with one of the sponsoring companies of the program.

Need-Blind Admissions

Need-blind admissions means that a student's and family's financial need is not taken into account by the college in its decision to admit or deny the candidate. Need-blind admissions became common practice in the late 1960s in response to increased federal support of collegiate financial aid programs. In recent years, the withdrawal of federal dollars from grant programs and the rising costs of providing a high-quality education have forced many colleges and universities to move away from the need-blind system.

Need-Sensitive Admissions

The policy that many colleges and universities have adopted, if they have been unable to afford a need-blind financial aid program, takes note of a student's ability to contribute to the cost of his or her education in the admissions decision itself. The practice of need-sensitive admissions has a number of modes:

♦ a college can be sensitive to need when taking students from the waiting list—and not take those it cannot afford to pay;

♦ it can be sensitive to need for candidates who are at the margin of the accepted group and among those with modest credentials accept only those who can pay;

♦ it can admit candidates with marginal credentials for acceptance but not offer them the aid necessary to meet their financial need. This practice is known as *gapping* because there is a gap between what the College Scholarship Service determines is the Family Contribution (see page 184) after receiving the PROFILE and what the college or university offers the student.

♦ a college or university can also decide to make the ability to pay a small factor in the admissions decision itself and then, with the savings realized by admitting students who can contribute something toward their education, proceed to award financial aid packages that meet the full need of all admitted students.

As a rule of thumb, students and parents should make sure to inquire about each institution's financial aid policy—in some detail! Ask the financial aid office to explain how students are packaged and examine any sample packages that may be available. Make sure that you find out about the merit scholarships at every school you are applying to. Make certain that you don't have to apply for them separately and that they are included in the regular process of computing your financial aid package.

Preferential Packaging

This is the name of the practice of giving more desirable students more favorable aid packages. Some colleges give increased grants and reduced loans to qualifying students whom they very much want to attract or, conversely, give higher loans and lower grants to students who are less desirable to them. The practice of varying the ratio of loan to grant according to admissions desirability is the essence of preferential packaging.

LOAN PROGRAMS

Perkins Loan

The Perkins Loan is a federally subsidized loan carrying a 5 percent interest rate. No interest accrues while the student is enrolled at least part-time.

Repayment begins nine months after the student leaves college. Students may borrow up to $3000 a year and must pay back the loan in ten years.

Subsidized Stafford Loan

This is a federally guaranteed loan given by local banks. Once a student's need is determined by the numbers on the FAFSA form, the student may borrow up to $2625 in the first year and $5500 in the senior year, up to a maximum of $23,000 for four years of undergraduate education. The amount borrowed, minus a 3 percent origination fee and a 1 percent insurance premium, is applied to the student's term bill. Repayment with variable interest begins six months after the student ceases to be enrolled and ends ten years later, when the loan must be paid in full. The interest rate is 7.43 percent, with an 8.25 percent cap rate for the life of the loan.*

Unsubsidized Stafford Loan

If your need is too small to qualify you for the Perkins or subsidized Stafford loans, you can still apply for an unsubsidized Stafford Loan. The loan amounts are the same as for the subsidized Stafford: $2625–$5500 and $23,000 maximum, but interest payments begin at the inception of the loan. Most lenders allow the interest to be capitalized (added to the loan), while the borrower is in school. The interest rate is currently 7.43 percent, with an 8.25 percent cap rate for the life of the loan.

PLUS Loans

Its full name is Parent Loans for Undergraduate Students, and it's the federally guaranteed loan program available from private banks and lending institutions. They are guaranteed by the federal government and are not related to the need of the particular family. PLUS loans may therefore cover the entire cost of the student's education, minus any financial aid awarded. After paying a guarantee fee and an origination fee, repayment begins 60 days after the loan is granted. The current interest rate for PLUS loans is 8.38 percent, with a 9 percent cap rate for the life of the loan.**

---

    * The interest rate for the Stafford Loans is set each year and is based on annual Treasury Bill rates plus points for overhead cost.

    ** PLUS loans are similar to Stafford Loans in that they are based on annual Treasury Bill rates, with points added for overhead cost.

SLS/Supplementary Loans for Students

Although this program no longer exists under this name, some financial aid officers still refer to it. When they do, they are describing an unsubsidized loan program for independent students or students whose parents have not been declared eligible for a PLUS loan. This program is a variation of the Unsubsidized Stafford Loan Program. Qualifying students may borrow up to $4000 in the first two years of college and $5000 in the second two.

ROTC/Reserve Officers' Training Corps

ROTC is a scholarship and educational program offered by the three military services of the U.S. government. In return for scholarship aid that amounts to the cost of room and board plus a stipend in some cases, students have to serve for a period of years on active or reserve duty in one of the military services.

SAR/Student Aid Report

When you submit your FAFSA to the federal processor, you will automatically receive a Student Aid Report in four to six weeks. The SAR has three sections. First, it will verify your citizenship, social security number, address, age, and your intention to be a full-time student. Second, it will provide you with a tear-off correction form so that you can furnish or correct any of the information requested by the federal processor. Third, the SAR will tell you if you are eligible for a Pell Grant by means of a Student Aid Index. If your index number is below 2100, you are eligible, depending on the cost of the school, and you should be sure that the colleges to which you apply receive a copy of the SAR letter. Note that many colleges are able to make changes to your SAR through an electronic link to the Federal Processor. Ask.

AID APPLICATION FORMS

Applying for financial aid is a great deal easier than the number of abbreviations might suggest. You should begin no later than November of the senior year in high school. At that point, if you think you will be a candidate for financial aid in college, you should go to the office of your guidance counselor and obtain a copy of both the Financial Aid PROFILE application and the FAFSA. When you receive the actual PROFILE form, discuss it and the FAFSA with your family. Remember that the PROFILE form will be required by many private colleges and scholarship programs.

The FAFSA will be required by state schools and will also be necessary if you intend to participate in any of the federally sponsored scholarship programs. Your parents have the sizable task of completing both these forms; however, you should familiarize yourself with them because once you are in college and have discussions with financial aid officers, the details of these forms will come up. Once the forms are complete, the PROFILE—with its fee—should be sent to CSS and the FAFSA to the federal processor whose address is printed on the envelope you received with the form. Parents and students should be very mindful of the deadlines on these forms. Sometimes colleges or universities with modest financial aid resources have to limit aid to students who file their forms late.

Filling out the PROFILE or FAFSA

Students and their families should strive for accuracy when completing their respective portions of the PROFILE or FAFSA. They should make sure that they have Social Security numbers for the head of household and the student and that these are entered properly. Students who are not American citizens may still qualify for aid if they are permanent residents or if they live in certain U.S. territories.

If your parents are divorced, most institutions will require completion of the Divorced or Separated Parent's Statement. You should obtain a copy of this form along with your PROFILE and FAFSA from your guidance counselor. Fill in the name of the parent with whom you have lived for the past twelve months, and send the form to the absentee parent.

The reason for the Divorced or Separated Parent Statement is that many colleges and universities look on financing college costs as a shared responsibility. These schools believe that the student, both parents, and the college or university itself have a responsibility to provide funding for college costs. It is often said that students, parents, and school are the three legs of the financial aid stool. Therefore institutions will ask both parents to make a contribution to their child's college expenses, even though there has been a divorce. The colleges will combine the incomes of both natural parents as a basis for a financial aid award. Some may look at step-parent resources as well.

Parents completing the PROFILE and the FAFSA are asked to furnish information about the number of their dependents for the current calendar year and the number of children they are supporting in college.* Most of the financial information requested on the forms can be taken from the parents' tax return (Form 1040 or 1040A); however, other information, such as the value of real estate, bank deposits, and stocks will have to be gathered separately.** Parents will also be asked to project their earnings for the year in which the applicant will enter college. In each case, they should not include any money earned by their son or daughter under any current financial aid program, nor should they project such earnings for the following year. The purpose of the form itself is to determine need on an annual basis and to help college officials decide how much aid to offer.

In cases in which Social Security benefits are involved, only those benefits that applicants and their parents receive should be included, not those received by other dependents in the family. Married students who rely on their parents' support to meet living expenses are required to include amounts received for welfare or child support, any unemployment insurance, and any living or housing allowances, whether received in cash or not. They must also report the earnings of their spouse.

Medical expenses that are not reimbursed by any insurance plan can also be included to offset other income, as can the amount paid for the private elementary or junior high school education of other children in the family. These amounts are then projected for the next calendar year. Then total income, taxable income, and nontaxable income are computed, and the federal income tax for the year is subtracted in order to arrive at the true family income.

The PROFILE form goes further than the FAFSA and asks students and parents to break down wages (including summer earnings), savings, checking account balances, dividend and interest income, trust funds, and home value. The PROFILE also has a section for institution-specific questions. In other words, when you designate College X on your application, your PROFILE may have a specific question about your financial situation that College X wants to know.

The college or university looks at all the family assets and follows its own formulas for computing value and for protecting certain assets like

---

* The PROFILE will ask for the purchase price, actual value, and amount of the mortgage on the parents' primary residence.

** When assembling a student's financial aid offer, not all colleges or universities treat the tuition expenses for siblings in secondary school, or for that matter, parents in degree programs, in the same fashion.

homes, businesses, and farms from having undue influence in reducing need. Schools also look at student assets, and you can normally be expected to contribute 35 percent of your assets toward college costs in the first year and a similar percentage thereafter.

Parents are normally expected to contribute 3–4 percent of their assets each year, but often this can be reduced by allowances for the age of a parent or a concession for the cost of an older sibling in college.* (The latter frequently reduces a parental contribution by half.) Business losses or loss of work in a given year are also considered in the calculation of Family Contribution.

The rest of the PROFILE and the FAFSA is fairly straightforward. Parents must report taxable income, wages, interest income, dividends, and various sources of nontaxable income, such as Social Security benefits. (Remember for the PROFILE, this is for two years.) Parents must also provide detailed information about the expenses they bear for the education of their other children. Child support, alimony, and the income of the parent with whom the child does not live are requested of divorced families.

Having done all this, applicants (parents) then code the FAFSA so that all the schools and programs to which they are applying receive copies of the determination of the Family Contribution. The PROFILE is merely mailed back to CSS.** Applicants and their families automatically receive a copy of the report (from CSS or the SAR from the Federal Processor) four to five weeks after the PROFILE and the FAFSA are filed. They will then be able to estimate how much aid may be forthcoming from the colleges to which students have applied.

Note: *It is a good idea to keep track of all the pieces in the financial application process on a chart similar to the one for the admissions application shown in Chapter 5. It should go without saying that it is imperative to keep copies of everything.*

EVALUATING YOUR FINANCIAL AID AWARD

When you are finally admitted to college and are deemed eligible for financial aid *and* receive your financial aid package, then you should follow

---

* This assumes a middle-income family.

** Remember that the FAFSA is free but that the PROFILE must be accompanied by a fee. The fees for 1995–96 are $15.50 for the first college and $9.50 for each additional college.

Sample Award Letter

June 13, 1995

Dear:

Thank you for submitting financial aid application materials for the 1995-96 academic year. We have reviewed your application and prepared this estimate of your eligibility for assistance to help you plan for your educational expenses.

This award is based on the information you have submitted thus far. You may need to submit some additional information, as previously requested, to finalize your award. *If this additional information differs from the information we currently have on file, your eligibility for financial aid may change.*

Direct costs for the 1995-96 academic year include tuition and fees of $20,746 and double-occupancy room and board charges of $5,970. You and your family are responsible for the difference between the school's charges and the amount of aid available for direct costs. In addition to these expenses, you should plan for the cost of books, supplies, travel, and other personal expenses. We estimate that books should cost approximately $575 per academic year. This will vary depending on the course work you choose and the availability of used books.

Financial Aid Available for Direct Costs:	Fall	Spring	Total
College Scholarship	$4,521	3,319	7,840
Federal Perkins Loan	1,581	1,294	2,875
Subsidized Federal Stafford Loan	1,313	1,312	2,625
Total of Aid Available for Direct Costs	$7,415	5,925	13,340

Students are expected to work during the summer and contribute at least $1,500 toward their educational costs and are expected to have funds available for books, supplies, and personal expenses when they arrive on campus. You are also eligible for campus employment. Our college has a Student Employment Office to help you find a position, but we cannot guarantee the availability of jobs. You may earn up to the following:

Federal College Work Study	$ 775	775	1,550
Total Financial Aid Award	$8,190	6,700	14,890

Please read all materials enclosed, then sign and return the Acceptance Form within two weeks. The Acceptance Form is used only to monitor financial aid commitments and does not obligate you to attend this college.

Sincerely,

Associate Director of Financial Aid

Sample Alternative Financing Options Sheet

A number of alternative financing programs are available to assist families with meeting the expense of financing an Coburn education. Listed below is a small sampling of such options. Coburn College does not recommend one program as being better than another. The decision to participate in any of the programs discussed should be based solely on the unique circumstances in each individual household.

Payment Plans:

Coburn College Budget Payment Plan

♦ yearly institutional expenses paid in monthly installments
♦ monthly service charge of 1% on outstanding balance
♦ balance due must be cleared by close of semester
♦ additional information is included with the August and December billing statements

**Knight College Resource Group
(formerly Knight Tuition Payment Plan)**

♦ available payment plans range from one to four years
♦ information will be sent to all students in early summer
♦ for more information contact Knight College Resource Group, 1-800-225-6783

**Tuition Management Systems, Inc.
(formerly Tuition Plan of New England, Inc.)**

♦ subsidiary of Chemical Bank
♦ for more information contact Tuition Management Systems, Inc., 1-800-722-4867

this simple guide for interpreting your award. Your financial aid package will probably be stated in a letter format with two columns of figures—the one on the left stating your estimated expenses for your first year, and the

Options Sheet *Cont'd.*

Loan Programs:

Extra Credit Loans

- maximum loan amount is 100% of college costs
- variable interest rate = treasury bill + 4.5%
- two repayment options available
- for more information contact College Credit, 1-800-874-9390

Home Equity Loans

- possible tax advantage, please consult with your tax advisor or the Internal Revenue Service
- for more information contact any bank, credit union or other lending institution

Option 4 Loan Program

- loan amounts from $2,000 to $15,000 per annum
- variable interest rate = treasury bill + 3.5%
- repayment period may be extended up to 15 years
- for more information contact United Student Aid Funds, 1-800-LOAN-USA

PLUS Loans

- maximum loan amount = cost of attendance - financial aid received
- variable interest rate = treasury bill + 3.10% (not to exceed 10%); current interest rate is 6.64%
- repayment usually begins 60 days after loan is disbursed
- for more information contact any bank, credit union or other lending institution

one on the right stating the resources from which those expenses will be met. The resources column is headed by the parents' contribution, then the student's contribution from assets, summer earnings, and other sources such as a tuition benefit or outside scholarship you may have won. These numbers are then added together and the difference is what the college or university has agreed to provide.

Options Sheet *Cont'd.*

SHARE Educational Loans for Families

♦ available to all creditworthy applicants
♦ loan amounts from $2,000 to cost of education - financial aid
♦ two interest rate options available
♦ option to defer principal payments while student remains enrolled, or pay fixed monthly payments including both principal and interest
♦ repayment period ranges from 4 to 20 years, depending upon amount borrowed
♦ for more information contact Nellie Mae, 1-800-634-9308 or 1-617-849-3447

TERI Supplemental Loans

♦ loan amounts from $2,000 to cost of education—financial aid
♦ current interest rate range is 7.5–8.0%
♦ credit line option available
♦ repayment period up to 25 years
♦ for more information contact TERI, 1-800-255-TERI

Achiever Loan

♦ loan amounts vary from $2,000 to cost of education: less financial aid
♦ variable interest rate is treasury bill + 4.5%
♦ three repayment options available
♦ for more information contact Knight College Resource Group, 1-800-225-6783

But you are still not done! Now you need to look at the way in which the institution plans to fund the difference between your family's contribution and the total cost of the education. This difference is normally covered with a combination of grants and loans. When scrutinizing this section of the financial aid package, the key point to keep in mind is the difference between price and cost. The price is what an institution charges the customer: tuition, fees, room and board. The cost is what the family will actually have to pay to send the student to a particular school: price, plus travel expenses, books, incidental expenses, and interest on loans. The more the college or university provides by way of grant money, the lower the cost to the student and family. Conversely, the higher the loan component of the financial aid package, the higher the cost and the long-term expenses for the student and family.

In the financial aid package, there are *four* categories of aid possible:

1. **Outright grant**—money that does not have to be repaid. Grant monies may be based on need, or merit, or both. Grant aid tends to be highest in cases where students have a high need. (But such students often receive large loan amounts too; this will vary by school.)

   As the Family Contribution (i.e., the amount a family is able to pay for college costs, as computed by CSS) rises, the grant portion declines and is eventually replaced by loans and Work-Study.

2. **Federal loans**—Stafford and Perkins Loans that you the student will be expected to take on. You should definitely consider the cost of repaying these and other loans as a part of your decision whether or not to attend a particular school.

3. **College or private loans**—such as TERI or SHARE that you or your family would be required to take. Here again every family's circumstances are different and you will need to discuss these loan offers with your parents. In cases where a middle income family does not qualify for grant aid and still finds the cost of a college education high, college and other kinds of loans may be an attractive way to finance the next four years.

4. **Summer Earnings/Work-Study**—the amount of money that you are expected to make at a job during the summer and during the course of the academic year. Note that the amounts may vary from one financial aid offer to the next. A lower Work-Study or Summer Earnings amount means a lower cost to the student, if loan and grant amounts are the same as another school. So look at these amounts carefully.

Interpreting the Family Contribution

In some cases students and families are surprised by the size of the Family Contribution they are expected to make. There could be several reasons for this:

♦ Families may have asked a college for an early evaluation of their financial aid status and may have received a tentative indication of an award. Now that the final award has been made, students and their families should remember that the former was an estimate.

♦ For economic reasons or recruitment purposes, some colleges and universities may increase or decrease the expected Family Contribution as computed by CSS. Since the FAFSA and the PROFILE ask for different information, schools relying on one and not the other may produce a different Family Contribution.

♦ In addition, college and university financial aid officers have some discretion in interpreting financial aid data furnished them by a family and in setting their own expectations. For instance, schools may differ on the amount they expect students to earn in the summer, or in the amount they allow for the purchase of books and supplies in computing the student budget, or in the number of hours they expect students to allocate to College Work-Study. These different policies will cause financial aid offers to differ among schools.

♦ Students and families should also be prepared for colleges sometimes to suggest a Family Contribution in excess of those arrived at by the CSS. In such a case, the institution may have adopted a policy that views certain assets such as savings, stocks, bonds, and rental property differently from CSS. Social Security benefits and giving credit for merit scholarship awards from noncollege agencies also can lead to differing offers among schools.

♦ Remember that these policies are not designed to single out a particular student or family. Rather they are designed to stretch the institutions' financial aid resources as far as possible. Some students and families may not receive as much aid as they want, but they should understand that most colleges assume that applicants and their parents have a responsibility to pay as much as they can reasonably afford toward the cost of higher education. The colleges in turn have the same obligation to pay as much as they reasonably can to support the students they accept. Their respective offers to a particular family may differ, yet their common goal remains the same.

CONTINUING FINANCIAL AID WHILE YOU'RE IN COLLEGE

Keep in mind as you review award packages that in your first year of college, you can be expected to contribute 35 percent of your assets toward your college expenses and 35 percent of the balance of your assets for each year thereafter. Most colleges will expect around $1400 from summer earnings. This will be included as part of the Family Contribution. Generally, the amount of the student's contribution from summer earnings increases over the course of four years. About the same amount can be expected from your campus job, which will be figured as part of your financial aid package. It's in your best interest to try to develop a marketable skill so that you can increase your summer and on-campus earnings as you move through college.

Is aid ever cut back once you're in college?

One of the myths that makes the rounds at colleges and universities is that financial aid packages may be deliberately changed (decreased) by the institution from one year to the next. This myth is contrary to all practice, but it is true that many schools do increase the summer earnings expectation slightly from one year to the next. Some may also increase the amount of loan indebtedness that they feel a student can carry from one year to the next. Of course, tuition and fees generally increase slightly as well. This combination may fuel the myth. However, students and families do not need to worry about any unexpected increases in what they will pay. It would not be in the schools' interest to take advantage of families they want to serve and students they want to transform into grateful alumni/ae.

Hardship situations

On the other hand, if your family experiences a sudden and adverse change (perhaps a parent lost his or her job or there were big medical bills to pay), apply to the Financial Aid Office for help. All schools have special resources set aside to deal with an unexpected drop in family and student resources.

QUESTIONS FREQUENTLY ASKED

Dealing with the details and decisions about paying for college is no simple matter. Having gotten this far in your reading you know a great deal, but you may still have some questions. Here are some of the most common ones:

What happens to my award after the freshman year?

Each spring the financial aid office asks families to complete a new PROFILE and FAFSA and, once these forms are processed, they determine the award for the next academic year. If your family's circumstances have not changed appreciably, you can generally expect that the college will meet your need as in the past year. Remember though, if you have a merit scholarship as a part of your aid package, you will have to live up to the conditions of that award in each and every college year.

If my family's situation changes, is there anything that can be done?

Your family should write a letter explaining what has happened and, in cases of a decrease in income, appeal for more assistance. Colleges often maintain small contingency funds for this purpose.

When my brother and sister enter college in two years, what happens?

Your family's need will undoubtedly be greater then, and most colleges will try to meet it by reducing the Family Contribution by one half for each child entering college. In this connection, if you did not qualify for aid when you entered college, perhaps, with your brother or sister enrolled, you will qualify for aid. By all means complete a PROFILE and the FAFSA and apply.*

I may get a local scholarship when I graduate from high school. What happens then?

You will be asked by your college to report all outside scholarship awards. Because the task of the financial aid office is to maximize the use of its funds—in other words, give them to as many students as possible—you may be asked to apply your outside scholarship to the school's financial aid award. This means that your college may reduce your loan and/or your grant by the amount of the outside award. If this is done, remember you are still benefiting from the outside aid and so is another student, who is now receiving aid originally earmarked for you.

What happens if I cannot procure a nonsubsidized Stafford Loan at a local bank?

This is very unlikely. Contact the Financial Aid Office right away for assistance if you cannot procure a Stafford Loan at a local bank. The college will help you find a lender.

---

* Remember, if your parents' income rises as your sibling enters college, then their parental contribution will rise and financial aid will decline some. If everything stayed the same, then their parental contribution might well be reduced by half.

What is a dependent student? An independent student?

Most financial aid programs are based on the premise that the student is living with his/her parent(s), and that they are providing the primary support. In that situation both students and their families have the primary responsibility to pay for educational costs. However, if you are truly independent of your parents, financial aid will be computed differently. To be considered independent, you have to be at least 24 years old; you may not have lived with either of your parents for the past year, nor received more than $750 per year from them, and not been claimed by them as an income tax exemption for three consecutive years prior to the academic year for which you are requesting aid. If you are judged to be an independent student, you may be eligible for higher levels of Stafford Loans.

Do I have to accept the Work-Study job offered to me as a condition for my other scholarship and loan aid?

Absolutely not. If you can make an equivalent amount during the summer, or your family can provide you with equivalent funds, that is satisfactory. Your other aid remains intact. However, you need to have solid plans for making up the difference in your contribution toward paying your college bills. The same holds true for summer work. It is an expectation, and if you can meet it through other means, fine. Your financial aid will not change.

What if I need aid and am not awarded any?

This is when PLUS loans and an array of college-sponsored loans can help. Colleges often have relationships with banks that will make short- and long-term loans. Colleges and universities also offer various tuition-payment plans that allow parents to spread out education costs for 10–15 years and make monthly payments. Financial aid officers will also be able to advise parents on low-interest loans from SHARE, sometimes called Nellie May, for the New England Education Loan Marketing Corporation (1-800-634-9308), and The Educational Resources Institute (TERI). Consult your financial aid office (1-800-244-TERI).

The chart on page 188 shows the different ways in which colleges and universities package financial aid and the resulting cost to the family. Set up a similar chart to compare the financial aid you are awarded.

Before comparing the financial aid offers of the colleges that accepted you, you and your parents may want to consider some general advice

SAMPLE FINANCIAL AID PACKAGES

	COLLEGE A (Small, selective private college)	COLLEGE B (State college, moderate size)	COLLEGE C (State university, large)	COLLEGE D (Large, selective private university)
Tuition and fees	$ 19,425	$ 12,500	$ 6,000	$ 20,400
Room and board	4,190	4,200	4,000	5,100
Price	$ 23,615	$ 16,700	$ 10,000	$ 25,500
Miscellaneous (books, supplies, etc.)	1,500	1,500	1,500	1,550
Total budget for attendance	$ 25,165	$ 18,200	$ 11,500	$ 27,050
Expected family contribution (including student assets)	−5,000*	−4,000	−4,000	−5,500*
Difference to be financed	$ 20,165	$ 14,200	$ 7,500	$ 21,550
Financial aid package Grant (gift money)	$ 13,465	$ 4,000	$ 2,000†	$ 14,250
Loans (to be repaid)	4,000	4,000	4,000	4,500
Work-Study (campus job)	1,400	1,300	Not promised	1,450
Summer Earnings	1,300	1,200	1,000	1,350
Total financial aid awarded	$ 20,165	$ 10,500**	$ 7,000**	$ 21,550
Cost of Attendance (Total budget minus financial aid)	$ 5,000	$ 7,700	$ 4,500	$ 5,500

* Colleges A and D require PROFILE and FAFSA. Colleges B and C require only the FAFSA.
** Note gap between aid and amount to be financed.
†In-state resident grant.

provided on the chart above. You also need to keep in mind that a difference in price does not necessarily mean a difference in value to you personally. You may still want to go to a more costly school, simply because you believe you will fit in better there and have a more productive experience than at a less costly school. Or the reverse may be just as true.

♦ **First, pay careful attention to the relative amounts of aid included in each offer, as well as to the bottom line, which is how much families are expected to contribute.** Obviously, high grant and loan offers should command careful attention if the schools are of equal quality and cost. (Colleges A and D are examples.)

However, if the school's tuition and fees are high to begin with, the high grant may have less net impact than a slightly lower grant at a much less expensive school (A and B). Or, when one school costs less than another overall and both have made equal grant offers, you should consider attending the less expensive of the two, where your loan and Work-Study commitments would be smaller. (Note the differences between College C and College D.)

♦ When schools of roughly equal quality and cost offer different levels of support, you should strongly consider the school offering the larger financial aid package.

♦ **Second, examine the loan structure in detail.** Federally supported loans are generally less expensive than those from private banks or the university itself. The same holds true for state guaranteed loan programs. Students who are considering going on to graduate school will not want to incur a heavy loan burden for their undergraduate education and may therefore favor an undergraduate college that offers them a large scholarship grant and a relatively low interest loan program backed by federal or state money. If you decide to take on a federal loan commitment, remember that you can postpone repayment if you go on to graduate school full-time. (Colleges A and D may well do this.)

On the other hand, families may be eligible for various parent loan programs offered by some private colleges and not available at public universities. These loans enable families to spread out the cost of educating their children over a period of up to fifteen years. (See the discussion of SHARE and TERI loans on page 187.)

♦ **Third, be wary of financial aid offers with an extensive Summer Earnings/Work-Study requirement.** Some schools expect students to earn in excess of $3000 during the academic year. This is easier said than done, especially when withholding taxes are taken out of earnings—and students are working at the minimum wage. The low skill level of some students may dictate that they work only at jobs paying the minimum wage and requiring long hours, at the expense of study time and extracurricular interests.

A WORD ON LOANS

One of the significant changes in the world of financial aid in recent years is called *direct lending*. Schools that participate in this federally supported loan program (there are about 150 of them at this writing) are encouraged to offer a series of long-term federally supported loans. The reason for the extended payback arrangement is simple: to help students and families to stretch out the burden of college costs.

The new federal program has three options in addition to the standard ten-year payback plan:

♦ an extended 30-year option (versus the more usual 10 years)
♦ a graduated payment option that increases your payments over 20 years, as you earn more money, and
♦ an income-contingent plan that allows borrowers to set their payments at a percentage of their income. Under this option, borrowers make their payments for 25 years, and if the loan is not repaid in full by then, the balance is forgiven.

If you're considering these and other plans, take a hard look at the amount of interest you will have to pay over these extended periods. For instance, look at this example:

> A future engineer who borrows the maximum allowed for four years of undergraduate school at the maximum of 8.25 percent would owe $17,125 at graduation. This would require a payment of $210 a month for ten years. The interest paid would be $8010. To finance the same amount over 30 years would only cost $129 a month, but the interest portion of the overall cost would be $29,190, more than three times the amount for ten years. ("Student Loans," *The New York Times*, 2 April 1995.)

A recent poll of college financial aid officers revealed that many of them think that students are not looking carefully enough at alternatives to long-term loans. They begin by borrowing more than they need because loans are easy to procure. Then they compound their difficulty by extending the payback periods, not realizing that they will be encountering other large financing costs while they are still carrying their college loans. One young reporter was very happy to have paid off his student loan in ten years, because he wanted to buy a house ten years out of college. He found that the $87 per month that he had been paying on his student loan now was freed up, enabling him to carry $20,000 more on his mortgage.

WAYS TO REDUCE TUITION AND FEES

♦ **You can accelerate your course of study in college.** This may be done by taking Advanced Placement examinations in various subjects in the last two years of high school. Many colleges and universities grant advanced standing on the basis of these tests, and qualified students are thus able to meet the requirements for graduation in three and a half years or less, thus saving a large chunk of tuition and fees. For a more detailed explanation of the AP exams, and also the International Baccalaureate, see page 166.

♦ **You can consider schools with cooperative education programs**, whereby you may attend college for one semester and then work in your field of interest for the next semester. Work and study may also be arranged on an equal-time basis so that you could work while going ahead with your college education. Naturally such programs prolong the span of your undergraduate education, but they do make it affordable and often lead to direct job placement upon graduation.

♦ **You can consider schools that offer extensive merit scholarships.** If you can qualify for one of these scholarships, you can save your family and yourself money. (See previous discussion under Terms and Their Abbreviations in this chapter.)

♦ **You can establish yourself as an independent student.** Remember the definition of independent student, above. The requirements are rigorous. However, if you can meet them, you may be able to save yourself considerable expense, especially at a low-tuition public university.

Because many public colleges and universities have been inundated with students seeking admission because of low tuition, some have added to the requirements outlined above. They may require proof of residence for the past six months or they may ask for a voter registration card or a local property tax receipt as proof of independent status. They may also require a state driver's license and/or a state income tax return (if applicable) from students who declare themselves independent. So it may or may not be advantageous for you to declare your independence. You should ask lots of questions of the financial aid and admissions offices at the school you want to attend. Make sure you construct a financial scenario for both dependent and independent status before making your decision.

COLLEGE PAYMENT PLANS

As you plan for college, you should also take into account the form of payment to the colleges. Parents need to look at the entire four-year period of their child's education and weigh the various forms of payment colleges offer them.

If you are well-off, you may want to take advantage of the tuition prepayment plan offered by some colleges. Under these plans, you pay the whole four-year tuition (usually not including room and board) at the beginning of the student's freshman year. You are assured of the fixed cost for the four years, while the college gains early access to additional funds.

If you have to borrow money to pay tuition, most colleges insist that you secure a Stafford Loan and/or a PLUS loan first, before you apply for college funds. Institutional funds are generally seen as a last resort before applying for institutional loans. Normally any funds an institution sets aside for parental borrowing are administered by a private agency appointed by the college.

You should also look closely at the schedule of payments the school offers. You will undoubtedly be able, for instance, to pay tuition charges over a twelve-month period rather than on two separate dates. You probably can take advantage of an extended payment plan as well and schedule your payments over four, six, or even ten years. Colleges will have information about payment plans in their brochures.

Parents in many states—Ohio, Michigan, and Minnesota are examples—have state loan programs available to them. Your guidance office or state department of education will know the address of the appropriate state agency.*

Behind the state agencies lie the private agencies and banks that specialize in education financing. The Richard C. Knight Agency (53 Beacon Street, Boston, MA 02108; Tel: 1-800-225-6783) and the Tuition Plan of New England (Donovan Street Extension, Concord, NH 03303; Tel 1-800-258-3460) are well-known. These institutions pay student charges as they come due in return for a fee, which is incorporated into the monthly charges that families pay to the agency.

FOR MORE INFORMATION

Here is a list of financial aid publications you may find useful:

American Legion, *Need a Lift?* Indianapolis, Ind. Published annually. Useful brochure for children of veterans, particularly those who wish to pursue a technical or military career.

Alexander A. Bove Jr., *Free Tuition: How to Beat the Soaring Cost of College Through Smart and Legal Tax Planning.* Boston, Mass.: Financial Planning Institute, 1993. Provocative survey of numerous ways in which families can cut their college tuition costs. Written from the point of view of a tax lawyer, the advantages and disadvantages of each method are spelled out. This volume is an especially useful guide as families try to navigate between the Scylla and Charybdis of tightening federal tax laws and declining federal aid to the college-age student. However, changes in the tax law itself and in its interpretation have to be kept in mind when reading Bove's book.

College Board, *Costs and Financial Aid Handbook*, published annually by the College Board. $16. Financing tips as well as the tuition, fees, and other costs at over 2,800 colleges.

---

* As an example, the state loan authority in Massachusetts offers loans at 12.5 percent, for 75 percent of the student's college costs. Payments extend for fifteen years. To borrow $5000 would cost the borrower $35.59 the first year and result in monthly interest payments of $61.62.

Coopers and Lybrand, *Early Planning for College Costs.* Available from P.O. Box 46, Rockville, Maryland 20850. Coopers and Lybrand is a large accounting and consulting firm with vast experience in advising clients on planning for college costs.

Alan Deutschman, *Winning Money for College,* 3rd ed. Princeton, N.J.: Peterson's Guides, 1994. First complete guide to competitions students can enter on their own. Contains facts, figures, and advice on how to win contests ranging from public speaking to essay writing to scientific experiments.

EXPAN: Software program for college guidance and application, produced by the College Board. Some high schools currently have this program, and you can learn much from the sections devoted to college costs and financial aid. There are financial aid worksheets that can be printed out and taken home to your families for consultation. Ask your counselor about the location nearest you. You might also want to ask about College Cost Fund Finder, a new software program from the College Board that enables you to search for scholarships that support your particular skills and to work on spreadsheets that automatically calculate the expected Family Contribution that you and your parents will have to make toward the cost of your college expenses.

Elizabeth Hoffman, *Financial Aid for College Through Scholarships and Loans,* 5th ed. Rye, N.H.: Richards House, 1989. Complete explanation of terminology, with helpful worksheets for estimating college budgets and financial aid awards. Long and valuable listing of privately funded sources of scholarship aid, including churches, businesses, trade unions, veterans' groups, and minority and ethnic organizations.

Robert Leider and Anna Leider, *The Ambitious Student's Guide to Financial Aid.* Alexandria, Va.: Octameron Press, 1988. Listing of lesser-known sources of merit scholarship and need-based aid that is not tied to a particular university or college.

NACAC, *Test Prep, and Financial Aid Services: A Consumer's Guide.* The National Association of College Admissions Counselors publishes this handy pamphlet, providing tips on the use of scholarship search services, financial aid, and financial planning services. Available in lots of 100. Ask your counselor to order some. 202-836-2222

Peterson's Guides, *Paying Less for College.* Princeton, N.J.: Peterson's Guides, 1994. A 591-page tome containing a wealth of information. One section devoted to profiles of the nation's colleges: cost, percentage of students on aid, and no-need and specialized scholarships offered. Another section consists of directories of colleges offering athletic and merit scholarships and co-op and ROTC programs.

Peterson's Guides, *College Selection Service.* Princeton, N.J., Peterson's Guides, 1995. This software is available in many high school guidance offices and libraries. It includes a complete file of scholarships, grants, loans, and internships and information on corporate and state scholarship awards. It is a good place to begin the quest to understand the financial aid system and to explore sources of funding.

Peterson's Guides, *Peterson's Financial Aid Service.* Princeton, N.J.: Peterson's Guides, 1995. For a number of Apple and IBM personal computers, this software parallels the popular *Paying Less for College* but has additional sections on estimating Family Contributions and calculating financial need. Another useful section enables the operator to group colleges by cost and type. There are also sections on federal and state aid programs, sources of private aid for college, and merit scholarships available from certain colleges. You can also group the scholarships by application deadlines, which is quite handy.

T. Rowe Price, *College Planning Package.* Free kit helps project college costs and suggests ways to meet them. 800-638-5660.

U.S. Government, *Federal Benefits for Veterans and Dependents.* Washington, D.C.: GPO. Published annually. Booklet providing a comprehensive summary of benefits available to veterans and their dependents. Especially precise when it comes to service-related disabilities and the benefits that pertain to them.

U.S. Government, *The Student Guide—Financial Aid from the U.S. Department of Education: Grants, Loans, and Work-Study 1994-95*, Washington, D.C.: GPO, 1994, 800-433-3243. Detailed description of rules and regulations surrounding Pell Grants, PLUS loans, Stafford Loans, and the other federal aid programs for students. Guidance offices have this 81-page brochure.

Peterson's Guides, *USA TODAY Financial Aid for College.* Princeton, N.J.: Peterson's Guides, 1995. *USA TODAY's Financial Aid for College* is your first step to getting the money you need for college. You will find clear and simple explanations of state and federal programs, tips for getting a head start on paying for college, the easiest way to calculate your ability to pay for college, and more.

Peterson's Guides, *USA TODAY Getting into College*. Princeton, N.J.: Peterson's Guides, 1994. *USA TODAY Getting Into College* looks at issues from both student and parent viewpoints and provides advice from high school counselors, college admission officers, and parents who have been through the entire process.

EIGHT

For Parents Only—The Myth of College and Success

I think all too often we get trapped by the externals—believing that a college education will somehow deliver a product called happiness to our children, whereas in fact, the college experience leads to a subtler outcome we might call enlightenment. And that enlightenment touches not only our children, but us as parents too.

Dr. Charles Ross, psychologist at Oberlin College

Parents have always had confused feelings about taking their child to college because of several myths that cling to the complicated process of choosing a college and leaving home. The difficulty was no less prevalent in late February of 1860 when Abraham Lincoln packed an old carpet bag with several shirts and a black silk suit and boarded the eastbound train from Springfield, Illinois. The ostensible purpose of his trip was to make a visit to his son Robert, who was then a senior at the Phillips Exeter Academy in New Hampshire. His hidden purpose was to test the political winds in what was probably the most critical election year in American history. Only his stated purpose need concern us here, for it demonstrates one of the fundamental myths about college choice that beguiles parents to this day.

Abraham Lincoln and his wife, Mary Todd, had sent their son east to a preparatory school the previous fall so that he could gain admission to a prestigious college. Believing in the myth of prestige, the Lincolns wanted their son Robert to gain much of what his father had been denied in life. Even though the elder Lincoln was now 51 years old, he still spoke with a Midwestern twang. "Mr. Chairman" came out "Mr. Cheermun"; "are not" was still sometimes "ain't." Lincoln and his wife hoped that Robert would meet the right people at Exeter and acquire a social patina. They hoped that, through his own efforts and the network of friends that he would make at Exeter and later at Harvard, Robert would rise quickly to the top of American society. They were not to be disappointed. In the years that followed, Robert Lincoln rose to prominence as a Chicago lawyer, chairman of the board of the Pullman Palace Car Company, and later a cabinet officer for President Garfield.

The recurrence of similar experiences over and over again in American history has led parents to believe the myth that college is the key to the future, to financial success, to social prominence, and to self-fulfillment. Yet college really plays a subtler role—by exposing students to the broad questions that have defined the social sciences, the humanities, and the scientific traditions we have inherited. A strong and broad college education helps students understand the major ideas, individuals, and works of art and science that have shaped our tradition and our world.

Robert Lincoln's education was the beginning of his understanding of the challenges he had to face: his father's premature death, his mother's protracted illness, and the rampant and irresponsible capitalism that engulfed the country during the Guilded Age.

Related to the myth of prestige is the myth that college is the adolescent's karma, a happy and foregone destiny that all young people must embrace in order to move from youth to maturity. College as karma sees the four-year undergraduate experience as a happy interlude before taking on the responsibilities of adulthood.

Parents whose children are facing the decision of whether or not to attend college have a responsibility, to themselves and to their offspring, to probe for the real reasons behind their desire to see their children get a college education. Often they will find that they believe that college is the key to social and economic success for their children. Sometimes parents who subscribe to this myth foist it on their children, who may then go off to college for the wrong reasons and end up bored, or unhappy, or worse.

COLLEGE AS THE FULFILLMENT OF PARENTS' ASPIRATIONS

If you are one of those parents who see your own fulfillment when your child is accepted by the *right* college, you are in the grip of another familiar myth about going to college. That myth is what one might call the halo myth. You are trying to compel your son or daughter to attend a specific college, particularly a prestigious one, because you believe that their success will have a halo effect and reflect glory on you.

One father, who insisted that his son apply to Harvard—where the boy had no chance of being admitted—told me that he did so because he himself had not had the chance to go to a prestigious school. And this came from a psychologist! So the boy dutifully applied to Harvard and several other prestigious colleges and was turned down by all of them—an unfortunate episode that didn't have to happen.

In thinking about the right college for your child, you need to distinguish his needs from your own, lest you both fall victim to confusion about whose needs are being fulfilled. Consider for a moment the untenable position in which the psychologist had placed his son. Children do not want to lose their parents' love, so they quickly learn to do the *right* thing to please their family. This young man, in an effort to please his father, suffered a significant loss of self-esteem when those prestigious schools all rejected his application. He had been encouraged by his father to put himself forward, to strive toward the apparently unattainable, but the rationale was not his. He could not own the ultimate decision because the needs of the father had been substituted for those of the son. If the psychologist father had looked honestly at the discrepancy between his own needs and those of his son, they might have made a better selection of colleges. The father should have considered the son's educational needs in guiding his choice of college: his areas of academic interest, his learning style, his extracurricular interests, and the kind of social environment in which he might prosper.

It was that father's job—and it is your job as a parent—to hold an honest conversation with your child, to understand his real motives for wanting to go to college. This question is best explored as a part of a discussion about which colleges the child wants to select and why. For that conversation, here are some questions to consider. As you read them, remember that your child may not have answers to all these questions yet because he may not have visited a particular school or interacted with one of its students or graduates. Nonetheless, the questions need to be answered at some point before an application is filed:

♦ How does his particular college choice meet your specific goals and aspirations, both in academics and in extracurricular interests?

♦ What kinds of students attend the college? Are they going to be people who your child will want to know the rest of his life, or at least some of them? Is the student population diverse in its social makeup?*

♦ How do students treat each other in class and on the playing fields and studios? Is there genuine interest in and tolerance for diverse points of view? Is there a genuine sense of a caring community on campus?

♦ How involved are the faculty in forming the undergraduate experience, both inside and outside of the classroom?

Parents who brush aside the answers to these questions and push their children toward a particular college that they happen to favor run a great risk. You can often tell that this unconscious process is under way when you hear the dead giveaway—the use of the plural pronoun "we," as in "We are applying to Skidmore." When parents hear themselves using "we," they should be aware that they are controlling the process too much.

EDUCATION AS A COMMODITY

Another view that frequently overshadows objective parental decision making about college is the myth that education is something that can be purchased like a *commodity*. As with any consumer item, the argument runs, the price of the college or university reflects its value. Good schools are expensive and therefore prestigious and valuable. Poor schools are not expensive because they are less valuable and produce a lower-quality product.

Recently a parent in a wealthy suburb was asked by her daughter's guidance counselor, "Why won't you let Jeannie apply to the state university?" The answer was, "I am not spending $9000 a year for my daughter to go to the state university when she can get twice as good an education for only 50 percent more at one of the 'prestige' colleges!"

There is an equally simplistic flip side to the commodity myth. It goes, "Why should I spend $25,000 a year to send my son to a so-called 'prestige' college when for half the price he can have a good time at the state university?"

Parents espousing the commodity point of view invariably know the price of things but not necessarily the value of them. They somehow equate

_____
* See George Matthew's case in Chapter 1.

the quality of the educational experience with the money being expended rather than basing their approach on the question "What type of educational institution is best for my child?" Ironically, the parents who are most often conscious of price are frequently the least concerned about value, ignoring the elements that add value to an undergraduate experience, such as the quality and accessibility of the faculty, the academic and social support systems that undergird the learning in the classroom, and the college's mission—its sense of itself. As long as parents are determined to "buy the best," whatever that may mean to them, their children will experience enormous difficulty in making a rational college choice. Commenting on the "new consumerism" of today's parents, Richard Hersh, President of Hobart and William Smith Colleges, remarks:

> Today's parents are consumer-minded and want reasonable assurance of value for the big sums of money involved. In today's economic climate, value in education is defined by concrete results, saleable skills, a job. Parents tend to think of a liberal arts program as a lot of money to have a good time for four years. That is a luxury unaffordable in the 1990s.*

COLLEGE AS UTOPIA MYTH

I have also known parents who advise their child to go to a particular college on the fallacious premise that it is *good*, and *good* colleges ultimately lead to the *good* life. These parents view the chosen college as a kind of utopia. Some parents talk about *good* colleges as if they actually know what that means or, for that matter, as if anyone knows what that means. In the face of their neat division of the world into good and bad, the rest of us can only wonder how they recognize their *good* college. Do they read the various college guides and make their decisions based on the information there? Do they count how many of the students of College X go on to graduate school, particularly to medical schools, or the number of scholarly treatises published by its faculty? Are they influenced by the economic dimensions of the school: the endowment per student, the scholarship aid, the physical plant, the size of the library, or the number and quality of sports facilities?

---

* Richard Hersh, "What Our Publics Want and Think They Don't Get From a Liberal Arts Education," AAHE Bulletin, November 1994, p.9.

A variation on this utopia theme can be seen in those parents who regard college as a place where their child can spend four more years of innocence before encountering the harsh realities of the everyday world. Parents who see it this way don't view the college years as inaugurating a new period of independence for their child but rather see college as temporarily taking over parental responsibility. They think that somehow the idyllic atmosphere of home can be transformed magically to a bustling campus where the academic and social life will magnify the core values of the family and the home community. Nothing could be further from reality, and often the utopian view is shattered abruptly when the student arrives on campus. Setting aside this myth of utopia, along with the others mentioned, will prepare parents to help their child make reasonable and healthy decisions about college life.

CHOOSING IS KNOWING

In order to make sensible college choices, you have to know your child as an individual.

♦ What are your child's needs, both personal and academic?
♦ What are his talents, both expressed and still to be realized?
♦ What kind of people does your child relate to best? How does your child bring out the best in these people?
♦ What is the nature of your child's relationship to you as parents?
♦ Are there stepparents or noncustodial parents involved in your child's life? What is their relationship to the child, and how might that relationship impact the college choice?

The answers to these questions need to be found in discussions between parents and stepparents and between parents and their child. The key is to identify the child's interests, talents, and expectations and to make your own thoughts known. Then you set off together to find a set of colleges where the child will find an interesting challenge and ultimate success.

Imagine the beneficial effect of such a candid and supportive discussion on an only son who is small, retiring, moderately able, and scientifically inclined. To send that young man to a large, prestigious liberal arts school, where he would in all likelihood be socially and academically out of his depth, would be a mistake. He would probably fare much better in a small liberal arts college with a strong program in the sciences. Once he and his parents can agree to that strategy in a series of honest discussions, the young man can relax and get on with finding the right school.

In a different way, a similar family talk could help focus the aspirations of a bright and versatile young woman who made the National Honor Society, was captain of the field hockey team, and was elected vice president of her class. She might be the type of person who would thrive in a large and cosmopolitan university. (One young woman like this, who had done very well at a small, demanding preparatory school where she was well-known by most of the students and faculty, told her counselor that she wanted to attend a huge university that offered her "the luxury of my anonymity.")

Talk with Your Child

So sit down and talk with your child. Ask her what *she* hopes to achieve in college. Make sure you tell her what *you* hope she will achieve. And try to be flexible. Academics need not come first. Does your child wish, for example, to continue her current extracurricular and creative activities while in college? If so, is she applying to colleges where these talents will be overwhelmed by the precocity of other students or to schools where her talents will sparkle beside those of others?

The high school track star who has already set the New England record in his event should not apply to a school where he will be far better than everyone else on the track team. That will not be any fun for the others on the team during the next four years, nor will it provide much of an inducement to the young man to set even higher goals for himself. The track star needs to find a school where he can compete and succeed at his level. You parents are perhaps the ones who will have to tell him that. The coach from the small college where he will be a record breaker certainly will not.

You should also talk to your child about career plans, especially when these involve the professions, such as medicine or law. It may be a good idea to encourage your child to take some of the interest and skill inventory tests described in Chapter 1 and to discuss the results with her guidance counselor. If a child's mind is already too firmly made up, a little practical experience can help reduce a fixation on a particular career. Perhaps the fervent premed should spend a year working in an emergency room or a lab before embarking on her college career. If that is not possible, she might take some courses outside her field in order to broaden her perspective. To narrow her career choices too soon and only apply to schools with strong premed programs might be a costly mistake that could lead to disillusionment in college.

Help Her Help Herself

Even professional schools are catching on to the significance of a broad liberal arts experience, and you may want to point that out to your precocious daughter. As an observer of the committee selecting candidates for the intensive six-year medical program at a major Midwestern university commented: "The ones who get through are invariably the ones who have something other than sheer excellence in science to offer. They have dropped out for a year to work in a nursing home, they have managed to make the Olympic skating finals while getting Bs in organic chemistry, they have written and published poetry, they have done something that will give them a broad perspective as a doctor six years from now."

When you focus on your child's career interests, try to help her to understand how a broad base of liberal arts courses and extracurricular experiences in college will enhance her credentials for the career she eventually plans to pursue.

As sensible parents, you will also realize that beneath the educational and career questions your child faces in making the decision to attend college lies an array of psychological issues that must be reckoned with. On the simplest level, the college admissions process brings young people and their families face to face with the conflicting forces that the imminent departure for college brings to the surface. As parents you have tried to bring a sense of closeness and nurturing to your child. You have tried to impart values and self-discipline and to socialize your son or daughter within the family structure. Now, with the prospect of going off to college you are faced for the first time with helping your child leave home and to live independently and happily away from you and other family members. You are being asked to send a two-part message: "We love you, but we want you to be independent." The authors of a recent book on parenting call this delicate process giving your children "roots and wings."*

---

* Barbara M. Newman, and Philip R. Newman, *When Kids Go To College: A Parent's Guide to Changing Relationships*, Columbus, Ohio State University Press, 1992, p. 3.

CHILDREN FEEL THE STRAIN, TOO

The anxiety is not all on the parent side either. Children at this stage often test the limits of family customs and values and risk parental disapproval at the same time that they need and want parental approval very much. As parents, we seek control over life's circumstances and we plan to avoid failure. But our children often demand their right to fail or make mistakes, and we must give it to them—for living with one's mistakes is part of accepting the consequences of one's independent actions. It is a part of the autonomy our children are seeking.

At the end of a meeting with her guidance counselor, a versatile and able high school senior was heard saying, "I don't know why, but I am just terribly anxious about all this." Indeed, many young people have had this same feeling! It shows the genuine fear that they feel as they move into the real world for the first time. The stress the young woman expressed stems from her sense that for the first time she is moving out of a world in which the competition had been essentially controlled—by teachers, coaches, and family—into the real world, where the forces that decide the outcome of events are much more uncertain.

It is understandable that such a young woman might be terrified of not gaining admission to the prestigious college where her father studied. She has always achieved her goals until now; she is an honors student, captain of one sport, star of another, and has a handsome boyfriend. Now things are different, and even the best-laid plans—her own, her guidance counselor's, and her family's—might go awry.

What she needs to hear from her family is how sensible planning can reduce the risks of failure to an acceptable level, along with the message "We love you, no matter what." By seriously investigating all the colleges recommended by her counselor and applying to colleges of varying difficulty, she will learn that a fine education can be found not only in the eight Ivies or the Little Three or the Big Ten, but in countless other places as well. When she reaches this realization, the young woman and her family will be able to relax a little and deal more easily with the normal stresses of applying to colleges.

SO MANY CHANGES AHEAD

How much easier the college planning process would be if the only anxiety were in not knowing to which schools one would be accepted! But, of course, there are many unknowns, many changes to come.

Her Relationships with Peers

In helping to plan your child's applications to college, you need to understand that she is also learning to deal with shifting peer relationships. She is leaving behind the security of high school relationships and often the homogeneity of many American high schools for the uncertainty of roommates and a society where she knows there will be others who do not share the same views and values. Often students deny the changes they know to be around the corner and set up the senior year in high school as a benchmark against which all future relationships will be measured. Then as they enter and experience success in dealing with some of the challenges of college life, relationships with high school friends shift, and they find themselves questioning the benchmarks they had established for themselves, leaving them behind.

The senior high school year can also bring out competition between students like never before, and this can be unsettling and alienating. One college applicant considered the high admissions standards of Stanford, a school that he and a number of his friends wished to attend, and said to his college counselor, "Perhaps I shouldn't say this, but after knowing Bob for four years, I really don't think that he has worked hard enough to deserve Stanford." Needless to say, that relationship cooled considerably when Bob was admitted, and his fellow student, who thought he had worked harder and was more deserving, was not.

Her Relationships with You

Relationships between parents and their children are likewise altered by the entire college admissions process. As children struggle to assert their own identity they often put great distances—literal and figurative—between themselves and their parents. "I want to go to school in California," a girl from Connecticut insisted. "Out there I will be free from my parents' wanting to know what I am doing all the time." She then added, "Besides, my mother wants me to take a lot of prenursing courses, and I am not sure yet that that is what I want to do."

When you hear these kinds of fallacious arguments, you need to remind your child to choose a college that will help her build on her accomplishments and focus on her chosen career. She should not choose a school because she believes it will give her more freedom and distance from you.

You need to recognize too that applying to college will often renew a child's interest in his or her family's special history. The process may be organic or prompted by an essay question on the application. Formulating a clear understanding of family history is part of the identity formation of the young person.* Each family's history is different; it stems from ancestry, race, religion, folklore, legends, and customs that have been handed from one generation to the next.

Students at this stage are also thinking about the commitments they will want to make in college and the traditions of your family history that they will want to carry on and those they will set aside. Take their requests for recollections, pictures, clarifications, and dates seriously, for they are but a part of the larger process of moving from dependence to autonomy and taking along the right baggage.

Invariably the college admissions process brings closer that day of final separation of children from their parents. What parents are learning is how to support their child while simultaneously letting her go, to control less and to worry more as one parent put it to me. It is a delicate dance—support, advise, step back, give space and time for the child to decide, then begin again—support, advise, step back, begin again. . . .

THE CAMPUS VISIT

Once a student and family have agreed on six to eight colleges to investigate seriously, all of you must make plans for visiting those campuses. You may be one of those parents who will want to accompany your child on these visits, or you may not wish to do so. A family should do what is natural within its tradition of decision making. If the child has always acted independently and responsibly, then he or she may prefer to go alone. If on the other hand your family tradition is one of democratic decision making in which you and your children have decided things together, then at least one parent should accompany the child to some of the schools chosen.

College visits can serve to alter a tradition, too. Consider the boy who has never ventured far from home on his own. College visits, his father decides, come at an important juncture, so he sends his son off to investigate colleges on his own. The boy makes all his appointments and finds his way, but he runs out of money by the time he reaches his last college. At that point the young man decides to approach the nearest father

---

* Erik Erikson, "Identity and the Life Cycle," *Psychological Issues I*, Monograph 1, p. 102, as quoted in Newman [1992], p. 18.

figure for a financial infusion. That person happens to be the director of admissions. The boy is a little embarrassed at having to request a loan, but he compensates for this by repaying it as soon as he returns home the next day. In this true story, the swiftness of the repayment and the forthrightness of the young man impress the admissions director; when the boy's fine grades and glowing school recommendation come through, he has little trouble gaining admission to the college. Without the independence thrust on him by a thoughtful father, this young man might never have had the chance to show himself as a person of sound character, a trait held in high esteem by many selective colleges.

What Do You Do During a Visit?

When you do decide to accompany your child on college visits, what do you do? Sit in the stuffy car and try to pay attention to a boring detective novel? Or go to the other extreme and try to make the visit count by going right into the waiting room and attempting to have a word with the admissions officer, in hopes of getting some idea of your child's chances of admission? Obviously, you should do neither. Instead, heed these suggestions:

- ◆ **Don't make the arrangements yourself.** Let your child make all the arrangements for the visit: estimating the travel time, setting up an appointment for the tour and the interview, and procuring printed information about the college before making the visit. You would be surprised how helpful appointment makers in college admissions offices can be when it comes to answering all of these questions—including how far it is to the next school you want to visit.
- ◆ **Time it right.** Try to plan your visit to the campus when the college is in session. Campus visits should not be planned during a college's vacation or special event, such as winter carnival or homecoming. At such times the campus is likely to look like a ghost town or a big party and it will not give an accurate picture of day-to-day college life.
- ◆ **Stroll around campus on your own.** Plan to conduct your own exploration of the college while your child is visiting. During the interview you can take the campus tour run by the admissions office or you can visit the facilities that are of special interest to you. Visiting colleges when they are in session will enable you to talk to students in a frank and casual way. Sometimes this is easier done when your own son or daughter is not present. Students can be asked all manner of questions

ranging from the quality of the food to whether or not they would send a son or daughter to this college, and why. You can pass along the answers you get to your child.

♦ **Sit in on a class or two.** Attend a class and try to pick a subject you know something about so that you can judge the sophistication and clarity of what is being communicated to the students. If you feel natural doing so, introduce yourself to the instructor afterwards and ask for comments on undergraduate education at the institution. Other questions might focus on how often instructors see students individually and for how long, what type of papers students write, whether the students are serious and productive, whether students and faculty ever collaborate on research, and what success the particular department has in placing promising students in graduate school.

♦ **Read campus bulletin boards.** This particular rule of thumb (useful for the applicant, too) was given to me by a father who had taken each of his five children on the college tour. "Always look at bulletin boards," he said. "They tell you what is going on and what the issues are, and they give you some idea of the vibrancy of the place." If you don't find a bulletin board in your campus rambling, check the entrance to the student union, the bookstore. Still no luck? Then ask the first student you pass. Also remember that there are electronic bulletin boards on many campuses. Sometimes admissions offices have computer terminals that you can use to access all sorts of information about a school, not just campus events.

♦ **Eat in the cafeteria.** Having a meal on campus is also a good idea, but not just to sample the food. Use it as an opportunity to observe how students interact and how the faculty and students relate to one another. For instance, be conscious of segregation or cliques in which the members of one particular group eat together and seem to exclude others.

♦ **Visit a dormitory.** In the course of your tour of the college, you should, by all means, see where students live. If the admissions tour does not include a dormitory room, you should ask to see one. The physical condition of dormitories, the environment as defined by lighting, color, and noise, and the security arrangements will all be very important to your child. After all, your son or daughter could be calling it home for the next four years. You will also want to ask about the various living options for students, such as theme houses, co-ops, and off-campus living.

♦ **Find out about support systems.** Where do students go if they have a problem? Assume that a student has difficulty comprehending the subject matter of an introductory chemistry course. To whom does he turn? Say there is a perennial problem with loud noise and partying in the dormitory—how does your daughter seek assistance in resolving that? Is there a network of adults and older students who can help freshmen through the adjustment of leaving home and living on their own? How does the advising system work, academically and socially? Can someone describe the interface between the advising system and the counseling system?

♦ **Get a feeling for the campus environment.** How does this college or university operate as a community? Is there an atmosphere of mutual respect between students and faculty and particularly among the students themselves? What happens when there are conflicts among students? How do those get resolved? Is there any evidence of intolerance or political correctness on the campus?

♦ **What's the school's mission?** How does it see itself serving its students and preparing them for the challenges of the twenty-first century? Perhaps this is not a question you ask anyone directly, but it is one you want to be able to answer nonetheless. Together with your other answers—all hopefully positive—you can feel confident in supporting your son's or daughter's interest in the school.

After visiting a small New England school, one mother wrote, "I'm glad I came. There's a chemistry here you can't explain. Whatever happens after this visit, my husband and I will feel that we were involved. We had our eyes and our ears opened, and consequently we know what our son is getting into."

Stay in the Background

You may be one of the parents who wonder whether you should seek a word with your child's interviewer at the conclusion of the interview. The best advice is to stay in the background. If for any reason the interviewer wants to speak to you—many schools have a protocol calling for this—you will be informed. The conversation will probably be informal, with your child in attendance. You should try not to be overzealous. At the same time, if you have specific questions about the curriculum or support mechanisms, now is the time to ask them.

Remember also that questions about financial aid are properly addressed to the financial aid office, and you may wish to make an appointment to visit there while your child is having her interview. Because of the decline in the college-age population, combined with a substantial *buyer's market* for students and their families, colleges have to compete for the good students, and parents are a part of the recruitment strategy. You will most likely receive a very warm welcome from the financial aid offices that you visit.

WHAT'S YOUR ROLE AT APPLICATION TIME?

When all the college visits are complete, you will want to discuss your impressions with your son or daughter—but be careful not to overly influence his or her impressions; let your child draw his or her conclusions about the schools. The final choice should include a range of schools, from those that are sure to accept the student, through several intermediate choices, to the one that represents his or her—not your—highest aspirations. In the process of arriving at this final list, try to keep the quality of education constant throughout and alter the other criteria—size, location, cost, special programs—to suit the level of admission difficulty.

Now that the selections have been made, it's time for the student to work out the final application strategy with his or her college counselor. What is the parents' role at this stage of the process? You must walk a fine line between giving too much assistance and too little. Specifically:

- If your child needs guidance in filling out applications, you might help establish a schedule for completing each one so that they all reach the colleges at the proper time. In setting a schedule, group the applications according to their complexity, beginning with the simpler ones first. Remember not to take any liberties with due dates!
- If your child comes to you with a question about what to write about for an essay question, it is acceptable to make a few topical suggestions. But resist the temptation to help shape and edit the final copy. Students need to know this from the outset. Sometimes teachers and peers will agree to read and react to application essays, and this is the course you too should follow.
- When students need assistance with the cost of postage, photocopying, and the application fees, parents can play a helpful role.

While rendering this subtle and symbolic assistance to your son or daughter, you should never communicate with the admissions office on his or her behalf. Once the student applies—and even before—colleges and universities believe that the primary relationship lies between the student and the school. So communication from parents, even about routine matters, is interpreted as intrusive and can be detrimental to a candidate.

A few years ago, I had just finished what I thought was a fairly eloquent speech on behalf of a candidate to the shrewd dean of admissions at a major eastern university. By way of response he picked up a letter from the candidate's file, held it between his thumb and forefinger, and waved it slowly back and forth in front of my face. "What does it say?" I asked. "It is not what it says; it is who says it," he replied sardonically. "This is a letter from Daddy's office, all neatly typed by Daddy's secretary on the office word processor, and the boy just signed it." Sure enough, it even bore the father's business address. The dean continued, "We are considering the kid, not poppa or momma, and we want to hear from the candidate!"

By helping your child at the margins of the application process, with your patience, with your resources—perhaps your son or daughter could print out his or her application on the office laser printer—and with your encouragement, it is possible to play a useful role during the application process without taking a direct hand in it. Your job as parent is to make sure that your child gives his or her best effort to all the college applications, and leave it at that.

To Use or Not to Use Influence?

In his short story "Babylon Revisited," Scott Fitzgerald entices his readers into his story with the line: "Let me tell you about the very rich, for they are different from you and me." Fitzgerald goes on to paint a picture of the decadent 1920s, in which influence often overwhelmed creativity and money too often defined human worth. Today we live in an era of much higher public and private accountability. The inappropriate use of money and influence is a very sensitive issue, and, as a result, some parents worry that their child's chances of admission might be jeopardized if they use any connections they might have to the business or political or academic world on his or her behalf.

Here are a few typical questions, similar to those my colleagues and I have been asked over the years about using influence, with some suggestions for appropriate conduct.

Question: Should I write to the director of admissions and tell him that my child definitely wants to go to Coburn as I did?

Answer: No, the child should do that.

Question: The other day at lunch my old client Clint Jones begged me to let him put in a good word for my daughter Luanne at Siwash. Says he knows the president from graduate school days. Should I let him do it?

Answer: Probably not. It doesn't sound like Clint and the president have kept up their relationship over the years. Moreover, Clint hardly knows Luanne at all. What new perspective could he shed on her candidacy through this obvious attempt to capitalize on an old acquaintanceship? It might upset the applecart completely.

Question: My son came home the other night and said that out of the blue his boss on the construction site where he worked last summer offered to write a recommendation letter to his colleges. Should I encourage him to have the letter sent?

Answer: Definitely yes, for it will cast a new perspective on the boy both as a person and as an employee—a perspective that the college would not be able to obtain from any other source.

Question: A good acquaintance of mine in college and in graduate school is now president of Hawthorne, where my daughter definitely wants to go to college. My friend and I have drifted apart over the years, since my husband Jack was transferred so much in the service. We only exchange cards at Christmas. But I really think she would want to know that Louise is applying. I would if I were in her position. What should I do?

Answer: This mother's instinct is correct! She should write a short, informative letter so her friend at least knows that Louise is applying. After all, there isn't much either can do after the decision is made, so the time to act is now.

Using Influence Appropriately

Questions and answers of this sort suggest a few guidelines concerning the use of influence on the college admissions process. Keep the following points in mind before any letters are sent, calls made, or other endeavors considered:

♦ **The person writing a letter should know the child well** and be able to cast a different light on the candidacy from that available through any of the usual sources, such as school, teacher, or employer recommendations, or the application itself.

♦ **If recommenders are basing their influence on connection to a college, that connection should be strong.** Being an enthusiastic supporter of the college's athletic teams and an annual contributor to the Dean's Fund is not usually strong enough. Being a trustee, a high administrative officer of the school, or a major donor is another matter.

◆ **Parents should not solicit letters or phone calls.** The subtlest form of influence is notification. They should let influential people know their child is applying to a particular college and allow the conversation to end there. Trust the judgment of the person whose help you seek. Many people with great influence maintain it by not involving themselves constantly in the internal workings of the school's admissions office. Instead, they write occasionally and reasonably, in support of candidates. In such a situation a few simple words will go a long way.

◆ **The integrity and intelligence of the college should be respected.** Parents can assume that anything their children have written down on an application has been factored into the admission decision. Alumni status is the most obvious example. Professional status and corporate ties are others. Most colleges have a system for assessing the potential financial worth of their candidates and keep in mind the possibility that some of their future assets may eventually flow to the college. Most admissions deans and development officers confer about applicants who could prove financially or politically beneficial to the college. At a given school there might be six to a dozen candidates who end up as *must takes* because of this, another twenty or more in the *highly desirable* category, and perhaps a longer list of students in the *it would be nice to have* category. Into these categories go students who come recommended by university officials, politicians, or other prominent individuals.

As parents, you should know that generally the college or university admissions office establishes a weight in the admissions scale for *special influence* applicants. So influence does count, but seldom will it overwhelm other factors in the decision-making process such as an abysmal high school record or very low test scores. You should also know that once the admissions office has made its decision, presidents and boards of trustees uphold these decisions rigorously. Long ago college presidents, development officers, and alumni chairpersons learned that it is far more equitable to have an autonomous, thorough, and professional admissions staff making the final decisions than to meddle excessively themselves, even though they could do so if they chose. It's wise therefore for you to understand the autonomy of the admissions office as you lay plans to employ or not to employ influence in the college's decision.

A TALK WITH THE GUIDANCE COUNSELOR

At some point during the college choice process, you should make an appointment to meet with your child's guidance counselor. This visit probably should come after your son or daughter has had one or two meetings with the counselor and after both family and student have attended a college information night in which members of the guidance office, often assisted by college admissions officers, explain how the process of applying to college and seeking financial aid actually works. You should also do some research on some of the colleges yourself, so that you know both schools and process. Then seek a conference with your son's college counselor. This conference should include the child and focus on the division of responsibilities among student, parents, and counselor.

You need to be sensitive to the fact that some counselors may misinterpret such a visit as a form of subtle pressure on them or the school to produce certain *results* for their child in the admissions process. Such are the drawbacks of our consumer-oriented society and the sometimes excessive involvement of the public in the operation of some high schools today. To avoid such a misunderstanding, make it clear to the counselor that you want to meet purely to get information and learn how you can best support the counselor's efforts and his or her professionalism. Ideally the visit will help the counselor get to know your family better and to bring to light information and viewpoints that may be useful to him or her in representing your son or daughter to colleges.

The frustration parents may feel at not being able to communicate certain information to colleges can often be allayed in a conference with their child's guidance counselor. A good counselor will pick up on information that will be helpful—or detrimental—to the student's candidacy.

One memorable conference with a counselor began on a somewhat negative note, but then stabilized. Very valuable information was imparted in a conversation that went like this:

> "It is too bad that the colleges won't be able to learn how much Ginny has overcome. She is too proud to say anything herself." The counselor looked confused. "Would you tell me what you mean by that?" she asked the parent. Ginny's parent explained that Ginny had been born with a hip defect and could not walk until she was four. At that point the doctor had

recommended that Ginny take up swimming to strengthen her lower body and legs. She did this, and, in her tenacious pursuit of the sport, she not only eliminated her limp, but she became a champion intermediate freestyle swimmer as well.

When the guidance counselor added this moving and significant information to Ginny's school recommendation, her candidacy, which was in every other way a modest one, took on another dimension. The admissions director at one selective college with a fine swimming program said, "We'd like to take a chance on Ginny; there are heartstrings in her folder."

Conversations with guidance counselors can clarify a whole range of topics that often puzzle parents and for some reason cannot be explained by their sons or daughters: how many times to take the SAT? how many colleges to apply to? or how to present extracurricular activities more effectively in the application?

Once the counselor knows your child's personality, abilities, and activities, he or she can also give you a realistic view of your child in relation to other seniors with similar credentials who will be applying to some of the same colleges. When an atmosphere of trust and respect is established by the parents, counselors are usually more than willing to assess a child's chances for admission at certain colleges and discuss tactics that might be employed. The conversation should end with agreement on the overall strategy that family, student, and counselor will undertake and who will do what and when.

The conversation with a counselor in the guidance office begins a three-way dialogue that will continue over the telephone, in the corridors of the high school, and perhaps even at a chance meeting at the supermarket as the application process rolls ahead. The rapport that you establish with the counselor will give your child a sense of emotional support. She will see that there are several adults ready and willing to support her and advance her cause.

Information In, Information Out

As the application process takes its course, counselors are sometimes given tentative evaluations of candidates by the colleges. The inferences counselors draw from these conversations can be relayed to students and parents. Then both can make tactical adjustments. Even if no tangible feedback comes from the colleges, counselors can help with any bureaucratic difficulties that may arise. (For instance, when a college sends notification that the high school has not sent in the student's transcript and recommendation, even though the student knows that these documents have, in fact, been sent!)

Counselors can also respond to parents' questions about the use of influence. Whether a particular family contact can help or hinder the child's application is a question best put to a counselor, who has an overall view of the student's chances at a particular college and of how that college responds to pressure of that type.

Throughout your dealings with your child's counselor, make sure that you make it clear that you want to understand the counselor's position and are appreciative of his or her efforts on behalf of your child. Remember that many counseling budgets have been cut in recent years and that counselors' jobs involve much more than just college counseling; they are often over-worked and understaffed. By the same token, counselors appreciate the understanding and involvement of a supportive family. Making the effort to meet with your child's counselor may mean much in the admissions process.

On the other hand, guard against overplaying your hand with the counselor. Steadfastly refusing to take advice on such points as:

♦ limiting the number of applications to "top" colleges,
♦ attempting to go over the counselor's head by talking to the principal or superintendent,
♦ secretly relying on an outside source, such as a private counselor, or
♦ leaving the counselor in the dark about certain tactics being employed

all serve to undercut her authority, eroding the potential goodwill and, through lack of coordinated efforts, jeopardizing your child's chances of admission.

SHOULD YOU HIRE AN INDEPENDENT COUNSELOR?

The increased pressures associated with college admissions today have led some parents to seek the services of a private counselor. Many of these indi-viduals are well trained and know the vagaries of the system well enough to avoid making outlandish predictions on behalf of their clients' offspring. In many instances they can provide much-needed assistance. For example:

♦ After a visit to their child's guidance counselor, a parent finds that the school's guidance department is not able to provide accurate and individualized college counseling.

♦ Their child needs special testing for values clarification, career preference, and academic tutoring as well as coaching for standardized tests that the high school is simply unable to provide. In this case, a private counselor's services are called for.

♦ There are a number of questions about financial assistance that the high school counseling office is unable to answer.

If you decide to hire a counselor, make sure that she is registered with the Independent Educational Counselors Association or a similar professional group. This will ensure that she has proper counseling experience and/or training and adheres to professional guidelines when representing your child to colleges and universities and helping in the preparation of applications and other materials. Make sure you interview two or more counselors before deciding on one, and be sure to include your child. In such arrangements chemistry as well as expertise is important.

IF YOU FEEL COMPELLED TO INTERCEDE

Counselors—public and private—aside, there are no substitutes for mother and father in the college search and application process. You have a vital and unique role to play in your child's college search. This means engaging in ongoing dialogue with your son or daughter, making genuine compromises from time to time, and letting your child make a mistake or two in order to learn. Help your child all the way along: in visiting colleges; researching schools through directories, college brochures, and videos; talking with teachers, alumni, and students on campuses; and just *being there* for the young person as he or she moves ahead with this challenging and exciting process.

Sometimes, however, just *being there* isn't enough. You might find your child in a special situation in which your involvement could make a big difference. You could, for instance, learn that your child has not been accepted at his top-choice college; he's been put on a waiting list instead. Despite your efforts so far to stay on the sidelines, you feel compelled to write an impassioned letter to the Dean of Admissions. Or you have learned that your daughter's first-choice college is headed up by your best friend's former college roommate. A positive word from her to the college president could make a difference.

Getting involved in either situation could be risky. Consider any such action seriously before you take it, keeping in mind that:

♦ The college admissions process is a once in a lifetime event and since it will not happen again, occasional extraordinary behavior is acceptable.
♦ The admissions committee can always deal with new information, especially if it is positive. (By contrast, they do not react well to old, regurgitated information.)
♦ "It is your kid!" and you have certain liberties as a parent.

The sample letter on the next page was written by the father of a young man seeking admission to a prestigious university with very high admission standards. After checking with his son's counselor, the father wrote his letter on plain stationery (that did not call attention to his status as a prominent diplomat).

The letter has both style and substance. The tone is properly deferential. Mr. Foss sympathizes with the pressures that are heaped on the director of admissions after the letters of acceptance have been sent out. While he does not reiterate all of Dan's accomplishments and abilities, he reminds Mr. Twombley of his son's ability to contribute to the musical and theatrical life of Hanover. He mentions his leadership in the Student Council—a point that will not be lost on a selective school seeking to identify the leaders of the next generation.

In addition, Mr. Foss makes the point that Dan is a mature and thoughtful young man who knows what he wants to do once he gets to college. His letter also emphasizes, subtly, Dan's unusual educational training in Europe and in America. Finally, Mr. Foss shows his understanding of what kind of university Hanover is, what it stands for academically, and what kind of students it wants to attract. The core of his argument is really that Dan Foss and Hanover are a perfect match, and college admissions is really a process of matching dynamic students to appropriate institutions.

The tone of the letter is reasonable, too. Dan is depicted not as a perfect candidate but as an intelligent, serious, and ethical human being who enjoys his moments of solitude and relaxation.

Also, the letter is not too long!

14 rue Cardinal Richelieu
75007 Paris
France

Mr. Dwight A. Twombley
Director of Admissions
Hanover University
Middlemarch, Connecticut 06590

Dear Mr. Twombley:

My son, Daniel A. Foss, is currently on the waiting list for admission to the class of 2000 at Hanover. Since his most fervent wish is to attend Hanover and be a member of the first class of the new millennium, I would like your permission to speak on his behalf.

From Dan's application you know that he has lived in Paris and attended French schools for the past five years. Last September he returned to the United States to spend his senior year at Saint James Academy. Saint James has been an ideal decompression chamber for Dan's reentry into the academic and social world of the United States. At Saint James, Dan achieved high honors for the first semester as well as for the current marking period. He has also been an active member in the theater there, and he has continued to play his beloved clarinet in the Saint James jazz band. He was elected as his class representative to the Student Council. His mother and I are very proud of Dan's record in all respects. We know the school is too.

My plea for Dan is based mainly on the fact that Hanover magically combines all the criteria that he set in selecting his ideal college. He wanted an institution with a tradition—one that had retained its academic integrity over the years and that still supported and respected individual accomplishment while stressing the centrality of community.

Perhaps because of his European background and his familiarity with the streets and boulevards of Paris, Dan has always insisted on an urban school, preferably one in the East. He also wants a school that is fairly large and able to attract a genuinely diverse student body. To Dan there is something in the Hanover ambience that appears more cosmopolitan, less stylized, and yet more individual than other colleges of comparable standing.

Since Dan is very interested in international relations, he wants to prepare for that field by majoring in government and French Literature at Hanover. His strong preparation at the hands of his French teachers in the International Baccalaureate curriculum has prepared him well.

I sincerely believe that Daniel would prove to be a responsible if not prominent person on the Hanover campus, both making a solid contribution to the community and deriving solid benefits from a Hanover education.

Moreover, Dan's classmates will find him a thoroughly enjoyable, warm, and kind young man. He is a mature and thoughtful eighteen-year-old, with a great deal of self-reliance and a sincere desire to learn. He is quite happy in himself and enjoys his moments of relaxation and solitude.

Recognizing that you and the admissions committee have many wonderful young people to choose from, I earnestly hope that you will review Dan's case and deem him a worthy gamble. You will not be disappointed.

Yours sincerely,

George A. Foss Jr.

HELPING OUT WHILE LETTING GO

There is absolutely no question that parents have an extremely difficult and delicate role to play in the college decision-making process. There is no routinely *right* way to handle all of its challenges. There are only some simple words of advice that may help families find their own answers in the college admissions experience.

First, separate your own aspirations from those of your children. Obviously you want your sons and daughters to be the best that they can be. To do that you have to let them make most, if not all, of the crucial decisions about college. Parents who say things like "We are applying to College X" are seriously mixing up their own lives and goals with those of their children. The point is to live for your children—not through them. Set examples for them, support them, and counsel them. Don't direct them, insulate them, or control them.

Second, you need to remind yourself that the college search and application process should be a journey from adolescent dependence to adult independence. Many children may not see it this way, but the progression toward independence is part of the college admissions process. This means that you have a dual responsibility: to educate your children about the realities of the admissions process and to inform them about the responsibilities that come with the immense freedom they will enjoy from the moment they step onto a college campus as freshmen.

Third, also remember that, deep down, children do want the advice of their mothers and fathers. They may not always want to act on it, however. They may stumble on occasion, but they want and need that advice all the same. The job of parents is to allow their children to make their own judgments and to support them when errors are made. This helps them forge their independence. Remember that guiding your child through the college admissions process may be one of the most difficult challenges you will face as a parent during your child's critical years of young adulthood. To allocate time to the enterprise and to try to help your son or daughter attain important goals could make it also your most rewarding experience of these years!

The difficulty in the end comes down to that of "roots and wings," of balancing the conflicting goals of security, traditions, and home against the aspirations for freedom, exploration, and separation.

As you look on the college admissions process ahead, view it as one of your last major opportunities to educate your child. In the brief time between the summer before the senior year and the college decision time in April of the following year, you have a chance once again to teach your child the things you value most: family, community involvement, ethics, spirituality, and the importance of education to a useful life. You can show how much you trust your child to fashion his or her own values in response to those values just mentioned. That those responses to these values will be different you both know. It will be the quality of that difference that the child's education will help define. It will be his education that will enable him to act reasonably and humanely in the not-so-reasonable-or-humane outside world. It will be her education that will solidify the self-esteem that you as parents have made sure to succor. It will be education that places the capstone of a fruitful and permanent adult relationship between you and the child you can parent no more.

NINE

Acceptance, Rejection, or the Wait List: What to Do Now

Students need to realize that the challenge these days is not only admission, but also finding the right match; that is sometimes the tougher problem.

David C. Murray, Vice President for Admissions & Financial Aid,
DePauw University

If an application is accepted by the college of choice, a student rejoices; if it is rejected, he's tearful. Emotions swirl, often obscuring the most important question in the long run: Which college is really the best match for me?

IF YOU'RE ACCEPTED

When you are accepted by a college you will naturally feel a sense of relief that you have gained admission, but you should not take the position that admission has validated every feature of your scholastic record and your moral character. The admissions process is an imperfect one; it relies mainly on information prepared by students, counselors, and teachers. Occasionally students look better on paper or a computer screen than they do in fact. This is especially true for students who test well. College admission officers are all too frequently influenced only by high test scores and high school grade point averages.

So if you consider yourself a winner in the college admissions sweepstakes, walk humbly and share your joy by extending a friendly hand to those who are not as fortunate, keeping in mind these words of Ecclesiastes:

I returned and saw under the sun that the race is not to the swift, nor the battle to the strong, neither yet bread to the wise, nor yet riches to men of understanding, nor yet favor to men of skill; but time and chance happeneth to them all.

WHICH COLLEGE TO CHOOSE?

For some of you, this is an irrelevant question. Maybe you've always wanted to go to State U. or Small College, and when it accepted you, you gave a shout of joy and mailed back your room deposit the same day. All well and good.

If You're Not Your First Choice's Choice

If you were rejected by your first-choice college, try not to indulge your disappointment. Excessive concern about the outcome of admissions decisions can undermine the self confidence you've worked so hard to build up. Families and guidance counselors frequently advise students to reach for a top college in the application process. They do so to ensure that candidates set high goals and put in a maximum effort. Even if you do not actually achieve that objective, you've still gained something important. In your striving, you may have found new reserves of skill and inner resources of strength.

This kind of emotional and spiritual growth cannot be measured but it is very real and should not be forgotten just because a selective college has sent a rejection letter.

As you and your fellow seniors rush home to find out how colleges have decided your fate, you should ponder these ultimate truths:

True education is not to be found in a particular college or university, nor in any combination of colleges and universities around the country. It is a process in which individuals pursue their own interests and perfect their own abilities under the discerning and compassionate eye of interested and competent teachers. The truly intelligent person is the one who is able to make the most of the entire college experience. Acceptance and rejection are ultimately of little consequence as you learn and become a thoughtful contributor to our society.

But if you are like many college applicants who don't have a single favorite school, you may be in the happy position of having several acceptances to consider and a big decision to make. If you have applied selectively—that is, to several colleges of varying difficulty—you may have at least three acceptances to consider.

Most of the criteria you established when you put your final list of colleges together—academic programs, location, size, extracurricular activities, and cost—are also important now, as you make your final choice. Difficulty of admission is no longer an important criteria, however. Remember that and don't leap to the conclusion that the college you should attend is the one that was the most difficult for you to get into.

Rather, you need to discover where you would be happiest, and that means a place where you are likely to succeed, not struggle.

By extending and revising your original criteria somewhat, you will be able to make a wise decision. The revised criteria are:

1. curriculum and course requirements;
2. student faculty relationships, both inside and outside the classroom;
3. student life; special programs—athletic, overseas, or extracurricular; and
4. cost.

Before applying these criteria, you should consider how to gather information that you need most about the schools that accepted you.

Another campus visit
The first and most useful means is to make another campus visit. Return to the campuses of the schools that have accepted you and study them again. Often the admissions offices will assist you by arranging for class visits, a night in a dormitory, and free meals while you are on campus. Some schools have special programs for students who've been accepted. If a campus visit is impossible, call the admissions office and get the telephone numbers and Internet addresses of students and faculty members to whom you can address your questions. Scholarship students and their families may have questions for the financial aid office.

Find out that phone number, too. Most colleges have toll-free telephone numbers and calling hours for the month following the date on which acceptances are sent out. During these hours accepted candidates can pose questions directly to college administrators and students.

Frequently colleges will offer to identify students who live close to a candidate's home so the candidate can contact them directly.

Your guidance counselor

Guidance counselors can be extremely helpful as an information resource now. Remember their role is not just to get you into college—it is also to place you in a college that is suited to your individual needs. Counselors and faculty members who have attended schools that have accepted you can provide special insight and raise questions for you to consider before making your final decision.

Friends and peers

Peers, with all due respect, are the third and least valuable source of information. Talk with friends who already are at college, then turn to peers who have also been accepted at one of your colleges. Ask your friends who, through visits or personal contacts, have had an opportunity to learn more about the school than you. The best peer information comes from friends who actually attend a college you are considering. They obviously know the school well and can answer specific questions you have relative to your list of criteria.

REVISITING YOUR ORIGINAL SELECTION CRITERIA

At this point in your selection process you need to revisit some of the selection criteria presented in Chapter 2, with a slightly more critical eye. This time around you can compare each of your schools closely with one another. Now you are not merely interested in what is available; you are interested in the total "product," so to speak—how the academic and the social opportunities will combine for you over the next four years.

Are the curriculum and course requirements right for you?

To begin this process, pick up the catalog of the school you are investigating and examine its curriculum more closely than you may have done earlier in your college research. Does it still meet your specific needs?

Is there sufficient depth? Let's say you wish to focus on computer engineering. Are there sufficient courses in this field to enable you to develop a specialty? Is computer engineering a department or just a major? What difference will that make to you?

Turn next to the distribution requirements. Here you face a real dilemma, because you want to have enough breadth both to take courses relevant to your major and to explore other areas in which you have a keen interest. At the same time, you do not want to be controlled by excessive distribution requirements. If, for instance, you have to take three courses in the humanities, three in the social sciences, and three in the physical sciences, will the requirements prevent you from keeping up with your interests in Spanish and music while majoring in computer engineering?

The only way to determine whether a college will allow you enough breadth is to make a mock schedule of your four-year program. Do this for each college that has accepted you. It may seem like a lot of work, but you've got a big decision to make, and the work is worth it.

As you create your schedule of classes, remember that a curriculum that has lots of distribution requirements may not be restrictive if the college runs on a trimester system and if it offers a good number of courses that satisfy those requirements. (See Chapter 10 for a detailed explanation of planning your course of study in college.)

You also need to bear in mind that when you complete your undergraduate experience you want to be well trained in a particular area and have had a healthy exposure to the liberal arts. In other words, your expertise has to be coupled with a capacity for independent thinking and broad awareness of other subjects if your education is to be truly valuable.

How is the quality of teaching?

Apart from examining the catalog description of the courses you would have to take, as well as those you might want to take, you will need to find out about the quality of teaching in those courses. Statistics about class size can tell you something, but an actual campus visit to attend several classes can be very revealing. Ask the admissions office to arrange for you to talk to professors in your field of interest so that you can address specific queries to them. While on campus, ask if there is a confidential guide to courses and teachers prepared by students. Its frank appraisals will tell you what to expect in terms of grades, work load, and individual assistance in a particular course.

Will they give you course credit?

There is also the question of credit for previous work done in high school or at a college. You need to ask the colleges what credit, if any, is given for exceptional high school preparation or Advanced Placement (AP) study. If you have been enrolled in AP courses in your high school, you should have already found out whether or not your college choices give credit for them before taking the relevant AP tests in mid-May. Some colleges will grant no credit for AP, so students are obliged to remain in college for the full four years. Other colleges grant placement but no credit, meaning they will allow students to move into advanced courses on the strength of their AP test results.

In contrast there is a third approach to AP and previous college courses that many schools have adopted recently. Often called an Accelerated Degree program, it grants credit in the fullest sense and enables students with four AP tests to save a whole year's work and expense in college. This may be appealing to some students who are looking for ways to reduce the cost of a college degree, to those with established career goals or fields of interest, or to those who want to be exempt from some distribution requirements in order to explore the curriculum.

Still other colleges have their own tests for advanced standing and you need to find out what your opportunities for such placement would be, based on your current high school courses.

These questions can all be answered by professors and department heads when you visit the campuses of the schools that have accepted you. Faculty at most schools will be available for your questions, and if you can't make a return visit, contact them by phone or e-mail.

Are there good student-faculty relationships?

Talk to both faculty and students directly. Ask faculty members how much time they spend with students outside the classroom, in the lab, on field trips, socially. Do they have students over to their house? Are they advisers to any extracurricular activities on campus? In other words, do they take their out-of-class commitments seriously? Use your good judgment in these exchanges with faculty, ask them open-ended questions and see if they will tell you what you want to know without pressing too hard and making them feel uncomfortable.

Ask students similar questions. Do they feel they have access to faculty? Are office hours adequate? Does access to faculty by e-mail really work? Most colleges and universities are wired so that students and faculty can stay in touch via their computers. At some schools homework and papers are even transmitted to an instructor this way. The work is then graded and sent back over the wires. It's paperless!

Is the campus atmosphere to your liking?

You also want to get some feeling for the level of political correctness on campus. Is there a genuine openness on the part of faculty to novel and different ideas, or is there a closed mindedness in some areas of teaching and learning? Are the opinions of students taken into consideration as a formal part of the tenure process? Because of a growing interest in how well students are learning, many colleges and universities have extensive course evaluation procedures. Do the schools you're considering care about the outcomes of your education?

If you learn, for instance, that professors begrudge students time outside the classroom or do not place much stock in student opinion about their course content and teaching methodology or that the school does not keep good records of what happens to its graduates after graduation, then you may want to consider another institution of higher learning.

What's the quality of student life like?

There are at least two parts to this question: the way students look on education at their particular college, and the way they interact with one another. Talk to students on campus about this. Ask them how well their college experience has lived up to the expectations they had when they arrived.

If you sense some disillusionment—and there probably will be some—try to find explanations for it. Does it originate with the undergraduates themselves? Were they unrealistic in their expectations of the college to begin with, or are there institutional problems? Think about how you might avoid similar pitfalls. For instance, if you should end up with an uninterested adviser, would there be a way to change advisers?

Is there help when you need it?

Is there an unofficial advisory system through which students can get answers to questions they face? Are there resident advisers (RAs) in dormitories, and how well does the RA system work? Are there support programs for multicultural students and learning-disabled students? Is there a learning assistance center for help with study skills and writing problems? Is there an active counseling system? Are there popular and accessible professors to whom students can turn in times of stress? How well does this invisible system of advising work?

What are students' priorities?

You will also want to know just how serious most of the undergraduates at each college are about their education and their personal and professional development. "What are the first words that come to mind when you're asked to think about your experiences here?" is one question that you can pose.

If certain answers keep coming up—"Too much work," "Great parties," "The teaching is great," "Girls have it tough," "The winters are awful"—then you know what to expect, should you decide to matriculate there. Each of these responses should then be examined more carefully and weighed against your own needs and preferences.

As you go from college to college, your questions will become sharper and your imagination will begin to suggest ways that you might cope with the challenges described to you. Bear in mind that no school is perfect, and no single response is universally true for all the students at a given institution. Talk to as many students as you can before making up your mind.

Do students show respect for each other?

As you carry on your investigation, focus on how students at a particular college treat each other. Do they respect each other's differences in personality and interests, or are they insensitive? Take an especially good look at the dormitory situation. Are there periods during the evening when people try to keep the noise down to a dull roar so that others can study or sleep? What is the accepted practice for entertaining visitors in rooms overnight? What happens to roommates who are not particularly social and like to have some private time? Are their rights honored by their more social roommates? Try to spend a Saturday night in a campus dormitory to observe how the different personalities interact and whether students seem to enjoy themselves and each other.

How's the library?

The library is something else to check out. Can students who have work to do find privacy there, or is there much talking and socializing going on? Quite apart from the seating capacity of the library and the size and availability of the reserve collection, are the rights of users respected there? Many college students have never been away from home before, and you may be shocked at how they interpret their freedom and do as they please, often at the expense of the rights and interests of others. Responsible students will want to find a school where relationships among undergraduates are not only harmonious but respectful and where an appreciation of individual differences, a sense of fun, and a serious attitude toward learning all coexist amicably.

Are there special program opportunities for you?

It's also wise to explore in greater depth the extracurricular programs that initially attracted you to the particular college or university. When, for example, promising swimmers visit a campus before making their final decision, they should talk to the swimming coach about their prospects for making the team in the fall. It may well be that many more swimmers than predicted have accepted the college's offer of admission, thus raising the level of competition for the team. Consequently, a student who swims may opt to look more closely at one of his or her alternative schools. Or take the example of fewer swimmers attending than predicted. In this case a candidate may be so superior to other freshman swimmers that he or she would not be challenged sufficiently by teammates over the coming four years. Or, another example: The orchestra may be unexpectedly flooded with oboists this year, or the radio station with sports announcers.

In order to be assured of a reasonable opportunity of using your skills, you should assess the situation before signing up to attend a particular college. Coaches, advisers, deans, and even admissions officers can be of assistance here.

They realize that the college experience does not consist of study alone, and they want their students to be happy and productive on the athletic fields, in the studios, in the entire variety of undergraduate activities that make a campus vibrant.

How's the career planning for grads?

In your efforts to distinguish among the schools that have accepted you, one special service deserves particular attention. Though it perhaps held only passing interest for you when you were applying, the career planning and job placement office at your college will be very important to you. Many students enter college with less than a clear idea of what they want to study and an even dimmer notion of what they might wish to do with their lives when they complete their undergraduate education. An effective and involved career planning and job placement officer can be of inestimable help as you seek to clarify your objectives and crystallize your career plans over the four undergraduate years.

Does the career office do its job well?

The career office of the college or university should be able to tell you how many graduates went into various fields last year and what the average number of job applications per student was. A few offices will have statistics on their "satisfaction rate"; that is, how the students who used their services felt about them. For information about how a given college's graduates are viewed in a particular field, you will need to turn directly to employers in that field. However, you can get an idea of what companies employed last year's graduates of a school you are considering by looking at the alumni job directory maintained by the career office.

Make a special point of finding out whether the career office has a testing program that enables students to discover the areas in which they have special interest and talent. Does the office offer a course, or informal advice, on decision making and career preparation to first- and second-year students? What sort of reference library (printed and electronic) does it maintain?

Can a freshman drop by to receive some preliminary advice? Are speakers invited to the campus to describe particular fields of expertise? Are there field trips or educational media accessible to undergraduates who are surveying the world of work and trying to determine what area they want to enter? Are there internship opportunities so that students can gain practical experience in the world of work before deciding on a particular field? Sometimes there are opportunities for students to obtain paid employment in their field of interest and to combine work and study. This is called a co-op option and can help many students pay their way through school.

Is there counseling for grad school?

How about graduate school counseling? Does the career office or the Dean's office offer a program of instruction in completing applications, attending interviews, and assessing offers? How well is this college's placement office regarded by its counterparts in other colleges and by the various companies and graduate schools that have contact with it? How do its instructional materials compare with similar materials at other colleges?

What will it cost?

Finally, there is the question of financial aid and/or the cost of your education. (This has been discussed in Chapter 7 in some detail.) What you need to remember is that financial aid offices do not exist only for those students who are on scholarship. A majority of families find it hard to bear the high cost of a college education today. When it comes to distinguishing among the costs of several accepting institutions, you should ask financial aid and admissions officers for advice about the costs you and your family will face over the next four years.

The first thing to understand is the billing system of the particular institution. When are bills due? What are the various charges/fees for student activities, laboratory use, exceeding the average number of course credits, meal plans, dormitory charges, and the like? Families need to know what the actual numbers are going to be and when the money will be due to the school.

Are there both short-term and long-term payment plans available? Are there tuition prepayment options? How much is it reasonable to expect students to earn on their own during the college year? And over the summer? Nonscholarship students who have to monitor their expenses carefully may want to know what access they will have to campus jobs and loan programs administered by the school. In particular, will scholarship students be given preference in the assignment of on-campus jobs?

Compare financial aid packages

Compare costs and aid packages awarded to you from all the schools to which you've been admitted. This is called comparison shopping, and every good shopper should do it when making expensive purchases. It's only fair that you know just what you'll be paying for; a college education is an expensive purchase. You and your family could conceivably be investing more than $100,000 over the next four years, and you will want to do it in the most sensible way possible. See Chapter 7 for a detailed discussion of how to compare financial aid awards.

Colleges do not want you and your family to miscalculate either. You can help avoid that unhappy circumstance by having a detailed discussion of your resources with a member of the financial aid office at the outset. Colleges want to make sure families understand and appreciate all the opportunities available for financing the cost of a college education. So any visit to a college prior to deciding which school to attend probably ought to include a stop at the financial aid office.

Final Decisions

If your schools are beginning to blur during this final analysis, don't be alarmed. After all, your original choice of colleges was based on similarities in academic program, location, size, cost, and quality of student life. Your final decision should be a difficult one if you chose wisely in the first place!

As you look over all your notes, reexamine your criteria, and talk to your family once again, don't be reluctant to fall back on your gut feelings. Although you may not realize it, your instincts are really informed instincts at this point. If you can see yourself happy at one particular school, then you probably should make the decision to attend that school. If one college seems to have a good sense of itself, an idea of what it does well and what it needs to do better, and if the students at the school are both happy and reasonably serious and respect one another's differences, then your chances of being happy and productive at that school are probably ensured.

In the end, even if you think you are making a visceral judgment, you're probably not. If you feel that this school is where you really want to be, then go there and be content with the fact that you've made the right decision.

IF YOU'RE PUT ON THE WAIT LIST

Because students apply to many colleges and can go to only one, colleges have to compensate by accepting more applicants than they can actually accommodate. It's a risky business—colleges do not want to accept more students than they have places for. So they hedge their bets with wait lists. A wait list response can mean one of at least three things:

1. **Academic.** You didn't have as strong credentials as others but could be accepted provided some of the students who have been sent acceptance letters decide not to come.
2. **Financial.** You are acceptable, provided that some of the accepted students elect not to come and thus return their financial aid awards for others to use.
3. **Political.** You are not acceptable but were placed on the wait list to avoid giving offense to an influential individual or group, such as a parent who is an alumnus.

Wait List Actions to Take

Being placed on a wait list is in some ways more agonizing than an outright rejection letter. You must prepare yourself for this ambiguous response and react as quickly as possible. Try not to get your hopes up too high. Act quickly, and take the following steps:

1. **Secure your place at one of the institutions that accepted you.** Return the reply card, and make a deposit. Colleges understand that some of the students who originally accept their offer ultimately will not come. The deposit is a means of dealing with this inconvenience.

2. **Find out what your status on the wait list means.** Are you near the top? Is it a political decision? Is there a financial dimension to the wait list decision? What is the major obstacle you have to overcome to gain admission to the college? (Your counselor should be able to help you here.)

3. **Rally your support.** Make an ally of your guidance counselor; he or she can serve as your intermediary with the college and give you much-needed advice. Mount a campaign to enlist others in your quest. Remember you need not behave like you did when you were an applicant. Now all bets are off, so to speak. Undertake your campaign with a good deal of gusto and humor. You have to show enthusiasm and commitment.

   Get a letter of support from a teacher who knows you well but who did not write in support of your application in the course of the regular admissions process. Go back to your neighbor across the street who graduated from the college you want to attend and who offered to write it in the fall. You were too proud to accept his help then; ask for it now. Call the relevant coach or department head at the college yourself. This will enable you to get a sense of the nature and degree of support you will need.

4. **Write a letter to the Dean of Admission or to the person in the admission office you know best.** In the letter: a) Reiterate your interest in coming to the school. Make it clear that you will come if accepted; b) Address your deficiency, such as a weak sophomore year, and note your improvement since then; c) Affirm your interest in contributing to the life of the college, and mention your special talent, academic, artistic, athletic, extracurricular, in so doing.

5. **Send in your recent grades and a document of your accomplishments,** such as new athletic times or honors received.

6. **Make sure your financial aid application, if you have one, is complete.** Colleges and universities invariably send out all their scholarship dollars to the students they accept, and then as the funds are declined by students who go elsewhere, they become available for wait list candidates. If your financial aid file is not up-to-date, then you might

be passed over in favor of another student whose file is, or you may be admitted without funds, and by the time you complete your file, the funds are exhausted. In this case your letter of acceptance can represent a hollow victory.

7. **Develop a schedule for your various actions, either in writing or on your computer.** Remember to have columns for follow-up; i.e., check to be sure that other people have done what they said they would do for you.

Call the Wait-List School

After you and your supporters have submitted all material, ask your guidance counselor to telephone the college again to reiterate your interest. Or you can call yourself. The call also can be made for the purpose of gathering information or to ask if the wait list is beginning to move, for example. You may learn that your candidacy may still be viable but that the admissions office had questions about X or Y. In this instance, you or your guidance counselor can address the weaknesses that prevented your application from being accepted outright.

Some questions you might ask are: "Where did I go wrong? Were my scores too low? If so, can these be offset by another teacher recommendation in math or English? Was the essay portion of the application weak? If so, may I write another?"

Should Parents Get Involved?

Only as a second recourse should parents become involved in wait list actions. One can easily imagine that a college would be reluctant to admit to a loyal alumnus that his daughter is really on the wait list simply because it did not want to offend him by rejecting her application, thus jeopardizing its receipt of his financial support in the future. Likewise, the college admissions office will not want to tell a family or a student that the athletic coach who had earlier virtually promised the candidate admission was overruled in the final deliberations of the admissions committee, and that, to save face, the committee opted to place the applicant on the wait list.

As the conversation proceeds, here are some other questions you may need to have answered:

♦ What new information would you like to see concerning me? I have additional and better sprint times from last Saturday's meet. May I submit them? Or the tape of a recent recital?

♦ Would it help me to write a letter to the Dean of Admissions restating my sincere desire to come? The answer to this almost frivolous question almost doesn't matter, for the question makes it clear that you would definitely accept an offer of admission if tendered by the college. Remember that the one thing admissions officers don't want to do is accept people from the waiting list who then won't come!

Once you have asked about the projected schedule for admitting candidates from the wait list, you are ready to conclude the call and start on your wait list. As you carry out the actions on your list, remember that the colleges will admit students in batches from the wait list, taking the most critical cases first, then proceeding at intervals to accept groups of diminishing size until the class is filled. Normally the process takes a month to six weeks; sometimes it even extends into early summer, especially when financial aid data is incomplete. You may have to make several calls to the admissions office to see what is happening with the wait list.

Risk Being a Pest

Being placed on a wait list allows you to take stock of your own feelings about a school. If you are only marginally interested in a college that has wait-listed you and think it might be only a little better than others that accepted you, drop it and forget the whole waiting list campaign. If on the other hand you decide to campaign for admission to a particular school, go to it—risk overkill.

Most colleges do not rank the people on their wait lists because they know that they are going to have to respond to various pressures in accepting them. They realize that wait lists are political in every sense of the word. Admissions directors are beset from every quarter: by coaches—their best-laid plans gone awry—who need two more divers or quarterbacks; by development officers who want them to accept a candidate whose father is on the education committee of the state legislature; and by influential guidance counselors who are asking, "How could you not have taken Jennie?"

In this somewhat chaotic situation, you should realize that your own chances may be slim because of various demands and institutional priorities that have to be met. Whether you like it or not, the swimming coach cannot present a team without any divers, and the guidance counselor who sends the college fifty good candidates each year has to be heard, and perhaps even accommodated. Nonetheless, the candidate who presents himself or herself vigorously and who is not afraid to take a few risks and overstep a few of the conventions often has a chance.

NO ACCEPTANCES?

Time and chance do play a large role in the admissions process, and if you are one of those whose applications are rejected, you have an important responsibility to yourself not to allow the colleges' decisions to serve as a definitive evaluation of your worth as a person, or even as a scholar. "If only I had been a better athlete; if only my mother had gone to the college that I wanted to enter; if only I had studied harder, been born rich or, better yet, poor, or lived in Alaska." The litany of "if onlys" is both mournful and unproductive and imposes a false simplicity on the college admissions process.

In the unhappy event that you are not accepted by any of the colleges to which you applied, an agonizing reappraisal is called for. Working directly with your guidance counselor or with one or more of the colleges that rejected your application, you must find out what the weaknesses in your application were.

Step #1: Work on remedying your deficiencies.
Once these are uncovered and addressed, you can move ahead with your efforts to gain admission to another college. If your scores on the Subject Tests were weak, you should consider taking those tests on which you think you can do better on the May test date. Perhaps you might look for colleges that don't require them!

If your academic average was insufficient from the colleges' point of view, you should make a last-minute effort to finish the year in the strongest fashion possible. Being frank with teachers—telling them of your difficulty and taking on projects for extra credit—will help produce better results for new colleges to consider. Again, you should look for some new schools that are not as academically demanding.

Remedying the defects in your candidacy is only one part of a multipronged response to a complete lack of acceptances.

Step #2: Work closely with your college counselor.
Your guidance counselor can ask the colleges some of the embarrassing questions that have to be asked; e.g., "Didn't you think she worked up to her capacity? Did you think her parents played too large a role in her application?" "What was so bad about her essay?"

Once you, your counselor, and your family have had a frank discussion of what went wrong, then you can try to remedy the situation. There are several routes that your counselor or you working on your own can follow.

APPLYING TO A NEW COLLEGE

Your next step is to initiate an application to a new college in late April. Try to find a school that has openings and academic standards that you can meet. College counselors usually keep a list of schools that are approachable in April. In fact, your counselor may be on the mailing list of the National Association of College Admission Counselors, which publishes a list of spaces available in more than 500 colleges across the nation. You may want to call one of the schools you disregarded as a safety school.

Alternatively, you could approach some of the lesser-known private liberal arts colleges hard hit by the declining student population. These schools are seeking students and are more than willing to consider late applications. Your guidance counselor may be able to suggest some schools and advise which one would be best for you.

Sometimes schools in this category send information to a large number of college applicants in the fall, so now is the time to look through any "fan mail" you may have received and reevaluate those colleges that wrote to you.

If, for some reason, both you and your counselor are stymied, you can turn to the local or regional board of higher education. These institutions invariably publish on a monthly or biweekly basis the names of the colleges in the region that still have vacancies. The New England Board of Higher Education (68 Walnut Road, Wenham, Massachusetts 01984) is one of these; it lists the openings at member institutions—public and private, two-year and four-year. Then it lists vacancies in New England colleges according to boarding men, boarding women, and commuters. A telephone call to your regional board of higher education is definitely in order if you have no other way of obtaining information about local schools with vacancies.

Colleges that rejected you could be a source of information and advice. Call them up and begin by saying, quite simply: "I wish I could have come to your school next year, but I understand why that is impossible. I wonder if you could give me some help. Could you advise me what to do next? What would you do if you were me?" Once you have a list of schools with spaces, ask your counselor to call them, one by one, on your behalf.

Applying to a New Private Liberal Arts College

Let us assume for a moment you've selected a private liberal arts college. With the help of your guidance counselor (or your parents, if for some reason your counselor is not able to help), call the director of admissions of that college. After confirming that there may indeed be some openings this year, the person calling on your behalf should mention that, although you have not been accepted by the other colleges to which you applied, you definitely want to go to college in the fall and at that particular college, if possible.

The point should be made strongly that you have researched the school, are definitely interested in it, and would attend if accepted at this late date. Furthermore, you would very much appreciate being sent the necessary forms and being allowed the opportunity to apply for admission. The caller should summarize your high school record, both academic and extracurricular, and state that you are willing to come to the campus for an interview.

Before the conversation is over, the caller should establish that this is the *only* school you want to consider and that you would not submit any other applications if you received an indication that you *might be accepted.* Such an approach plays on the college's natural desire at this late point to consider applicants who are actually going to attend the school.

In the conversation, remember to bring up the topic of financial aid, if you are applying for it. It is helpful to have some idea of what the family contribution is because the admission director will undoubtedly have her eye on the checkbook, as the saying goes.

Applying to a New Public College

If you don't have a college acceptance in late April you should consider approaching public institutions in two different ways, either for September admission or for admission at another point in the year, such as the start of the second semester, which usually begins in January. Your state university, for example, has a special obligation to you and your family as taxpayers who support it. Your state school is also apt to be large enough to have room for just one more student in September.

Admissions officers at state universities can often find a place for candidates who are willing to forgo student housing and financial aid.

State colleges and universities frequently have some academic programs or schools that are underenrolled, and if students can adapt to the curricula of one of these schools or departments, their chances for admission are considerably increased. Often they will be able to transfer to the program or major they prefer at a later date. Some state universities will also admit students late if they agree to begin in the summer. Ask about this option.

In addition, most state universities have branch campuses where candidates can begin their work before transferring to the main campus later. Even though a state college might not have sounded attractive back in September, it may appeal to you now, when you know you've got no acceptances; you may find going to one will salvage some your self-esteem and, more important, allow you to get on with your education. Beginning work at a branch campus and finding a job in order to help your family with tuition expenses may give you a sense of independence that you would have otherwise been denied had you been accepted at your first-choice school.

It goes without saying that state or public universities are cheaper than private colleges, too. Furthermore, when you've established a fine record at the state school, you may want to consider transferring to a private college.

REAPPLYING TO A COLLEGE

Should you choose to reapply to a college that has rejected you in the past, you should find out why you were not admitted and what you can do to build a stronger case for yourself when you reapply. Here are some guidelines for you to follow:

1. If possible, you should let some time elapse between your rejection by a college and bringing up the topic of applying a year

later. Let the admissions director get the freshman class solidified. Mid-June is a better time than the day after you receive your rejection letter. July is even better.

2. **Seek a face-to-face interview at the college, preferably with the dean or director of admissions.**

3. **When you do bring up the subject of applying again, you should not be timid or embarrassed.** The admissions process is not perfect. Decisions are close; occasionally an injustice is done. Most admissions officers recognize this and see their role as counselors. They will be willing to help rejected students make a new and more realistic plan so that they are admitted to an appropriate college elsewhere. So in the course of your conversation with the admissions officer or dean, try not to give the impression that you feel that a college has made a mistake.

4. **Emphasize the learning experience you have derived from the college application process, and stress your seriousness about your education.** After volunteering what you feel were the weaknesses in your candidacy, ask the admissions officer to share his or her views of your case. Put the two together and ask for advice on how to strengthen your case upon reapplication. Show flexibility in your response. Perhaps you will be advised to take courses at a community college—something you never thought you would do. Be open to suggestions. And, yes, follow the advice you are given. In a way, the advice is a form of condition. When the condition is met, the obligation for the college to accept you increases.

5. **Confirm the advice you receive with another college just to make sure you have broadened your options.**

Whatever you do, make sure to have some fun or relaxation during the period between your rejection and your reapplication. Restore your spirit and your energy. Build your confidence, preferably in an activity that you enjoy and are good at.

TAKING A YEAR OFF

If you are one of those students whose applications were rejected at all their schools, you may well choose to take the year off and reapply for admission in September of the following year. You should make it your first order of business to think through what went wrong with your applications. You

If You're Planning to Transfer Later

If you elect to go to another college or university and then transfer to the school of your choice later, remember to:

♦ Take solid courses in the area of your interest.

♦ Ask for grades in the courses—no pass/fail.

♦ Remember you will need recommendations from one or two of your professors, so take an active part in your classes.

♦ Save your course syllabi to show to the registrar once you are admitted to your first-choice school. These will help with your placement in the proper courses.

♦ Participate in some activity outside your classes if possible, and try to gain recognition.

will need to be honest with yourself. Once you have some ideas of your own, contact the colleges in which you were interested, and ask them to review your folder with you.

As you prepare for these conversations it will be important for you to have some ideas of your own and not to rely on the colleges to do all of your educational planning for you. If your academic record was weak, for instance, then consider enrolling in your local junior or community college and taking two courses in your weak areas during the year. If your application lacked focus about potential career directions, then maybe you should take one of the variety of preference tests to see where your real strengths lie. Contact your guidance counselor for advice here. Ask about the Kulman Anderson Preference Test or the Campbell Interest Inventory. You can then follow this up with course work in your area of strength and perhaps a work experience that will acquaint you with the practical side of a field in which you have an interest or skill.

Discussions with guidance counselors and college admissions officers may have revealed more subtle weaknesses than simple academic deficiency or career uncertainty. You may, for instance, have demonstrated specific unimpressive personal traits.

Nonchalance about the admissions process itself, incomplete or frivolous responses to questions on the application, or lack of self-confidence displayed in the interview might have figured in the decision to reject your application. Naturally, these traits are harder to discern than academic or extracurricular weakness, and the college admissions officers may only mention them in passing. Keep your ears open. If an admission officer or school counselor does allude to something of this sort, try to deal with it honestly. Be open to criticism and try to develop a genuine desire to deal with your own imperfections.

Use the Year Off to Your Advantage

In cases where immaturity, indifference, arrogance, or similar qualities have become problems, you may want to consider using your year off to participate in an activity that could sharpen your sense of self-worth and appreciation for others.

Participating in Outward Bound, which requires several weeks of wilderness living, may be too radical a solution for you, but some kind of volunteer work that would bring you into contact with those less fortunate than you might be quite educational. It would broaden your perspective and might incline a college to look on you more favorably next year.

Everyone will have a different plan for a year off. Your plans will develop from a combination of advice from parents, counselors, colleges, and reflection on your own values and goals. Inevitably you will emerge from your adversity as a stronger person. When you do secure college admission the following year, your acceptance will be a lot less important to you than the educational and personal growth you have gained in the interim.

Making the Most of the Freshman Year

It is a period of unlimited freedom, the greatest you will ever have, but also a period of exciting responsibility. The trick is to balance the two effectively.

B. Ann Wright, Dean of Enrollment, Smith College

When Barbara Crowley decided to accept the offer from Hanover College, she knew that she had much planning to do. Choosing Hanover did not signal the end of the college admissions process for Barbara; instead, it marked the start of a new phase, one in which she would be required to make intelligent and informed decisions about her freshman year.

Barbara's first order of business was to select her courses for the fall term and send in her registration card to the college. So she sat down with the Hanover catalog one evening and began by surveying the requirements that she would need to meet in order to obtain her degree in four years. Once she understood the requirements she could construct her academic road map or course of study. Her father called it her strategic plan.

CHARTING THE ACADEMIC PATH

After perusing the college catalog, Barbara decided to sketch out the big picture for herself. She knew that she wanted to major in economics so that she could enter the business world when she graduated. She knew also that she wanted to take a broad range of courses while in college and avoid overspecialization—specializing could wait until graduate school. She also wanted her education to include a mix of practical experience and book learning. She decided to try to plan her freshman and sophomore years, considering both the summers and academic years. She began with three objectives: her major, a breadth of other courses, and practical experience.

The Hanover catalog stated that majoring in a given subject required taking at least eight courses within the department and at least four courses in a related field. In addition, each student had to take six other courses that represented a sampling of the three broad areas of knowledge: the social sciences, the humanities, and the sciences. Two courses were required in each of these areas, and no two could be taken in the same department. Thus a student, in meeting the distribution requirements, would be exposed to at least six different subject areas.

The college also had three other requirements: quantitative reasoning or math skills and expository proficiency. Satisfying these requirements meant choosing particular courses with an asterisk or a dagger—that demanded students meet a reasonable level of proficiency in math and writing.

The third requirement was called multicultural distribution and required the student to take nine hours of designated courses (including foreign language) that would expose the student to non-Western cultures.

Barbara now made three shrewd practical decisions so that she could reach her broad educational objectives. First, she decided to begin work on her major right away so that she could attain an advanced level of study and qualify for special programs by her senior year.

Second, she decided to meet her distribution requirements as soon as possible so she could benefit from the breadth of the subject matter. Completing these requirements would also give her the freedom to take more courses of her own choosing in her junior and senior years. *Keeping your options open* is what her father called it.

Third, Barbara decided to try to take courses that overlapped slightly, at least two per semester. Doing so made sound educational sense because it would cause Barbara to learn and compare the modes of inquiry of different disciplines, say, economics and political science. It would also provide Barbara with knowledge that could transfer from one subject area to another.

Barbara also decided that as a strategy, she would try to concentrate on the economic dimension of the courses she took outside her department, and thus inform herself about the relationship of economics and literature, economics and philosophy, economics and social history, and so on.

Advice From Campus

Before going any further with her planning years, Barbara had made a telephone call to a Hanover undergraduate, Ron Barrow, who lived in the next town. Ron was studying economics at the college and was just completing his junior year. The office of admissions had suggested that Barbara talk to Ron before deciding whether or not to attend Hanover. Barbara had found Ron's comments very helpful. This time Ron suggested that she take the course in research and methods in economics (Economics 90), even though it was not required by the department. In his opinion, Economics 90 should be a required course for economics majors and would be of inestimable value to Barbara when it came time to write her senior thesis.

Ron also suggested that she study the economy of one particular region intensively, and since this advice coincided with that of her father, who was a corporate executive of some experience, Barbara decided to follow it and tentatively chose Latin America as a focal point.

Ron advised Barbara to consult the "Confidential Guide to Courses and Instructors at Hanover." The Hanover guide was similar to those prepared by resourceful students at other colleges around the country. It listed each course in the catalog, giving its number, instructor, informal title, number of pages of reading required per week, number of papers assigned, and relative difficulty. An explanatory paragraph told what students ought to expect in regard to grading procedures, assistance from the instructor, exam questions, and the character of student/faculty interaction in the classroom.

The guide's analysis of Political Science 35—Political Economy of the U.S. went like this:

> **Political Science 35**, Political Economy of the U.S.: Money and Power—Prof. Peter Fowles. Two lectures and one seminar per week.
>
> Although this is one of the toughest courses at Hanover, it is a must. Fowles is inimitable as a lecturer; he has a broad command of his subject, gained from eleven years of perfecting this course, a real compassion for students, and practical experience in the field of economics as a consultant to several government committees. (He is currently helping the Ethics Committees of the House and Senate draft guidelines for Washington lobbyists.) You will have to do virtually all of the

200 pages of reading each week because Fowles has a way of referring to it on exams. Fortunately most of it is in inexpensive paperbacks, so extensive note-taking is not necessary.

Fowles and his two assistants expect you to ask questions in the seminars. And if you don't, they will. So do the reading on schedule and don't leave it until the end of the course. Fowles is not above stopping his lecture from time to time and asking a student if he has understood what has just been said. Who else would bother?

There are two short papers—one a description of how a particular institution operates politically and economically, the other an analysis of a policy question, e.g., "The Proper Role of the Federal Reserve Board in a Global Economy." There is also a stiffly graded hour exam and a final. However, the range of the questions on the final allows students to bring in their particular area of interest; it is not just another test. Fowles is going on leave the year after next so this is the year to take this course, one of Hanover's crown jewels.

January Term

After Barbara had digested the contents of the guide, she turned to the January term described in the catalog as a period in which students could study a particular topic in depth, working in a small group under the direct guidance of a faculty member, or as a period during which they could take some time away from the college to enrich their life in any way they saw fit. Many schools have variations of the January term, but if the one you chose does not, consider the long vacations and the summer months as opportunities to take courses of special interest at other institutions or to pursue internships and other forms of practical learning. (*The Ultimate College Survival Guide*, by Janet Farrar Worthington and Ronald Farrar, Peterson's, 1995, is a very thorough and readable guide on how to cope with college life.)

DRAWING UP A PATH OF STUDY

Barbara then proceeded to draw up a *path of study sheet* (see page 253). She made a series of columns: one for the fall semester, one for the January term, one for the spring semester. Then she added three columns in which she could keep both a running total of the major and distribution requirements she had met and an overall total of the credits she had accumulated at the end of each year. She did not fill out the entire sheet but used it to plan her academic path over the next four years.

The First Year: "Casting a Wide Net"

On her sheet Barbara wrote in some of the courses she wanted to take for the fall and winter—based on her study of the catalog and the confidential guide and on her conversation with Ron Barrow. Since she wanted eventually to enter the world of business, Barbara decided that for her first summer vacation she would seek a job that would acquaint her with the inside operations of a major business. She wrote in "banking" and thought tentatively of applying to her local bank for a job as a teller, messenger, or credit coordinator of some sort. Barbara thought it would be a good idea to pencil in courses in mathematics and computer science in her freshman year. She put a course in probability and statistics and a calculus course (Math 35) in the spring term because either one would meet a concentration requirement for a course related to economics. After writing these courses down on her course sheet, she indicated the requirements they met, recording "C" for concentration requirement and "D" for distribution requirement; then she entered her totals for concentration and distribution in the appropriate columns.

Barbara saw that the principle of overlap had led her to choose History 11 to go with her introductory course in economic theory. What about the fourth and final course for the fall semester? At this point Barbara decided to take the plunge into the broad lake of the liberal arts and elect a course in music theory and harmony (Music 30). She had always felt deprived of music in her home. Music was not of interest to her older brother or to her parents. On the other hand, some of her more interesting friends had musical interests of some sort. Barbara decided to investigate this unknown territory. The confidential guide said that Music 30 was a very popular course for nonmusic majors at Hanover and that the instructors, a wonderful German couple named Kleberg, were famous for being as interested in students who were just passing through to meet a humanities requirement as they were in avowed music majors. Barbara's decision to take Music 30 also gave her course of study the breadth that all liberal arts students should strive for.

January break and spring semester

Barbara did not take long to make up her mind about the January term of her freshman year. She decided to go skiing. She would then return to campus refreshed from her break. Her spring semester schedule would include a course in applied economics (Economics 12)—the second course of the introductory sequence in economics—and Professor Fowles's political science course. Barbara hoped that the overlapping study of economic and political systems (Political Science 35) would enhance her perspective in both areas. She also chose probability and statistics (Math 37), a course that she hoped would help brighten up her resume as she sought summer employment.

Barbara's last choice was an art history course, The Art of the United States (Art History 10), which would meet her third distribution requirement for her first year and, more important, satisfy her long-standing craving for some knowledge about the work of American painters. Barbara traced her interest in American art back to a visit she had made to the U.S. Customhouse in New York; she had been only a little girl at the time, but she vividly recalled her sense of wonder at the beautiful murals there. One of the reasons she decided to attend Hanover was the strong reputation of its art history department.

Second Year: "Gaining a World View"

As Barbara thought about her second year at Hanover, she reaffirmed her decision to focus on her major early on in her career at college. Thus she decided to take the course in corporate management (Economics 41), described by the confidential guide as "a heavy course, for majors only." She then elected to take a course in imperialism in the late nineteenth and early twentieth centuries (History 33). Barbara knew that the interface of literature and imperialism in the nineteenth century would be an interesting one, so she opted to take English 29, a literary analysis of the prominent Victorian writers of England.

Barbara also decided to complete her foray into mathematics by taking an intensive course in computer programming (Math 41). She knew this would provide valuable training for the kind of job she would be seeking two years later. Under the January term heading for her sophomore year Barbara wrote down a course called "The Ethics of Investment." It had received excellent reports from Ron Barrow.

In the spring of her sophomore year Barbara would capitalize on her study of imperialism and the ethics of investment and attempt a course in corporate finance (Economics 42). She also thought it would make good sense to enroll in Organizational Behavior (Psychology 15) at the same time since it was a distant cousin of Corporate Management (Economics 41). She then tentatively chose a course in research methods in economics (Economics 90). She would complete her distribution requirements with Ecology and Progress (Biology 37). The biology department had designed this course for nonmajors, and it was reputed to be not too hard. Barbara had three tough courses already and did not want to risk pulling down her grade point average by adding another. Following up on her idea of gaining a broad perspective in her chosen field, Barbara decided to seek a summer experience outside the field of business during the summer after her sophomore year.

Junior and Senior Years: "Focus and Breadth, Together"

Barbara had thus planned a sensible course of study for her first two years—one that enabled her to sample a broad range of subjects while getting a good start on her major. She realized that some changes might be made if her interests shifted, or if her academic adviser convinced her of the wisdom of following other paths. However, her careful planning would allow her quite a bit of flexibility in her final two years.

During that time Barbara decided to continue with her study of a foreign language, Spanish, and pursue a special concentration in Latin American studies within her major. Barbara's parents and high school teachers had convinced her of the importance of knowing a second language and through it becoming conversant with another culture. "Knowledge of another culture is the fundamental premise of a global economy," her high school history teacher had asserted.

Even though the junior year would be one of increasing focus, Barbara continued to explore courses beyond the social sciences. Music, art, and literature had always attracted her, and she would study all three. These and other courses would enable her to communicate with and learn from others who shared an interest in them. Equally important, Barbara would be broadened as a human being by her exposure to the humanities and the sciences. She would be more aware of the wider world beyond her chosen specialty than others who chose a narrower and safer route. This breadth of knowledge would help Barbara to put her own life and work in perspective and at the same time inform and enlighten the decisions she would have to make within her own field.

Having carefully considered both the benefit of a broad liberal arts experience and the practical benefit of strong preparation in her major, Barbara Crowley was ready to make optimum use of her opportunity to attend Hanover and eventually play a useful role in the complex world beyond college.

When she got through with her course of study chart, it looked like the chart on page 253.

WHAT COURSES SHOULD I SIGN UP FOR?

Every college has a slightly different way of advising students and registering them for classes. All will assign students an academic adviser, either during the summer before they arrive on campus or during the freshman orientation period just prior to the start of classes. If your school falls into the first category, it is perfectly reasonable for you to draw up a rough plan of study as Barbara Crowley did (it does not need to be as elaborate as hers!) and even call your adviser on the phone to ask for his or her opinion. This will allow you time to think about what your adviser says and perhaps to make some other choices before you come to campus. It will also enable you to get a fix on just how many of the required courses your school wants you to take in the first semester. There may be an unstated policy of taking a fair number of required courses, right away, before moving too far ahead with your major.

As you approach the advising system of your college, and your adviser in particular, remember that there may be differences between the way in which you are advised and the way in which your best friend is advised. Advisers are mainly faculty members; they are individuals. They may take a keen interest in advising students, and they may not. The important thing is to give them a chance. They know the institution much better than you do; they want to help. However, it is up to you to have some ideas and plans of your own as Barbara did, so that your adviser has something to react to.

If you do not get along with your adviser, you can usually change to another faculty member. Before doing that, remember to examine your reasons. If you are changing because you don't like the advice given rather than the personality, then you probably ought to stay with your original adviser. Remember, too, that at most schools your adviser will change once you have elected your major. At that point you will be assigned to a faculty member from the department in which you are majoring. Remember,

BARBARA CROWLEY'S PATH OF STUDY SHEET

Fall Semester	January Term	Spring Semester	Total Courses			Total Concen- tration (C)	Total Distri- bution (D)	Summer
			Fall	Jan.	Spring			
Freshman Year Economics 11. Foundations of Economic Theory (C) History 11. Western Tradition: The Greeks to the Enlightenment Math 35. Calculus (C) Music 30. Theory and Harmony (D) Freshman Writing Course (no credit)	Ski break at Christmas Work in depart- ment store	Economics 12. Applied Economics: Money and Banking (C) Political Science 35. Political Economy of the U.S. (C) Math 37. Probability and Statistics (D) Art History 10. The Art of the U.S.(D)	4		4			Bank teller, messenger, credit coordinator (work experience within the business world)
			8			4	3	
Sophomore Year Economics 41. Corporate Management (C) History 33. Imperialism in the Nineteenth and Twentieth Centuries (C) Math 41. Computer Programming (C) English 29. The Literature of the Victorians (D)	Ethics of Investment: U.S. and South Africa—A Case Study	Economics 42. Corporate Finance (C) Economics 90. Research Methods in Economics (C) Biology 37. Ecology and Progress (D) Psychology 15. Organizational Behavior (D)	4	1	4			Camp counselor, social service job National Forest Service (work experience outside the business world)
			9		9	5	3	
			17			9	6	

C = A course required for concentration. At Hanover College the requirement for concentration in economics is eight courses within the economics department plus four from related departments. Total: twelve courses minimum.

D = Distribution courses. Each student must take six courses to meet this requirement: two in different departments of the social sciences, two in different departments of the humanities, and two in different departments of the sciences.

finally, that many advising relationships between faculty and students lead to very close friendships that often last well beyond the college years.

Once you have your adviser's approval of your course of study, you can move ahead with registering for the actual courses. At many schools this is done electronically, and students actually do it themselves. At some schools you can enter your course selections via modem; at others you register on campus during a period of time reserved for members of your particular class. Once you have your student identification and your course registration number, follow the instructions for accessing the database, and enter the courses you wish to take. As you do, you will find out which ones are filled and what the alternatives are. It helps to have your overall course of study in mind as Barbara Crowley did, so that if a particular course is filled, you know which one to choose next. Often you have to make decisions fairly rapidly.

Your adviser can always be consulted again if you run into trouble at registration. Your adviser is supposed to know what the exceptions to the rules are and what particular departments do when their classes are overcrowded. Some departments, for instance, will add sections to the course, or they will offer the course at another hour or in a later semester. Your adviser will be your guide.

WHERE WILL I LIVE AND WITH WHOM?

As Barbara put the finishing touches on her plan of study, her mind naturally raced ahead to the social relationships she hoped to form on the Hanover campus in the next four years. Would she be radicalized by the politics on campus? Would she fall in love? Would she learn to ski? Would she feel lonely and lost and miss her family? Probably all of the above, she thought. Then she thought for a minute and decided to focus on the housing arrangements at Hanover.

The college offered single, double, and triple rooms. You could also elect to live in one of the smaller houses that were formerly private residences. Some of these had a particular theme, such as being organized around a particular culture or language or directed at a particular goal, such as social service.

Whether you picked a theme house or a large dormitory, you were still asked to fill out an elaborate questionnaire, indicating your choice of major, your extracurricular interests, musical and artistic tastes, political views, hobbies, and your own preferences for a roommate. The Housing Office uses the questionnaires to match roommates for entering freshmen.

Barbara Crowley made sure in her housing application to mention her allergies and state her preference for a nonsmoker. She requested one roommate and a double room because she wanted the chance to get to know her roommate well and not have to manage two or three other individuals in a triple or a quad. Barbara also wrote a short paragraph asking for a roommate who was quiet and serious about pursuing her academic studies and had an interest in the arts. She left it at that.

The Housing Office agreed to Barbara's request a few weeks later and sent her the name of her roommate for the fall. Following a suggestion from the Housing Office, Barbara wrote her roommate a letter of introduction. This overture led to an exchange of letters, and by the time fall term opened, Barbara and her roommate had gotten to know each other pretty well. They had divided the responsibilities for furnishing the room, thus saving a good deal of duplication of wall hangings, appliances, and even some general reference books. More important, they had established a tradition of discussing their needs and aspirations first, before acting on them! This tradition would help them deal with any controversies that might arise later.

On a larger scale, Barbara and her roommate, without being conscious of it, had come to terms with one of the biggest anxieties facing college freshmen—the loss of high school friends whom they may have known all their lives. Now they both realized that there would be new and different kinds of relationships to look forward to—ones that could be actively undertaken and not just be a result of living on a particular street in a particular community.

Barbara and her roommate had succeeded in placing their relationship on a solid basis from the outset and maximizing the chances that a strong friendship might grow from it. In so doing, they had prepared themselves to handle some of the usual challenges that college undergraduates face: how to make decisions about socializing and study in their room, how to respect an individual's right to privacy, and how to share their possessions equitably. Barbara and her roommate were thus able to avoid the sort of shock experienced by one undergraduate woman at an Ivy League school who, in the first week of school, returned to her room to find that her roommate was entertaining a young man. Because the young woman had to study, she sought refuge in the bathroom until 2 a.m., then returned to her room to find her roommate and the young man in bed together. This became a nightly practice, forcing the young woman to retreat to the common-room couch with her sleeping bag. Eventually she became so exhausted by the routine that her grades plummeted, and she had to go to the infirmary for a decent night's sleep.

Guidelines for Getting Along with Your Roommates

This incident suggests a few simple rules that will help your relationship with your roommate start off on a positive note and continue that way:

- **Communication.** Talk early and often about potential trouble spots. The first time your roommate entertains a visitor late into the evening, beyond the time that both of you normally go to bed or at a time when both of you have agreed to study, you need to take it up with your roommate the next day. "I think we miscommunicated last night. My recollection of our understanding was . . . What is yours?"
- **Space.** Try to reach a clear understanding with your roommate as to what part of the room is your space and what part is his, and what part is common to both.
- **Borrowing.** Having a discussion with your roommate about borrowing will be of enormous help. The sooner the better. If you have a car, you probably don't want others to drive it. The same holds true for your computer. But you have to bring those matters up and reach an agreement. Perhaps there are things you will willingly lend, such as athletic equipment and books. Make those items a part of your understanding too.
- **Shared Responsibilities.** You and your roommate need to share in the responsibility for keeping your room or apartment clean. When does that happen? You may have a refrigerator and food supplies and laundry soap that are shared and need occasionally to be replenished. Work out some orderly arrangement for that during your first days together.
- **Sensitivity.** Living away from home is not always easy. Coping with the stress of new relationships in college as well as new classes and a new environment isn't either. Occasionally your roommate (and even you!) will feel low and in need of encouragement. Try to provide that for your roommate and be considerate of his or her needs for quiet, for consolation, for diversion. In thinking about others, you will increase the likelihood that they will think about you and that together you will both be able to overcome most of the setbacks of the freshman year. (Letter to New Freshmen, Ohio Wesleyan University, April 1995)

If you and your roommate cannot get along, you should use the counseling system described below to try to understand the situation as best you can and to make use of all the steps that the college's counselors think are constructive. If that doesn't work, there is always next year—the opportunity to meet new people and room with them. (If necessary you can go to the Dean of Students and ask for a change or an intervention this year.)

DEANS, COUNSELORS, AND RESIDENT ADVISERS

When Barbara received her packet containing information about freshman courses and housing at Hanover, she discovered that the college had fine advising and counseling services for its students. The first line of defense was the resident adviser (RA) system, under which upperclass students living in the dormitory were assigned to advise students in lower classes and help to arrange dormitory social functions. This system worked reasonably well, Barbara found. Some RAs were concerned and careful counselors who could keep their relationships with advisees confidential. Others were less discreet and less skilled.

Beyond the resident adviser system lay the health services, the counseling center, the academic advisement and tutorial services, and, most important, the Dean of Students Office with its clutch of tireless and concerned deans. Barbara found that at Hanover one could turn to the counselors in the dean's office on any matter, from parking or laundry to a relationship that threatened to become overwhelming.

Students at many colleges seem unaware of the capability of these various offices to render immediate and useful advice and counsel. Some schools have spent thousands of dollars to make their counseling services first-rate. At the University of Chicago, twenty counselors operating from the dean's office, most of them full-time, oversee the relatively small undergraduate population of approximately 2,700 students. These counselors frequently give both academic and personal advice and follow the progress of their advisees throughout their four-year stay at the university.

Every college or university will have a counseling center that will help with such difficulties as homesickness, test anxiety, or problems with friends or family. Don't be worried about the distinction between what you might think of as an academic problem and a social problem. Consult someone in the counseling center, and get the advice you need.

Here is a good rule of thumb: *If you're thinking about seeking advice and counseling, then chances are you should. Counseling can help people in a variety of ways: to learn to make better decisions, to become aware of their feelings and needs, to improve interpersonal skills, to manage stress and anxiety, to improve communication skills, and to cope more effectively with life. "Remember, not to use these services is to undermine your progress."*

As you think about adjusting to college life, remember the university or college ministry. "The ministry center on campus can act as a good stabilizing point, because there is a connection between something from home and something from campus."**

As Barbara Crowley drove with her family to Hanover in the fall, she was only dimly aware of how much her educational experience in the next four years would hinge on her own self-awareness and the development of personal relationships with others. But she had studied the college's pamphlet for freshmen and familiarized herself with the various ways in which she could use the counseling system and get whatever kind of help she might need. She also resolved to extend herself to other people and to try to forge new relationships. Such an effort would offset the loneliness of being away from her home and friends. This openness to new relationships would ensure her an education in the broadest sense and reduce the vulnerability that most college freshmen experience.

TRANSITIONING INTO COLLEGE LIFE

If one were to visit any college campus during the beautiful days of September and October and ask passing freshmen to describe in a word the experience of their first few weeks, the response would undoubtedly be "freedom." It is only natural that a student's first reaction to college life is to laud the freedom from home, from family, from day-to-day assignments, from required sports, from required group activities, from a code of behavior that, if dutifully followed, wins respect from teachers and neighbors. Freedom, to ecstatic college freshmen in their first few weeks on

---

*Joyce V. Rhoden in "Use Your Campus Support Services," *Off to College* (Montgomery, Alabama, Guidance Research Group, 1992.)

** "How to Survive the Freshman Year," Chicago, Loyola University Press, 1988.

campus, usually means freedom "from" rather than freedom "to." At the same time, that euphoric feeling of freedom obscures what may be a confusing and even depressing experience for some.

Psychologists know that the transition that a freshman has to make in the first few weeks of college is extremely difficult. In many cases, going to college involves a complete break with the past and hence a real discontinuity in a student's life. The structure and routine of family life are left behind, the numerous ties to community groups and peer groups are severed, and, most important, the regular nourishment of self-esteem that came from family members and from the prestige and respect earned in high school is ended. A new life has to be started in college, new challenges divined, and new relationships kindled. New outlets for your talents have to be discovered. It isn't easy. A book like this can only scratch the surface of the freshman year experience and offer some kind words of counsel. It can set before the prospective freshman a sort of informal agenda to consider during the summer before the freshman year and in the early weeks of the fall.

If you want to go beyond what is presented here, read *The Ultimate College Survival Guide*, by Janet Farrar Worthington and Ronald T. Farrar (Peterson's, 1995). It does a very good job of describing in detail the freshman year experience and how to make the most of it.

A Little Fish in the Big Pond

"The Little Fish in the Big Pond" syndrome refers to a freshman's first exposure to a mass of other students who are as able, as resourceful, as funny, as good looking, as athletically or musically gifted as he or she is and to the problem of dealing with that experience. Often students become depressed when they realize that they are no longer the big fish in the little pond, but rather a little fish in a big pond.

Here's some help for dealing with that big pond:

♦ **Acknowledge the legitimacy of your own feelings of loss.** After all, stability, security, and success such as you have left behind cannot be permanent fixtures in our lives. Feelings of loss are a natural part of the process. It is important to accept these feelings, so you can continue to choose, explore, and move on.

♦ **Communicate your feelings of frustration and loss**—and of elation and joy—to others, be they roommates, resident advisers, deans, professors, or chaplains. When seeking advice, remember to search for questions rather than answers. Each person's solution is different, but the kinds of questions we ask ourselves are similar.

♦ **Try to make your college your new home,** with its own routine, relationships, activities, and support systems. Avoid cultivating fierce independence or separateness. Make sure you spend some time decorating your room, and make sure to bring those photographs to remind you of the good things you want to remember—and to which you will return at Thanksgiving!

♦ **Redefine your conception of success.** Lower those standards you simply cannot meet and set new standards that you can meet. Move around the limits imposed by grades or social relationships or athletic competition and look for new areas of interest and challenge. In doing so, try to avoid the feeling that you are betraying yourself. Who knows, you may discover that there are myriad ways of proving yourself or that you are better than some of your fellow students at some things.

♦ **Remember, finally, that frustration and a sense of loss are cyclical phenomena** for most people and that excitement and progress follow periods of despondency. If you encounter a low point, keep in mind that it may well be caused by exhaustion. The shift of responsibility from your high school counselor, friends, and family telling you what to do to your planning your life and taking responsibility for the outcome yourself is enormous. If nothing else, it is tiring. So relax, rest, and remember that temporary frustration is a part of the healthy process you are undergoing.

Making the Campus Work for You

On a practical level, the following tips can help you orient yourself and find direction amidst all the freedom of the first few weeks of college:

1. **Stay loose.** Do not seek out a single small group of friends and cling only to them. Social groups of various sorts will coalesce during the first few weeks, and you will naturally want to be a part of one of them. Fine, but try to avoid loyalty to just one group, for it may eventually fall apart and leave you stranded. By definition, a group has to exclude someone, and that excluded person may interest you. If you find that you are going to the dining hall with only one group of friends, one that you are doing all your socializing with, then break away somewhat. Try to go to the

dining hall with someone new, or even alone, once or twice a week, so that you will create the opportunity to meet different people from different backgrounds.

2. **Join at least one, preferably two, extracurricular activities during the first week of your freshman year.** Just do it on an "inspired" basis. Too often college students defer this type of decision. They say to themselves, "First, I've got to get my courses squared away, then get to know the people in my dorm, and then I will go out for the orchestra." Avoid this kind of thinking; enter extracurricular activities right away. One Harvard freshman told a professor, "You know, when I came here from high school, the first thing I did was join the orchestra, and suddenly I found a bunch of friends." This may sound calculated, but a little planning of this sort will ensure that you develop different bases of friendship in college—your classes, your dormitory, your extracurricular activities, and so on.

3. **Avoid adopting a particular personal style lest you become known only as a campus character or a member of a particular group.** This is particularly hard for minority and international students whose culture shock on coming to college is sometimes greater than that of other students. It is natural and necessary for them to gravitate toward one another. Even so, try to balance the reassurance of group acceptance with that need for individual identity.

4. **Try to get acquainted with one person or family that has no ties to the academic life of the college.** Often an older family will be anxious to meet students—you might meet such a family by doing odd jobs through the student employment office. In the course of casual conversation, such people can render helpful advice and support to a young person facing the challenges of adjusting to a new community.

5. **Try to make friends with an older student, preferably a senior, during the first weeks of school, and get to know this person.** These elder statesmen can give all sorts of practical advice on where to shop, which courses to take and to avoid, and, in particular, how to sort out some of the turmoil of the early weeks of your freshman year.

6. **Read a newspaper unconnected with the college at least twice a week.** You may want to buy the local newspaper to find out what the relations of the college with the broader community are. A local paper will also tell you what events are occurring outside the college and what the major concerns of the community are. Reading it will help you relate to the townspeople you meet. Or you may wish to subscribe to your

hometown newspaper, acknowledging that your home continues to have meaning and interest for you. Whichever you choose, read a noncollege newspaper. Keep yourself aware of the world beyond college. In so doing, you will develop a perspective on the challenges you face from day to day. You will also be able to relate what you are learning to the ebb and flow of world events.

7. **If you are a member of a church or synagogue in your home community, by all means retain that membership while at college.** Quite apart from the spiritual sustenance that religion provides, the opportunity to meet people outside the college and to have contact with the lives and concerns of others helps to put your own life in perspective. So if you don't belong to a church, resolve to attend a public gathering where major world issues will be discussed.

8. **Get to know your advisers.** The first person to get to know is the resident adviser in your dormitory, who is apt to be an upperclass student. RAs know the system; they are familiar with the behaviors of freshmen. It wasn't so long ago that they were freshmen too. They want to help. Seek them out. Your faculty adviser is assigned by the dean of the college to monitor your academic progress. You will need to visit your faculty adviser during his office hours or to make an appointment through the secretary of his academic department. You may also be able to contact your adviser through electronic mail. Try to do this if you can for routine questions. You may also use electronic mail to stay in touch with your teachers and avoid the formality of appointments for routine matters. As your contact with your faculty adviser increases, a close relationship may develop. If it does, you will be able to seek various kinds of advice from your adviser and hopefully get some useful answers.

9. **Set up a schedule.** The most important task for you to accomplish in your first several days at college is to prepare a schedule. Set up your life by the week: your classes, study times, sports, campus job, and social activities. You can do this neatly on the computer, and the resulting spreadsheet will confirm that you are mastering the skill of time management. If you can set your priorities down on a schedule, then you can avert the disaster of frittering away your time. Learning to discipline yourself so you can manage that seemingly endless free time effectively will help ensure the success of your freshman year.

Keeping a Healthy Perspective

In addition to keeping these bits of advice in mind, try to keep your sense of humor. Remember, everyone else is new too, and everyone else, to some degree, feels that he or she is no longer the big fish, but rather an infinitesimal minnow. What you need to do in your own way is to build a structure for your life that will make college your new home. That structure consists of multiple ties to various members of the college community and to the world at large: to the town and its people, through friendships you initiate yourself; to your home, through newspapers and contact with your family and friends; and to the more distant world, through newspapers, magazines, and contact with dignitaries visiting the campus.

By taking the initiative to establish these ties and by making use of the second structural device—a schedule that helps you manage your time—you can create a college life that has meaning, continuity, and joy.

REESTABLISH YOUR TIES WITH YOUR PARENTS

The pressures of new roommates, new friends, and new freedoms and the enormous amount of free time have an impact on your parents as well as you. "Freshmanitis" is a communicable disease, and your parents may become upset by your confusion and complaints. So in communicating with your parents, try to balance the good with the not so good. Remember that as you go off to college and during the college years, the relationship you have with your parents will undergo a dramatic transformation. Both you and your parents will need to work out your roles as mature and independent men and women. That, of course, will take a different form for each of you. Parents, for instance, may make the early error of trying to protect you from your mistakes, but they will soon recognize that their old role as supervisors and directors needs to be replaced by a new role as listeners and counselors.

Keep Communication Open

Frequent and healthy dialog between you and your parents will help your family play a positive and even crucial role in helping you adjust to college life:

1. **Students: keep the lines of communication open.** Being away from home, perhaps for the first time, should not mean that you drop all contact with your family, feigning independence. A weekly call or letter

or e-mail will keep your parents informed of your activities and your concerns. Show that you still care about your parents and other family members at home.

2. **Students: plan to show your parents some examples of your college work.** Let your parents know how you are performing, so that they know what is going on and can offer their advice occasionally. Remember your parents are paying for much of your college education, and they are entitled to see some of the results of their efforts and your labor.

3. **Parents: realize that colleges are shifting the burden of education from the institution to the individual and that this is a totally new experience for your child.** Colleges often speak of acting *in loco parentis*, but they have a different definition of that phrase than you do. Colleges give young people much more freedom than they ever had at home and that they may ever have in their lives. Students who have been used to parental direction (and protection!) up to this point in their lives now feel exposed and frightened at having to make decisions for themselves. Parents should empathize with this fear. They should try to help their children formulate the questions they should be asking of professors, advisers, and peers and use the college's dean of students office, counseling department, or the student's adviser to find answers for themselves.

4. **Parents: don't nag.** Understand that constantly exhorting your son or daughter to get to work will probably not achieve the desired result. Rather, take the position of a sympathetic listener who can help your child discover the sources of assistance that are available and the options that present themselves. Let your children hear the "echo" of their words.

5. **Parents: send care packages.** Remember to include the hometown newspaper and any recent family photos that may have been taken.

6. **Finally, both parents and students: realize that the trials and tribulations of the freshman year are short-lived.** Parents should temper their reactions to problems with the understanding that most crises are probably transitory. Indeed, some crises are necessary. Matriculation statistics show that over 90 percent of freshmen graduate with their class four years later, and an even higher percentage of students obtain degrees within five or six years after entering college.

DEALING WITH DIFFERENCES

There are many forms of differences that you will encounter in college. One is that of race. *Race relations* is a term used here to describe relationships between the majority community of white students and the minority communities of African American, Latino, Native American, and Asian students in a collegiate setting. There are also a variety of other minority groups in any broadly representative college community—women, athletes, musicians, learning-disabled students, and gay people, not to mention the various groups of ethnic Americans—but here we are concerned with the minority defined by race and the tensions that sometimes exist between the white majority and the minority racial groups.

Since the late 1960s, colleges and universities around the country have striven to increase the representation of American racial minorities in their student populations. In response to growing social awareness, governmental encouragement, and a genuine concern for a democratic society, colleges and universities have made enormous progress in recruiting, retaining, and educating members of racial groups that had previously been excluded from the mainstream of American education. Although tensions still exist and much needs to be done to improve the quality of race relations at many schools, few other countries have come so far in so short a time.

Because of this progress, minority freshmen will probably not encounter any outright situations of deliberate discrimination at most American colleges today. All students will, however, have to be mindful that residual prejudice may still exist in spite of the good intentions of students, teachers, and administrators. They will have to face the fact that inequities still linger and will have to work with leaders of the majority population to change them. Students of color may find that their college curriculum contains few courses about their group's history and development. They may find only a small number of their own race represented on the faculty or the administration of the college. African American students, the largest of the minority groups, may find no department of African American studies to help them explore their cultural past. Asian students may find that the major languages of the Far East are not offered in the school's catalog. Or the majority students may find that some of the courses offered in the traditional fields of history and political science are very critical of America's treatment of women and minorities and say little about the so-called mainstream of American life.

In discovering these situations, you need to recognize that colleges and universities today are reflecting the struggle of our national culture. We are not sure as a society how we want to deal with race and class and gender. Those are issues we are working out in our national politics, in our literature and our music, and on our college campuses. As you seek to explore your particular area of interest, remember to talk with your adviser and other faculty members who can help you find the answers to your particular questions. As you go through the process of exploration and find something that is apparently insensitive or unjust, you owe it to yourself and your college to try to change it.

Learning and Living Together

Majority students who have had little previous experience with minority students in high school may find that their collegiate situation is very different. Most white students will have attended high schools where they were in an overwhelming majority. In college they may find 10 to 20 percent of their class composed of people of African American, Asian, Latino, and Native American descent, not to mention other students of color and different ethnicity from countries around the world. Moreover, all these groups, minority and majority, will now have to live together on a 24-hour-a-day basis. In high school, different groups lived in different neighborhoods; now everyone is thrown together in a 300-person dormitory. Try to make the most of this situation and expand your contacts with multicultural students. Examine your own feelings about race and make your own exploration of race relations an integral part of your college education.

Remember that members of minority and majority communities approach the question of race relations from different vantage points. On the social side, white students may wonder at the need for the exclusive, racially based membership of, say, an African American Student Center or a Native American Club. They may take exception to being excluded from some social affairs put on by minority groups or from eating with them in the dining hall. Multicultural students may counter that they often congregate at meals and form their own clubs to build relationships with other members of their group and to support each other. Like white students, they are far from the neighborhoods where they were the majority. They say they have no antipathy for the white community, with whom they have daily and frequent contact in classes, in sports, and around campus. Some Asian students may tend to internalize their feelings, arguing that public behavior should be restrained and reasonable. No particular group response is right. Tensions are bound to exist.

Ways to Avoid Tension Caused by Differences

As you cope with these tensions, no matter what your race, you may find the following bits of advice useful:

1. **Avoid stereotyping.** Thinking in stereotypes about members of your own racial community or about members of communities other than your own leads nowhere. People are just too complicated. Take each person on his or her own merits, as you find them. Avoid plugging people into preconceived categories. To think someone said or did something because of his or her racial background is to rely on a mental stereotype. To do so is unkind, simplistic, and, in the end, anti-intellectual. As such, it runs counter to the purpose of the education you have come to college to obtain.

2. **Be yourself.** Avoid assuming a pose, just because you think it will help you win friends and simplify the complex questions of racial interaction for the moment. If you are a farm person from middle America, be proud of it, make no secret of it, and listen carefully to what you can learn from others. Don't make yourself out to be a cattle baron. If you are in fact the well-educated daughter of a Mexican-American dentist, avoid presenting yourself as an impoverished Latino from the barrio. This posturing complicates the challenge of meeting your brothers and sisters honestly and helping them to relate to members of the white middle-class community, with whom you may be more familiar.

3. **Avoid separatism.** Exclusive behavior only reinforces prejudice and eliminates communication. If you are moving only with members of your own racial group—to classes, to meals, and to various social activities—then you are succumbing to peer pressure and accepting social barriers that someone else has erected. Break out and meet people from other groups as soon as possible.

   Observers have noticed that separatism along racial lines is occasionally a subtle way in which minority college students force others of their race to submit to their will. The ultimate result of separatism is to restrict your circle of friends: If all your friends are from one particular racial group, then you have failed to realize an important goal of your college education—to understand various kinds of people and to make some of them your friends.

4. **Be wary of humor at someone else's expense; look at history.**
Steer away from facile attempts to harmonize race relations, such as employing humor. Jokes can be taken the wrong way and can perpetuate stereotyping. Leave such humor to the professional comics, lest it unintentionally fracture the delicate bond among the races at your college. When trying to understand another culture, read its history and note where its customs come from. Ask a friend from that culture to recommend a book that reveals its uniqueness.

5. **Know your college's grievance policy.** Acquaint yourself with the institution's grievance procedure for racial injustice at your college. If you have a question about the suitability of a paper's topic, the possibly prejudicial remark made by a professor, or a college policy such as a separate orientation for minority freshmen, ask the appropriate authority about it. You owe this to yourself. You will probably be satisfied with the answer you receive; if you are not, use the grievance procedure. Do not harbor your personal grievance and thereby confirm your own prejudice. Trust in the good intentions and real commitment of university officials who want to see inequities, however slight, corrected and justice done.

6. **Study our multicultural society/world.** Seriously consider taking in your first two years of college at least one course that has to do with cross-cultural relations. If the goal of your college education is to gain a greater understanding of yourself in relation to the world at large, it is both logical and necessary to take a course that probes the ways in which persons of different racial groups relate to each other. If a person completing a college education in America today has managed to do so without seriously contemplating racial and ethnic diversity within our society, that person is not adequately prepared to assume a position of leadership in this society we all share.

GRADE FRENZY

One does not have to be a college freshman to know that in American colleges today there is intense concern about career preparation. This has led to a virtual fixation on making good grades in order to gain admission to graduate and professional schools. Grade frenzy touches every college freshman in one form or another, yet it is to be avoided if at all possible. You should arrange to discuss course preparation for your chosen career with your adviser. Find out what the potential role of grades is in your admission to graduate school or the world of work. At the same time that you plan to take particularly difficult courses, balance them with other courses that are not as hard. Try to give breadth to your course of study; you came to college to take some risks and to choose courses in areas you know little about but nonetheless find intriguing. Don't avoid academic challenges just because you fear failure and the harsh judgment of a graduate school admissions committee. Many courses can be taken on a pass-fail basis, and the further such courses lie from the path of your major, the more appropriate to opt for pass-fail. Medical school committees are not going to be alarmed that you took music theory as a pass-fail course, or that you got a C in art history. Try to do your experimenting in the first two years of college so that if you happen to do less than well, your record for the last two years will clearly demonstrate your ability in your chosen field.

Grade-Frenzy Danger Signs
Beware these red flags:

◆ If you find yourself working on successive Saturday nights, it probably means either that you are too concerned about grades or that you are not planning your work efficiently. Discuss the situation with your adviser.

◆ If you are beginning to lose your friends because you say you have to study and cannot join them for meals or socializing, it is time to reassess your situation. Making friends and socializing are integral parts of your college education. You are crippling yourself socially and educationally if you can't keep old friends and make new ones and still get your work done.

◆ If you are tempted to do something that you know is academically dishonest—such as copying another student's results, lifting an idea for a paper without crediting the source, or, worse, cheating on an exam—then you are already in the clutches of grade frenzy. You need to take a break. Discuss your situation with an adviser or friend. Try to relax.

◆ If you reach the point where you are unable to carry on a major outside activity because of the urgency of academic studies, you have also arrived at the edge of grade frenzy. Pull back. Maintain your outside activity. Remember that one of the main reasons for pursuing an extracurricular activity is that it provides perspective. If you find that you can no longer maintain your activity, it has probably been serving that express purpose; i.e., acting as a check on overcommitment to your studies.

◆ Finally, think carefully about the system of grading itself. Excessive emphasis on grades by students, faculty, and graduate admissions committees often reduces the whole educational process to this one standard of measurement. Too great an emphasis on grades teaches students that the whole process of undergraduate education is a game of high grades in which creativity and experimentation take second place to playing back what the professor wants to hear or what the book says.

◆ You can be assured that discerning graduate schools will recognize the breadth of your course selection, the variety of your extracurricular activities, and the value of your summer jobs and travel, not to mention other indications of the vitality and maturity of your personality. But even if they didn't, you should recognize and respect these elements of your education and not succumb to the frantic quest for grades.

Several years ago a thoughtful and popular Dartmouth physics professor, Elisha R. Huggins, addressed the problem of grade frenzy at the end of his final exam:

> Normally at this time in the course I pass out a questionnaire to see how students feel about various parts of the course. This time I am going to reverse the process and instead explain my feelings about the Physics 34 students.
>
> Academically this was an outstanding class. In about eight years of teaching these courses I have not seen such consistently good performance on tests and such a high level of quality on projects. And on an individual basis there were a number of students who showed considerable originality and enthusiasm and were extremely enjoyable to work with.
>
> My main comments, however, are reserved for the majority (but not all) of the premedical students in the class who are sacrificing too much of their own personality and life toward the goal of admission to medical school. You know what kind of distortion this has caused in your attitude toward courses and other opportunities here at Dartmouth.
>
> I am aware of the pressures that medical school admissions policies cause—their overemphasis and distorted use of grades and lack of appreciation of human understanding. However, this is not the first time you will face a screwed-up system, and life is too short to take it as seriously as you have done this year. It is

possible to get into a habit of taking everything so seriously that you can never break away and see why it is worth living.

My comment is to let up a bit, look around at the opportunities that you have now and the next couple of years at Dartmouth, and if you do not break through the med school barricade, to hell with them. I can tell you that there are a lot better things in life than being an overly serious, uptight doctor.

A PARTING THOUGHT: USE YOUR FREEDOM WISELY

The diversity, the questioning, the uncertainty, and the waste of time and energy, the frantic and the relaxed times that often describe the freshman year are all reasonable elements of your education—they are a function of you, exercising your own freedom, your freedom to speak and act openly, and to grow in understanding and confidence. This new freedom is partly defined by the new ideas you encounter in books, in the lab, at the lunch table or over coffee, discussing a paper. Your new freedom is also defined by your increasing self-confidence, in using your influence on your roommates to abide by the agreed-on "rules of the room." Your freedom to say no to sex, alcohol, or drugs, and your freedom to say yes to going to a friend's home in Mexico for a vacation.

Your new freedom also flows from understanding that you now are in a position to govern your own destiny, to set the questions you will ask of a text, or of a person, or of a situation—and to listen and analyze the answers that come back—and then to take an action. This then is the joy of your college experience: the exploration, the freedom to learn to be independent, and ultimately to act responsibly for the good of all.

INDEX

ESSENTIAL GUIDES FOR TODAY'S COLLEGE-BOUND STUDENT

#1 Bestselling College Guide!
PETERSON'S GUIDE TO FOUR-YEAR COLLEGES 1996

Descriptions of over 2,000 colleges, with guidance on selecting the right school, getting in, and financial aid. **Includes CAP—College Application Planner, IBM-compatible software to help students select and apply to schools.**
ISBN 1-56079-481-X, 2,924 pp., 81/2 x 11, $21.95 pb, 26th ed.

PAYING LESS FOR COLLEGE 1996

"One of the best guidebooks around for families who want to compare the financial aid alternatives." —Smart Money
A one-stop information resource and financial aid adviser featuring in-depth financial aid data and money-saving options at more than 1,600 U.S. four-year colleges and universities. **Includes Financial Aid Planner, IBM-compatible software for estimating college costs and planning family finances.**
ISBN 1-56079-520-4, 720 pp., 81/2 x 11, $26.95 pb, 13th ed.

USA TODAY GETTING INTO COLLEGE

Pat Ordovensky
Provides parents and students with a concise overview of the entire selection, application, and admissions process. Includes the most commonly asked questions—and answers—from *USA TODAY*'s annual "Financial Aid and Admissions Hotline."
ISBN 1-56079-463-1, 160 pp., 6 x 9, $8.95 pb

USA TODAY FINANCIAL AID FOR COLLEGE

Pat Ordovensky
Explains the types of aid available, tells how to qualify for aid, and answers commonly asked questions.
ISBN 1-56079-568-9, 160 pp., 6 x 9, $8.95 pb., revised ed.

ULTIMATE COLLEGE SURVIVAL GUIDE

Janet Farrar Worthington and Ronald Farrar
Covers everything a college-bound student wants—and needs—to know about college life. It's a "get real" guide to campus life, written in lively, conversational language that hits just the right note with students. ISBN 1-56079-396-1, 256 pp., 7 x 9, $11.95

TO ORDER CALL: 800-338-3282
FAX: 609-243-9150

 **Peterson's**
Princeton, NJ

NEW ON THE INTERNET
Peterson's Education Center
A World of Information and News About College and More
http://www.petersons.com